Affect Theory, Shame, and Christian Formation

Stephanie N. Arel

Affect Theory, Shame, and Christian Formation

palgrave
macmillan

Stephanie N. Arel
Boston University
Boston, Massachusetts, USA

ISBN 978-3-319-42591-7 ISBN 978-3-319-42592-4 (eBook)
DOI 10.1007/978-3-319-42592-4

Library of Congress Control Number: 2016957388

Printed on acid-free paper

This Palgrave Macmillan imprint is published by Springer Nature
The registered company is Springer International Publishing AG Switzerland
The registered company address is: Gewerbestrasse 11, 6330 Cham, Switzerland

For Rebecca

Acknowledgments

I feel deep gratitude and joy that so many people have been willing to engage in my work. Several people have provided significant aid and ideas that have made this book possible. Among those who have contributed, I owe particular thanks to a few.

I profoundly thank Shelly Rambo, who supported this work at its infancy. She has given me consistent feedback on my writing and has provided countless opportunities for me to share and receive comments on my work. Her discerning insights into both the ideas and the writing, along with her commitment to my project, have been invaluable. Bryan Stone has, since the beginning of my matriculation at Boston University, been a trustworthy, insightful, and consistent mentor, guiding me at critical junctures while encouraging great freedom to explore my topic. My friends and esteemed colleagues Xochitl Alvizo and Kathryn House both contributed generously to the process of writing this book at pivotal points and have endured with me through it all. The Center of Practical Theology at Boston University supported this project since its insemination. Thanks also to Wesley Wildman, Anjulet Tucker, and Steven Sandage, faculty members who have met with me at different times to guide my writing, challenge me intellectually, and help me complete this text.

I am grateful for the editors at Palgrave Macmillan. I appreciate the generous support of Phil Getz and Alexis Nelson, who saw this process through to its fruition.

I had the opportunity to present many parts of this work to various groups. For this, many thanks go to the Body and Religion Group of American Academy of Religion and the Pacific Northwest Region of

American Academy of Religion, especially Anne-Marie Ellithorpe, who encouraged me through Chapter 5 with precise thinking on friendship, solidarity, and empathy. This same chapter garnered feedback and reflection by those at the Trauma and Lived Religion Conference, Amsterdam, Netherlands. I thank R. Ruard Ganzevoort for his reflections on trauma and Srdjan Sremac for his astute observations, and continual support, of the work on touch and shame.

Many thanks to the American Association of University Women whose fellowship supported this work at its earliest stages. I owe particular gratitude to several members of the Society for Ricoeur Studies, including George Taylor, Dan Stiver, Roger Savage, Todd Mei, and Joseph Edelheit, who have supported my interdisciplinary work integrating shame and trauma with philosophy since I began to undertake it. The 2016 Intercontinental Academia, jointly sponsored by the Israel Institute for Advanced Study at Hebrew University and the Zentrum für interdisziplinäre Forschung of Bielefeld University in Germany, provided a platform for thinking about trauma and shame in the context of human dignity. I appreciate the members' support and encouragement at the final stages of the project.

I am especially grateful to the participants—religious leaders, theologians, and a variety of healthcare workers and healing professionals—of the Journey to Healing International Conference, Belfast, Ireland, where I first spoke about shame in the context of war, addressing the experiences of women survivors of rape during the Rwandan genocide, US soldiers returning from war with posttraumatic stress disorder (PTSD) symptoms, and cultures, like those in Belfast and Bosnia, steeped in war and violence. Two priests from Belfast and a therapist of African victims of torture shared about deep wounds suffered in war, urging me to continue this work.

Thank-you to my family members and those who have been like family, supporting and encouraging this process: Denice, Garry, Courtney, YT, Steven, Christina, Chris, Sydney, Shianne, Sally, Nathan, Judy, Bill, Margena, Marian, Tiffany, Lynne, Laurie, Vanessa, Nancy, Garry, June, Amy, Doug, Jamie, Ronnie, Bill, Kathy, Arlene, Jessica, Nancy, Tonya, and Gina. A special thank-you to Andrew for his continual contributions to deepening this work and without whose unflagging support this book would not have been possible.

Finally, I dedicate this book to Rebecca Daugherty, who deserves more thanks than I can give her here.

Contents

CHAPTER 1

Introduction

Christian rhetoric and practice shape not only minds but also bodies.[1] The consequences of discourses, liturgies, and ceremonies intended for Christian formation are significant. Attending church to find solidarity, seek guidance, and connect with God, participants present themselves to be changed by worship. In the desire for spiritual growth, they expose their most vulnerable selves. Susceptible and open, they avail themselves to be modeled, and traces of the Christian tradition remain to emerge in their behavior, words, and deep-seated beliefs.

Christian adoration of God, no matter which denomination, includes a willingness, even a desire, to be shaped. Worship serves to offer a promise, alleviate pain, and offer hope. In the desire to connect with God and community is an entreaty to mitigate human suffering. Shame, one of the most ubiquitous and potentially damaging states, often plays a role in such suffering.

Complicated and painful, shame evinces human sensitivities and weaknesses. Yet, shame is a normal part of human life that shared and faced assimilates into the varieties of experience with little detrimental impact. However, not addressed, shame is interred,[2] stored in the body to function maladaptively in the Christian self. In the process of interment, messages about shame internalized as beliefs, values, and norms, or externalized through projection onto others, emerge viscerally as affects in the self. Present experiences of shame reinforce memories of past shame—burying

S.N. Arel, *Affect Theory, Shame, and Christian Formation*,
DOI 10.1007/978-3-319-42592-4_1

the affect deeper. Although interred shame is detrimental, the affect serves a very natural biological, neurological, and social purpose. Understanding the role of visceral, innate shame and its involvement in attachment phenomenon is critical for developing a responsible theological anthropology of shame.

The project of uncovering and highlighting where shame appears in Christian language and practice is a formidable one. Shame once recognized is often so painful it readily escapes our view. But envisioning shame as a part of the Christian self recognizes the whole self and lifts up the reality that theology both participates in and potentially disinters shame from the Christian self.[3]

A theological dimension to research on shame's role in self-understanding in the humanities and the social sciences fosters a recognition of how religion and culture together participate in shaping shamed bodies. Further, engaging affect theory and trauma studies with theological anthropology provides the analytic lens that lends itself to capturing the essence of shame carefully distinguished from guilt, deeply associated with embodiment, and closely related to attachment.

The affect of shame functions naturally in the body, relying on relationships of interest for its emergence, but also potentially interfering with secure relational bonds.[4] When a person meets with disapproval or disgust, shame innately motivates the turning of the head or the down casting of the eyes to reduce facial communication and prohibit exposure.[5] This behavior inhibits or restrains the affect of interest or enjoyment but does not completely eradicate it either. For example, a child shamed loses all muscle tonicity and drops to the floor, crying in pain, but also beseeching love from the caregiver in front of whom shame emerged in the first place. In toxic shame, an individual often seeks isolation, unable to tolerate high levels of others' affect and therefore refuting connection. Subsequently, reclusiveness and detachment replace social engagement and intimacy. This reticence as a result of shame poses a challenge for a Christian tradition built on the concept of communion and empathic connection, where a person's presence, even to touch, is a mundane expectation.

A reading of seminal texts well known within the Christian tradition demonstrates how shame persists thematically present in those texts in ways that cannot simply be assimilated into a discourse of guilt. Shame is not as easily recognized as guilt and has more pernicious effects, unless guilt itself goes unrecognized.[6] Moreover, in order to address the way in which shame functions in the formation of the Christian self, shame must be distinguished from guilt and engaged with differently.[7] In the Christian tradition, rhetoric, along with practice, explicitly and implicitly inters shame and forms "shamed" bodies while it establishes a Christian and/or Christianized self, bringing to the fore the different bodily expressions and distinctive impacts that shame and guilt have on the body.[8]

Christian interpretations of shame and guilt have laid the foundation for how each is theologically interpreted today. References to the role of shame in Christian tradition support a robust theological analysis of the relationships between shame, pride, sin, and guilt. Further, distinguishing shame as an affect opens up a discourse between theological notions of shame and the biological, neurological understanding of shame in self-development, self-delimitation, and notions of attachment. The shame experience emerges in major theological anthropological literature and Christian practice and, although sometimes mentioned directly, is more often than not veiled by other terms.[9] While often obscured, shame surfaces within a field of exposure, often either severing or indicating attachment. In order to repair its toxicity, shame must be uncovered, faced, and addressed, not simply distinguished by positive affect or eradicated by treatment modalities. Shame displays the self at its most vulnerable—that is, socially in relationship to another person, and theologically to God.

Distinguishing where shame appears in theological discourse, for instance, by pointing to where language concerning guilt eclipses shame, establishes an important step in unveiling how shame has unintended deleterious effects. Unveiling this shame to impede its pernicious impact is, thus, the aim of this book. To achieve this aim, a rich analytical engagement between discourses of shame as they relate to the body in the Christian tradition, grounded in both the psychological and philosophical conceptions of affect theory, facilitates the discerning and disentangling of guilt and other affects from the often accompanying but distinct affect of shame, entrenched but generally ignored in Christian rhetoric.

In addition, considering the intimate communication of touch inherent in Christian practice draws the body further into the discussion of shame. Tracing the relationship between shame and touch, especially focusing on touch of the face where affect initially emerges, draws out the potential of touch to disinter shame. Further disinterment evolves as the Christian self finds himself or herself intimately engaged with the other in an empathetic exchange. Yet, as is evidenced throughout, shame both emerges in the encounter with the other and can be modified by such an encounter.

Ultimately, examining how the affect of shame functions embedded but eclipsed in Christian texts and praxis demonstrates the potential power that theology has both to shame bodies *and* to address that shame, contributing to still growing areas of theological discourse, affect theory, trauma studies, and literary studies.

Dominance of Guilt in Christian Anthropologies

The Christian tradition and the Western world in general routinely focus on guilt as a response to wrongdoing. Guilt relates theologically to sin, remorse, penance, and forgiveness.[10] But shame is often subsumed under or concealed by these terms in theological language. Thus, theological discourse, widely accepted or renowned traditional Christian texts, and Christian practice fold shame into rhetoric about guilt, thereby obscuring the impact of shame, concealing its effects, and so forming the "shamed" Christian self. Religious discourse about sin, guilt, and reparation—that the Christian gains his/her greatest fulfillment in being empathetic while he/she is also sinful—produces a paradoxical character.[11] The most apparent impetus of this character appears to be guilt; however, guilt in this situation eclipses unconsciously interred shame.

Confusing shame with guilt in language and practices around sin compounds the paradoxical character, while exclusive focus on guilt ignores the experience of shame and prohibits healing from shame's detrimental effects.[12] The continual eclipsing of shame, buried by language about guilt and sin, leads in effect to the perpetuation of shame itself and its damaging evolution into withdrawal and/or violence since shame inhabits the self yet is generally disregarded.[13] Shame and guilt intertwine, persisting undistinguished in different types of theological language. Revealing how this occurs, while also showing how other terms conceal shame, not only exposes where shame operates as maladaptive but also discloses how shame figures in attachment and bonding. This duality in shame, that it both impedes and fosters attachment, along with its propensity to operate deleteriously in the self, illustrates the need for a more distinct theology of shame.

The recent developments in affect theory prompt a consideration of how Christian language confuses and conflates shame, guilt, and other affective experiences configuring "shamed" bodies, thereby interfering with human connection. After establishing shame's powerful role as an affect, examples from two theological texts known for their defense of the

Christian faith and influence on the development of theological anthropology demonstrate the embeddedness of shame—named or unnamed—in Christian beliefs. The first passage, by Saint Augustine (354–430), historically precedes and influences the second passage, by Reinhold Niebuhr (1892–1971). Then, turning to the moment in the Christian liturgy where touch and shame intertwine in the Ash Wednesday practice of imposing ashes on the forehead draws attention to shame more distinctly *on the body*. Last, this body becomes an avenue of shame's mollification. The final chapter examines the interplay of empathy, shame, and attachment, arguing that shame impedes emapthy, but reciprocally empathy attenuates shame. Thus, through empathic connection with another, as interpreted by the theological philosophical project of Edith Stein *On the Problem of Empathy*, we come to a greater "givenness" of ourselves.

In Christian theology, Augustine and Niebuhr assume roles as master diagnosticians of the human condition, and their widely known works on Christian ethics, composed at two pivotal moments in Christian history, are significant for this study. Both talk about sin, guilt, and shame, criticizing what shame theorists identify as unhealthy pride. Their theological platforms offer rich ways to think about how shame is consciously or unconsciously interred in the body, often functioning to sever connections. The study of shame in and through their highly significant and influential works is important for rethinking the theological meaning of shame in the current context.

The trajectory into shame in theological anthropology begins with Augustine. His idea of congenital sinfulness has become normative for Catholic and Protestant theologies. In one interpretation of Augustine, human nature has been so distorted by the biblical Fall that humans are born both sinful and incapable of anything but sin. In Augustine's view, evil is a product of sin, and sin's root is pride. Augustine claims that pride represents the desire to elevate oneself to the place of God and the inclination to deny one's status as a creature under God. In this view, at the center of a corrupt natural order, which erupts from the order of paradise after the Fall, lies a helpless, sinful, and shamed humanity disconnected from God. However, alternate readings of Augustine illustrate that he promotes an intimate, passionate, and visceral connection and attachment to God above all else.[14] Highlighting the concept of attuned attachment to God fundamental to Augustine's theological anthropology bears significance for analysis because of affect theory and the examination of attachment studies in trauma. Furthermore, Augustine has a unique reading of shame that incorporates shame's biological function with its social role of connecting the Christian self to the Christian community. Thus, Augustine's rhetoric constructs a Christian self in ways that are useful for showing how shame becomes interred and subsequently how it becomes repaired through empathy and secure attachments.

Niebuhr's sense of sin also starts with humanity's condition, and although the context is different from Augustine's (he was a Christian realist responding to World War II), his sense of sin is also central to the Christian self. For Niebuhr, sin occurs as the result of a tension between the possibilities of human freedom, or self-transcendence, and the constraints of finitude, or humanity's limitations and dependence on nature. Anxiety caused by human finitude leads people to try to secure their existence. Humans, made in the image of God, but paradoxically creatures of the natural world, struggle for ascendency in freedom. This freedom not only distinguishes humanity from nature and raises humans up beyond animals but also allows humanity to attempt escape of finitude, disregarding God. Niebuhr retains Augustine's emphasis on sin as a consequence of freedom, where sin illustrates humanity's desire to be powerful, rejecting God in ambition and pride. Insecurity and anxiety about finitude precedes the sins of pride (self-deification) and sensuality (the deification of another). Niebuhr presents humanity as participating in the sin of pride, characterized by excessive and inordinate self-love, defying finitude in "unbounded desire," or as participating in the sin of sensuality, escaping or losing the self. Both facilitate an escape from finitude.[15]

When referring to self-deification or deification of another, Niebuhr uses two images: (1) the individual puffed up in pride as *hubris* conveying "unbounded desire" and (2) the other as God, or the self as absorbed by the other, revealing the escape from or loss of the self. These images of humanity in sin correspond to the two poles of shame articulated by Donald L. Nathanson as outward violence and inward withdrawal.[16] For Niebuhr, pride facilitates these postures and, inherent in the Christian self, signifies humanity's effort to assuage anxiety about mortality and finitude. Niebuhr's writing focuses on guilt and enjoins reparation of pride. His diagnosis of the human condition in pride approaches an understanding of shame, yet shame goes unnamed. The realism and justice he advocates cannot be fully entered into by a Christian with interred shame; shame must be drawn out and faced to disallow for interpretations of his work that ultimately lead to shame's interment.

In conjunction with the textual analysis, examining an event in Christian practice in which shame and the Christian narrative intertwine at the moment of touch—the imposition of ashes on the forehead on Ash Wednesday—elucidates something about the praxis and the shamed body. The moment of touch during the liturgy serves as the corporeal manifestation of an affective encounter, drawing attention to the haptic in Christian practice especially insofar as shame, guilt, and sin collide at the moment the ashes touch the forehead, and even more significantly, when an officiate makes the sign of the cross on the forehead of the faithful, marking them as penitent. This especially intimate contact has implications both for acknowledging the Christian self, as a shamed self, and for the success of the Christian intent to join Christians together in mortification with the promise of renewal. The continual return in the practice to this event connotes interior conversion and restoration, goals that remain unachievable if shame remains interred.

Such conversion and restoration rarely happen in isolation. Christianity understands this and illustrates this understanding in its commitment to community and communion. People need other people, and part of the disinterment of shame includes these others. Engaging Edith Stein's philosophical and theological project on empathy facilitates a more explicit comprehension of what it actually means to commune with the other to dislodge shame. Stein interprets the self as essentially "psycho-physical" and spiritual. She identifies empathy, and its curtailment by shame, as a theological phenomenon, integral to the development of the person—here treated as the Christian self. Stein's work illuminates that developing empathic connections is pivotal to Christian formation of body, psyche, and spirit on individual and social levels.

The Significance of Shame

New research on affect and trauma confirms the need to challenge dominant theological conceptions and/or articulations of guilt and shame, especially those that encourage the elimination of shame or promise salvific healing. Although toxic levels of shame, which manifest, for instance, as low estimations of self-worth impeding development and attachment, addictive behaviors, character disorders, and/or psychosomatic illnesses, might be remedied, shame itself as a natural phenomenon cannot be healed in the sense of being eliminated. Rather, shame must be disinterred so that it can be tolerated and regulated by the self to serve its biological objective of social regulation and connection. The unique role that shame plays biologically includes delimiting the self while pointing to the need of repairing broken attachment bonds and reconnecting with the other to restore the relationship.[17]

Studies of shame outside of theology are extensive and expanding. Drawing on several arenas that deepen and broaden an analysis of shame provides multiple angles for theological engagement. The first arena is affect theory.[18] The study of affect represents an attempt to account for the ways in which individuals come to know the world, theorizing not only the body but also its capacity to act and be acted upon. Accounting for the very material engagements that inform human life, affect theorists acknowledge that people learn bodily. Thus, affect theory is a way of theorizing the relationship between the body and the mind differently, distinguishing it from the Enlightenment's epistemological legacy of dichotomizing body and mind.

Emerging out of a collection of concerns about the perceived limits of critical theories indebted to psychoanalytic and Freudian theory, affect theory critiques therapeutic "talking cures"[19] and expands into the natural sciences to ground a more body-based theoretical mode of analysis. Affect theorists' renewed interest in the "biological portion of emotion"[20] places emphasis on bodily experiences and recognizes the relationship of an affect to its object.[21] Affects are understood to be participating in an "ongoing process" that enlarges experience contributing to self-formation.[22] Examining affect theorists' commitment to explicating the interchange between material and human life reveals that shame plays a part in this interchange. Moreover, consideration of shame as a bodily affect upon which theology makes an impact is critical to the premise that interred shame functions in the formation of the Christian self.

Viewing shame through the lens of affect theory also clarifies for theology the important distinctions between guilt and shame. Even though Silvan Tomkins and Donald Nathanson associate the initial affective experience of guilt with shame, shame can be distinguished from guilt based on action, location, and rates of repair. Guilt results from wrong action, as an emotional response to a mistake or wrongdoing, whereas shame implies no standard of comparison that comes with having done something wrong or right. Instead, shame is internalized as some wrong inherent in the self. Shame points inward and is interred, while guilt points outward to an act.

Therefore, guilt can be repaired more easily than shame.[23] However, unaddressed or acknowledged guilt turns into shame, while shame unaddressed turns into more shame, or violence.[24]

The second arena of relevant literature includes trauma studies situated at the juncture of psychoanalysis and literary theory. Trauma theorists, such as Cathy Caruth and Shoshana Felman, expand terms like guilt and shame by bringing them into the realm of rhetoric and literary theory. This approach suggests that, "psychoanalysis and literary analysis are two different contexts for similar methodological insights."[25] While the former negotiates the contents of the psyche, the latter investigates the elements of the text. Both approaches explore and reveal multiple layers of meaning. Although examples of this style vary, a core assumption stands, situated at the intersection of psychoanalysis and literary theory: the psyche and literature (here theological texts), including rhetoric, language, and style, intertwine.[26]

In recent decades, the development of trauma studies, an interesting collusion of psychoanalysis and literary theory, has motivated theologians to address how theology accounts for trauma's destruction of persons and communities, while also challenging theologians to respond to trauma and surrounding debates in a more robust way.[27] In terms of shame, trauma theorists link the affect with withdrawal or violence, which manifests in the responses of burying memories, denying pain, hiding from the world, or lashing out at others.[28] Studies carried out by trauma theorists have challenged theologians to consider how theological rhetoric fails to respond to the internalizing of shame caused by trauma, thereby further shaping "shamed" bodies.

The literature that composes the third arena relates to *habitus* and the findings of neuropsychological and somatic research that show how shame becomes interred in the body and that this interment is destructive.[29] Gender theorist Elspeth Probyn argues that shame plays more than a social or cognitive role in human relationships, or it would be easily eradicated; shame also represents a particular *habitus*.[30] She refers to sociologist Pierre Bourdieu's concept of *habitus*, which both constructs a world and is inscribed on the body.[31] Bourdieu's research provides a way to consider an analysis of shame as a *habitus*, inscribed and interred through practice.[32] Building on Bourdieu's work, textual analysis of the passages by Saint Augustine and Niebuhr, along with an investigation into the moment of touch on Ash Wednesday and the capacity of empathy to both mitigate and be hindered by shame, demonstrates how rhetoric contributes to the formation of a paradoxical self, illustrating the Christian tradition's participation in creating "shamed" bodies.[33]

The idea of *habitus* as developed through repetition illustrates its dependency on memory and relates it to the idea that shame responses repeat and emerge in an interminable spiral. The experience of shame contributes to additional shame or rage: shame for feeling shame, or rage at feeling shame; each response elicits further shame. The spiral of shame,[34] neglected in theological literature that focuses on guilt, further illustrates shame as a *habitus*. This analysis seeks to show that theological discourse often exchanges guilt for shame, fusing or conflating them. Equating guilt with shame minimizes the effects of shame, further enabling its bodily interment and perpetual repetition.[35]

Christian discourse that eclipses shame with talk of guilt and sin is especially problematic in light of the negative physiological effects of toxic shame on the body. According to Rosemary S.L. Mills, experiences of shame induce or encourage a rise in cortisol and pro-inflammatory cytokine activity in the body.[36] This rise in levels of bodily chemicals negatively impacts the immune system and disenables maximal functioning.[37] Shame produces stress on the body, inhibiting the immune system from protecting the body from external pathogens and interfering with positive affect, which directs attachment. This physiological response to shame increases the intensity of the shame affect especially in cases of trauma where the body's natural response to extreme stress is magnified. As psychologist Judith Herman explains, the experience of shame is a "biologically stressful" event that acts like a sudden "brake" to an excited emotional state.[38] Typically, it stifles excitement in a form of hypo-arousal resulting in bodily postures that signal submissiveness, defeat, or withdrawal—bodily positions that primates also assume to signify acquiescence such as slumped shoulders, averted gaze, and bowed-down head.[39] The damage to human flourishing that shame potentially effects inspires research that, delving into texts and praxis, uncovers new theological understandings of shame.

Challenging shame's interment uncovers where shame is concealed and where it interferes with its original role as a moderator of social bonding. Through the lens of affect theory, along with work in trauma studies, an investigation of theological rhetoric's power to shape shamed bodies recognizes theology as a critical conversation partner in the dialogue about shame, especially insofar as theologians such as Augustine and Niebuhr have shaped the theological discourse and anthropologies that undergird Christian theology and practice.

Texts and Practice

A detailed examination of selected theological passages within the Christian tradition that have played and continue to play a key role in shaping the Christian character provides the heart of this analysis and draws from a variety of disciplines to better understand the dynamics of shame. Although a division is often made between the role and impact of text and practice, a practical theological approach interprets this "shaping" or formation in a more robust way. Theology's messages about sin and guilt impede a cognitive understanding of shame because shame often goes unaddressed. Thus, shame remains clouded by rhetoric about guilt and sin, even as Christian rhetoric communicates that shame or something like shame exists *on* and *in* bodies. Further, theological discourse, through the implication of the Christian as a lonely sinner, isolates the Christian in a posture of sin and shame, dismissing the possibility of repair since such restoration depends on reconnection. Finally, theology intends for an empathetic connection, which impeded by shame, cannot be achieved if shame remains interred in the self, in and on bodies. Disentangling the rhetoric of guilt and sin from shame in each text expands the idea that this rhetoric serves to inter the affect of shame, thus perpetuating the formation of "shamed" bodies.

Viewing shame through the lens of affect theory illustrates what is at stake in the theological conflation of guilt, sin, and shame. Theology must negotiate shame as visceral, affective, and neurological. An examination of Saint Augustine's *City of God*, Book 14, Chapter 17, initially demonstrates how language about sin, guilt, and shame form the Christian self by burying shame in the body and marking the body with shame. Then, considering Reinhold Niebuhr's *The Nature and Destiny of Man: Human Nature*, Volume I, primarily pages 251–260, advances a deeper analysis of the language of pride and sensuality as sins that incur, inter, and deeply repress shame. Yet while Niebuhr does not name shame, something like shame operates in his theology, often under the guise of other terms such as "anxiety" and "insecurity." Thus, Niebuhr diagnoses shame as part of the human condition, never using the term "shame" but eliding it with other terms.

Next, exposing the moment of touch as a collusion of the past and present in the Christian tradition at the location of the forehead fosters a multidimensional understanding regarding how Christian bodies are shaped in shame. This moment of touch represents an affective encounter that potentially reveals and accepts shame as a constructive part of the Christian self. The moment of touch also provides a window into an expansive theological premise regarding the importance of community and communal worship. The touch that recognizes and ameliorates shame in the Christian tradition values the other's worth and contradicts shame. Practices of touch rely on concepts of connection, attachment, and empathy. The theological philosophical project of Edith Stein, *On the Problem of Empathy*, elucidates this connection. Entering into the affect of another as a spiritual practice, in Stein's assertion, is an essential part of formation of a "psycho-physical" and spiritual self. But Stein shows that this development includes—not excludes—affect and bodily expression. Thus, this Christian self must still also tolerate shame, as shame indicates and severs attachment bonds that empathy facilitates. Pressing theologians to acknowledge shame liberates its interment and enables more positive affect which promotes the empathic connection essential to Christian formation. Recognizing shame allows it to serve its natural social role, fostering communion within the Christian community and influencing the rest of the world.

Practical Theology

Beneath the theoretical assumption that theological texts and moments in liturgical practice serve a formative function lies an additional presupposition that unconscious processes motivate behavior. This analysis consistently seeks to understand not only how shame is embedded within texts and rhetoric about guilt and sin, but also how shame, as an affect, becomes interred in bodies. Trauma theorists and affect theorists recognize distinctions between conscious processes—those that lie within awareness—and unconscious processes—those that lie outside of awareness. When what is unconscious conflicts with what is conscious, *dis*-ease results. The presumption that different levels operate within the psyche, as evidenced by conscious and unconscious processes related to shame, fosters the related presumption that multiple levels of meaning occur in discourse.

The theoretical assumptions that emerge in this text result in an analytical method that aligns with psychoanalytic and hermeneutic practices of disclosure as a means of what Elaine Graham considers the exposing and recovering dimensions of experience that go unrecognized.[40] Part of this process of exposition includes evaluations and challenges of the "sources and norms" often established by theological texts and scripture that impose a "unitary identity."[41] To do this effectively within the tradition requires a rereading of the past developed by Christian texts and traditions, examining how tradition shapes the Christian self and Christian practice. As Graham asserts, only after analysis of texts and traditions can lost voices be reclaimed and different realities be imagined.

The core pre-commitments (psychoanalytic and hermeneutic) that permeate Graham's work in *Transforming Practice*, and which also inform this theological investigation, are not foreign to literature and theology. Recognizing the importance of analysis that bridges these disciplines, while tracing textual patterns that emerge and reveal levels of meaning not apparent on the surface, illustrates a contribution of psychoanalysis and literary theory to theology. This manifests in what Heather Walton considers the investigation of the validity of "the concept of the rational, unitary and stable self from which all else in humanist thinking gains its bearings."[42]

Reading discloses what messages lie hidden in language, what words signify beyond their literal or even symbolic meaning, and what lies outside of awareness. The assumption that layers of meaning operate within Christian discourse permeates the analysis. This approach integrates the concerns of trauma theory with practical theological analysis, applying particular insights and methods of trauma studies to the reading of theological texts and practice.

Sources of the Study

Primary theological texts, shame studies including affect theory and trauma studies, and studies that consider theological anthropology as it manifests in Christian formation and body theologies serve as the sources for this investigation. Silvan Tomkins's and Helen Block Lewis's work on shame is foundational. Their early research on shame as an affect distinguishes shame from guilt.[43] Although other branches of psychology began to write about shame during the late twentieth century, many referring to Sigmund Freud's less direct work on shame (often articulated in terms of guilt),[44] the focus on affect theory, shame related to the body, and shame related to trauma continually concentrates on shame's biological, visceral, and neurological functioning. Donald Nathanson and literary critic Eve Kosofsky Sedgwick have contributed to more recent research on shame and affect theory both expanding on Tomkins's work into the fields of psychology and literary theory respectively. Work on shame also emerges in much literature on trauma theory where shame correlates with posttraumatic stress disorder (PTSD) symptoms, dissociation, bonds with the perpetrator, secrecy about traumatic experience, and failed efforts at attachment.[45]

The return to rhetoric to think about how it shapes Christian bodies requires use of scholarship both by and inspired by Michel Foucault and Pierre Bourdieu.[46] These scholars direct reading of the primary theological sources and their ideas underlie the theoretical approach. Work by theologians who consider how the Christian tradition approaches and negotiates bodies furthers my analysis of texts and their formation of bodies. Mark D. Jordan's theological anthropology and analysis of the construction of the Christian self serve as a model to this end, along with the work of Marcella Althaus-Reid, Lisa Isherwood, Elisabeth Stuart, Ludger Viefhues-Bailey, and Graham Ward.[47] In addition, literature that considers Christian practices and the body is growing and has value both methodologically and in the consideration of the shamed body in this dissertation. Karmen MacKendrick, Jean-Luc Nancy, Virginia Burrus, and Marcia Mount Shoop have also contributed to this genre.[48]

Limitations of Study

The specific focus and contribution of this project rely on the effort to reveal shame in traditional Christian discourse, showing how shame's interment in the body limits and even impedes Christian ideals of reparation and restoration in community. Research on shame has started to expand across disciplinary divides; however, this study focuses on the scholarship emerging from the fields of affect theory, psychology, trauma studies, and theology. Affect theory in both its psychological and philosophical conceptions frames this analysis of shame and its impact. Thus, the scope of the research does not include some anthropological and sociological research on the topic. The former would draw in a history too complex for this work, while the latter introduces a vocabulary situated around organizations and institutions distracting from a focus that necessarily considers the diagnosis of an individual according to rhetoric and words. For instance, there is no direct address to the empirical studies that followed Ruth Benedict's work, extending her notion of "shame culture" to Asian cultures.[49] This line of analysis also contributes to the growing body of theological literature on shame and pastoral care from multicultural perspective that deserves a more robust analysis in future projects.[50]

Further, the study, limited to the Western Christian context, draws on multicultural references to delineate shame experiences but does not make suggestions for treatment modalities in pastoral care.[51] Furthermore, while the research draws from scholars on race, gender, and religion it focuses more on these at the service of affect theory.[52] In addition, the working definition of shame does not completely capture the work done in social psychologies and psychologies of the self.

A further limitation emerges in the textual selections made for this study. Christian liturgy has a variety of instances where guilt, sin, and shame converge. However, the texts selected both assert a theological anthropology within the same intellectual history, where Augustine's claim serves as the basis. In fact, a consideration of Augustine is critical to the study as his theology undergirds so much of what emerges in contemporary considerations of the Christian body. More important, the examination of Augustine's and Niebuhr's contributions is conducted specifically in terms of affect theory and shame. In addition, working from the representative passages by Augustine and Niebuhr, and only one work by Edith Stein, limits a full reading of their work and theory, and so does not achieve an exhaustive study of their corpus. However, the purpose is to provide insights into their analyses of the human person.

The shame experience signifies an important phenomenon in human life and deserves more attention by theologians at multidisciplinary intersections. Neglecting shame happens too frequently in theological anthropologies and subsequently creates serious problems for the Christian self and self-formation, as shame lies at the root of pathologies, physical problems, and the ever-growing issue of violence. Shame acts as a motivator of violent behavior, but it is also key in forming secure attachments within the Christian community and to God. Theological anthropologies that address shame in this way will take a significant step toward the inhibition of violent behavior directed toward the self and others.

Notes

1. Rhetoric in this dissertation refers to persuasive doctrine, liturgical sources, and theological writing that forms the Christian self. This dissertation's frame concurs with Mark D. Jordan's method articulated in *Recruiting Young Love: How Christian's Talk about Homosexuality* (Chicago: Chicago University Press, 2011): "studying the effects of rhetoric means studying its circulation into lives" (xvi).

2. The concept of shame's interment or shame interred is one developed specifically for this book. Shame resides as a biological source or affect in the body. The word "inter" signifies the way(s) that shame becomes buried in the body, when it is overlaid by other terms and experiences that mask or bypass shame. Further, the interment of shame in the body becomes problematic, because in this case shame goes unnamed.
3. Michel Foucault's psychomedical disciplining of the self in his analysis of the panopticon in *Discipline & Punish*, trans. Alan Sheridan (1975; reprint, New York: Second Vintage Books, 1995) illustrates a kind of self-formation; see also Elaine Scarry, *The Body in Pain* (New York: Oxford, 1985), where humans have the capacity to make the world and the self; William T. Cavanaugh, *Torture and Eucharist: Theology, Politics, and the Body of Christ* (Malden: Blackwell, 1998), where torture creates human and social bodies; and Karmen MacKendrick, *Fragmentation and Memory* (New York: Fordham University Press, 2008).
4. Silvan Tomkins, *Affect, Imagery, Consciousness*, 4 Vols. (1962; Reprint, New York: Springer Publishing Company, 2008), 402–403; Donald L. Nathanson, *Shame and Pride: Affect, Sex, and the Birth of the Self* (New York: W. W. Norton & Company, 1992), 325; see also Helen Block Lewis, *Shame and Guilt in Neurosis* (Madison: International Universities Press, 1971), where she discusses repair and the reduction of shame through the therapeutic alliance.
5. Tomkins, *Affect, Imagery, Consciousness*, 354.
6. Nathanson, *Shame and Pride*, 147.
7. Recent research has shown that emotional and affective distinctions between guilt and shame hold across all or most cultures, whether Western or Eastern, even while the triggering events of shame or guilt differ by culture, see Seger Breugelmans and Ype H. Poortinga, "Emotion without a word: Shame and Guilt with Rarámuri Indians and Rural Javanese," *Journal of Personality and Social Psychology* vol. 91, no. 6 (2006): 1111–1122.
8. Antonio Damasio, *Descartes Error: Emotion, Reason and the Human Brain* (London: Penguin Books, 1994); June Price Tangney and Ronda L. Dearing, *Shame and Guilt* (New York: The Guilford Press, 2002); Alan Schore, *Affect Regulation and Repair of the Self* (New York: W.W. Norton & Company, 2004). It is important to note that psychological inquires, while founded on classic psychoanalytic theory, are informed by affect theory and are meant to prime readers, pointing to subjects for future research regarding shame and guilt.
9. Early work to reveal shame began with sociologist Ruth Benedict's distinctions of societies as either shame cultures or guilt cultures see *The Chrysanthemum and the Sword* (New York: Meridian Books, 1946). See also Bernard Williams, *Shame and Necessity* (1993; reprint Berkeley: University

of California Press: 2008); Jerome H. Neyrey, *The Social World of Luke-Acts: Models of Interpretation* (Peabody: Hendrickson Publishers, Inc., 1991); Peter Brown, *The Body and Society: Men, Women, and Sexual Renunciation in Early Christianity* (New York: Columbia University Press, 1988); Jacob Neusner, *The Social World of Formative Christianity and Judaism: Essays in Tribute to Howard Clarke Kee* (Philadelphia: Fortress Press, 1988); Mary R. Lefkowitz and Maureen B. Fant, *Women's Life in Greece and Rome: A Source Book in Translation*, 3rd ed. (Baltimore: The Johns Hopkins University Press, 2005); David Konstan, "Shame in Ancient Greece," *Social Research* vol. 70, no. 4 (2003): 1031–1060; David Kovacs, "Shame, Pleasure, and Honor in Phaedra's Great Speech (Euripides, Hippolytus 375–87)," *The American Journal of Philology* vol. 101, no. 3 (1980): 287–303; Charles Segal, "Shame and Purity in Euripides' Hippolytus," *Hermes* vol. 98, no. 3 (1970): 278–299; J.T. Hooker, "Homeric Society: A Shame Culture?" *Greece & Rome* vol. 34, no. 2 (1987): 121–125; Jean Delumeau, *Sin and Fear: The Emergence of a Western Guilt Culture 13th–18th Centuries* (New York: St. Martin's Press, 1990).

10. Friedrich Nietzsche, *On the Genealogy of Morality*, trans. Maudemarie Clark and Alan Swensen (Indianapolis: Hackett Publishing, 1998).
11. I use the word "character" to describe the self to avoid the limitations and inflexibility inherent in the idea of identity. Furthermore, "identity" presumes a more rigid categorization of the self, whereas character presumes some nature of the self that performed, alterable, and in process.
12. Helen Block Lewis, "Introduction," in *The Role of Shame in Symptom Formation*, ed. Helen Block Lewis (London: Psychology Press, 1987), 18. Lewis claims that fusing shame and guilt confuses them.
13. One of the more poignant examples relates to the term "survivor guilt" as a component of moral injury. Recently discarded by the DSM classifications, as reported in Jonathan R.T. Davidson and Edna B. Foa, eds., *Posttraumatic Stress Disorder: DSM-IV and Beyond* (Washington, DC: American Psychiatric Press, 1993), 92, "survivor guilt" has been categorized as a component of PTSD; shame, not guilt, is related to PTSD symptoms. Thus, survivor guilt is not guilt but shame as a consequence of having lived when others have died. See also Judith Lewis Herman, "Posttraumatic Stress Disorder as a Shame Disorder," in *Shame in the Therapy Hour*, eds. Ronda L. Dearing and June Price Tangney (Washington, DC: American Psychological Association, 2011). In this essay, Herman shows parallels between the experience of shame and trauma aligned with current DSM V categories of post-traumatic stress and dissociative disorders.
14. Virginia Burrus, Mark D. Jordan, and Karmen MacKendrick, eds., *Seducing Augustine: Bodies, Desires, Confessions* (New York: Fordham University Press, 2010).

15. Reinhold Niebuhr, *The Nature and Destiny of Man: Human Nature*, Volume I (1943; reprint, Louisville: Westminster John Knox Press, 1996), 185 and 283.
16. Nathanson, *Shame and Pride*, 24.
17. Silvan Tomkins, "Shame," in *The Many Faces of Shame*, ed. Donald L. Nathanson (New York: Guilford, 1987), 144; Schore, *Affect Regulation and Repair of the Self*, 152–171.
18. See Melissa Gregg and Gregory J. Seigworth, eds., *The Affect Theory Reader* (Durham: Duke University Press, 2010); Patricia Ticineto Clough and Jean Halley, eds., *The Affective Turn: Theorizing the Social* (Durham: Duke University Press, 2007); Lauren Berlant, *Cruel Optimism* (Durham: Duke University Press, 2011); Ann Cvetkovich, *An Archive of Feelings: Trauma, Sexuality, and Lesbian Public Cultures* (Durham: Duke University Press, 2003); and Eve Kosofsky Sedgwick, *Touching Feeling: Affect, Pedagogy, Performativity* (Durham: Duke University Press, 2004) and *Tendencies* (Durham: Duke University Press, 1993).
19. The "talking cure" emerges out of the famous case study of Anna O. presented by Sigmund Freud and Joseph Breuer in *Studies of Hysteria*, trans. James Strachey (1955; New York: Basic Books, 2000), 30. The term emerges during analysis conducted by Breuer with Anna O.; she mentions the use of the "talking cure," or what she calls the "chimney sweep," as her process of verbalization after being hypnotized. Freud describes what is developed into a technique as "sweeping the mind clean" through continual verbalization, which potentially reveals unconscious content thereby enabling recovery from presented symptoms in psychoanalysis. See Sigmund Freud, *Five Lectures on Psychoanalysis*, trans. James Strachey (New York: W.W. Norton & Company, Inc., 1961), 8.
20. Nathanson, *Shame and Pride,* 49.
21. Sedgwick, *Touching Feeling*, 99–101. Sedgwick differentiates drives in psychoanalytic theory from affects. Either a drive is operating or it is not; affects allow for more possibilities than "on and off."
22. Gregg and Seigworth, *The Affect Theory Reader*, 5.
23. Michael Lewis asserts that simple acts like apologizing assuage guilt, while shame generally requires therapeutic intervention, see *Shame: The Exposed Self* (New York: The Free Press, 1992), 75–77.
24. James Gilligan, *Violence: Reflections on a National Epidemic* (New York: Vintage Books, 1996), 110–114; Tangney and Dearing, *Shame and Guilt*, 3, 5, and 163–165.
25. Nicholas Abraham and Maria Torok, *The Shell and the Kernel*, trans. Nicholas T. Rand (Chicago: University of Chicago Press, 1994), 19.
26. Céline Surprenant, "Freud and Psychoanalysis," in *Literary Theory and Criticism: An Oxford Guide*, ed. Patricia Waugh (Oxford: Oxford University Press, 2006), 200.

27. See Kathleen M. Sands, *Escape from Paradise: Evil and Tragedy in Feminist Theology* (New York: Fortress Press, 1994); Jennifer Beste, *God and the Victim: Theological Reflections on Evil, Victimization, and Forgiveness* (Grand Rapids: Eerdman's, 1999); Serene Jones, *Trauma and Grace: Theology in a Ruptured World* (Louisville: Westminster John Knox Press, 2009); Shelly Rambo, *Spirit and Trauma: A Theology of Remaining* (Louisville: Westminster John Knox Press, 2010).
28. Tangney and Dearing, *Shame and Guilt,* 105; Judith Herman, *Trauma and Recovery* (New York: Basic Books, 1992), 56 and 189; Lenore Terr, *Too Scared to Cry: How Trauma Affects Children and Ultimately Us All* (New York: Basic Books, 1990), 62–63, and 113; Gilligan, *Violence,* 111.
29. See Schore, *Affect Regulation and Repair of the Self,* and Tomkins, *Affect, Imagery, and Consciousness.*
30. Elspeth Probyn, "Shame in the Habitus," in *The Editorial Board of the Sociological Review* (Malden: Blackwell Publishing, 2004), 245.
31. Pierre Bourdieu, *Pascalian Meditations,* trans. Richard Nice (Stanford: Polity Press, 2000).
32. "The Baltimore Catechism," The Baltimore Catechism Revised Edition (1941), accessed August 15, 2014, http://www.catholicity.com/baltimore-catechism/; "Mass: Ash Wednesday," accessed August 15, 2014, http://www.liturgies.net/Lent/ashwednesdayrc.htm.
33. Saint Augustine, Bishop of Hippo, *Concerning the City of God against the Pagans,* trans. Henry Bettenson (London: Penguin Books, 2003), 14–17; Niebuhr, *The Nature and Destiny of Man,* 251–60.
34. The shame spiral is expanded in Thomas J. Scheff, "The Shame-Rage Spiral: A Case Study of an Interminable Quarrel," in *The Role of Shame in Symptom Formation,* ed. Helen Block Lewis (London: Psychology Press, 1987), 109–149.
35. James Gilligan, "Shame, Guilt, and Violence," *Social Research* vol. 70, no. 4 (2003): 1165.
36. Rosemary S.L. Mills, "Taking Stock of the Developmental Literature on Shame," *Developmental Review* 25 (2005): 52.
37. Sally S. Dickerson, Tara L. Gruenewald, and Margaret E. Kemeny, "When the Social Self Is Threatened: Shame, Physiology, and Health," *Journal of Personality* vol. 72, no. 6 (December 2004): 1197–1204.
38. Judith Lewis Herman, "Shattered Shame States and Their Repair," presented at The John Bowlby Memorial Lecture, Saturday March 10, 2007: 6.
39. Dickerson, Gruenewald, and Kemeny, "When the Social Self Is Threatened," 1196.
40. Elaine Graham, *Transforming Practice: Pastoral Theology in an Age of Uncertainty* (1996; reprint Eugene: Wipf & Stock Publishers, 2002), 193.
41. Graham, *Transforming Practice,* 9; see also Elaine Graham, "A Remembrance of Things (Best) Forgotten: The 'Allegorical Past' and the Feminist Imagination," *Feminist Theology* vol. 20, no. 1 (2012), 59.

42. Heather Walton, "Re-Visioning the Subject in Literature and Theology," in *Self/Same/Other: Re-Visioning the Subject in Literature and Theology*, eds. Heather Walton and Andrew W. Hass (London: T&T Clark, 2000), 13.
43. Block Lewis, *Shame and Guilt in Neurosis*, 15–18.
44. See primarily Sigmund Freud, *Beyond the Pleasure Principle*, trans. James Strachey (1920; reprint, W.W. New York: Norton and Company, 1990) and Freud's later *Civilization and its Discontents*, trans. James Strachey (1929; reprint, New York: W.W. Norton, 1962).
45. Herman, "Shattered Shame States," 11 and 13; see also Léon Wurmser, *Torment Me, but Don't Abandon Me* (Lanham, MD: Rowman & Littlefield, 2007).
46. See Gary David Comstock and Susan E. Henking, eds., *Que(e)rying Religion: A Critical Anthology* (New York: Continuum, 1997); Gerard Loughlin, ed., *Queer Theology: Rethinking the Western Body* (Malden: Blackwell Publishing, 2007); Lynne Huffer, *Mad for Foucault: Rethinking Foundations of Queer Theology* (New York: Columbia University Press, 2009); Christopher Irvine, *The Art of God: The Making of Christians and the Meaning of Worship* (Great Britain: Liturgy Training Publications, 2006); Graham Ward, *Cities of God* (London and New York: Routledge, 2000); Jordan, *Recruiting Young Love;* Daniel Franklin E. Pilario, *Back to the Rough Grounds of Praxis: Exploring Theological Method with Pierre Bourdieu* (Leuven: Leuven University Press, 2005); Kieran Flanagan, *The Enchantment of Sociology: A Study of Theology and Culture* (Basingstoke: Macmillan Press, 1996).
47. Marcella Althaus-Reid, *Indecent Theology: Theological Perversions in Sex, Gender and Politics* (New York: Routledge, 2000); Lisa Isherwood and Elizabeth Stuart eds., *Introducing Body Theology: Introductions in Feminist Theology* (New York: T&T Clark, 1998); Ludger H. Viefhues-Bailey, *Beyond the Philosopher's Fear: A Cavellian Reading of Gender, Origin and Religion in Modern Skepticism* (Burlington: Ashgate, 2007); Graham Ward, *Cities of God* (London and New York: Routledge, 2000), *The Politics of Discipleship: Becoming Postmaterial Citizens* (Grand Rapids: Baker Academic, 2009), and *Christ and Culture* (Oxford: Blackwell, 2005).
48. Karmen MacKendrick, *The Word Made Skin* (New York: Fordham University Press, 2004) and *Fragmentation and Memory*; Jean-Luc Nancy, *Corpus* (New York: Fordham University Press, 2008); Virginia Burrus, *Shame: Martyrs, Saints, and Other Abject Subjects* (Philadelphia: University of Pennsylvania Press, 2008); Marcia W. Mount Shoop, *Let the Bones Dance: Embodiment and the Body of Christ* (Louisville: Westminster John Knox Press, 2010).
49. Ying Wong and Jeanne Tsai, "Cultural Models of Shame and Guilt" in *The Self-Conscious Emotions: Theory and Research*, eds. Jessica L. Tracy, Richard

W. Robins, and June Price Tangney (New York: Guilford Press, 2007), 209. Francis Inki Ha, "Shame in Asian and Western Cultures," *The American Behavioral Scientist* vol. 38, no. 8 (1995): 1114–1131.

50. Jacob Hee Cheol Lee, "Shame and Pastoral Care: Implications from an Asian Theological Perspective," *Pastoral Psychology* vol. 57 (2009): 253–262, 254. See also You, "Shame and Guilt Mechanisms in East Asian Cultures," Carrie Doehring, *The Practice of Pastoral Care: A Postmodern Approach* (Louisville: Westminster John Knox Press, 2006); Boyung Lee, "Caring-Self and Women's Self Esteem: A Feminist Reflection on Pastoral Care and Religious Education of Korean-American Women," *Pastoral Psychology* 54 (2006): 337–353; Neil Pembroke, *The Art of Listening: Dialogue, Shame, and Pastoral Care* (New York: T&T Clark/Handsel Press, 2002).
51. The following texts exceed the white American context to represent shame: Grace Cho, *Haunting the Korean Diaspora: Shame, Secrecy, and the Forgotten War* (Minneapolis: University of Minnesota Press, 2008); Salman Rushdie, *Shame: A Novel* (New York: Random House, 1983) where the narrator of the novel asserts on page 22, "Shame, dear reader, is not the exclusive property of the East;" Jasvinder Sanghera, *Shame* (London: Hodder & Stoughton, 2007); K.E. Supriya, *Shame and Recovery: Mapping Identity in an Asian Women's Shelter* (New York: Peter Lang, 2002).
52. See Joy DeGruy Leary, *Post-Traumatic Slave Syndrome: America's Legacy of Enduring Injury and Healing* (Baltimore: Uptown Press, 2005); Anthony B. Pinn and Dwight N. Hopkins, eds., *Loving the Body: Black Religious Studies and the Erotic* (New York: Palgrave Macmillan, 2004); Emilie M. Townes, *Womanist Ethics and the Cultural Production of Evil* (New York: Palgrave Macmillan, 2006); M. Shawn Copeland, *Enfleshing Freedom: Body, Race, and Freedom* (Minneapolis: Fortress Press, 2010); Kathryn Bond Stockton, *Beautiful Bottom, Beautiful Shame: Where "Black" Meets "Queer"* (Durham: Duke University Press, 2006); Kelly Brown Douglas, *Sexuality and the Black Church: A Womanist Perspective* (New York: Orbis Books, 1999); Erica L. Johnson and Patricia Moran, *The Female Face of Shame* (Bloomington: Indiana University Press, 2013); Patrick Moore, *Beyond Shame: Reclaiming the Abandoned History of Radical Gay Sexuality* (Boston: Beacon Press, 2004); Gershen Kaufman and Lev Raphael, *Coming Out of Shame* (New York: Doubleday, 1996).

CHAPTER 2

Interpreting Shame Affectively

As an affect that shapes bodies, the positive, negative, and cumulative effects of shame function in the Christian self. Examining shame through the lens of affect theory, as a branch of psychological and philosophical thought, while distinguishing shame from other experiential affects, uncovers the influence shame has on self-formation. The ubiquity of shame in our lives challenges us to not only disentangle it from other affects but also to examine where shame lies hidden in Christian rhetoric and practice. Formulating an affective theology of shame includes assuming that the body, a source of flowing and changing energy, has the capacity to act on and be acted upon by the world, in this case constituted by Christian tradition and practice. Revealing shame and its operations in specific theological writings and practice fosters an understanding of shame as a psychological phenomenon which rather than interred in the self needs to be confronted and addressed.

The idea of a corporeally expressed affective shame establishes the grounds from which to consider how shame operates in theological anthropologies: that shame originating in the body can become interred in the body. Interment occurs because shame's immediacy and potentially negative intensity inspires a conscious or unconscious judgment that the self, or part of the self, is corrupt. This judgment takes place through the eyes of a real or imagined other. Feeling exposed before another and shamed is a painful experience that often results in shame's denial. Denying or dismissing shame also recognizes the unbearable way that

S.N. Arel, *Affect Theory, Shame, and Christian Formation*,
DOI 10.1007/978-3-319-42592-4_2

shame corroborates a diminished sense of self-worth. The diminished self hides from or conversely lashes out at the other in anger. Thus, renouncing shame becomes an affect driven full-body response: the self goes to great extents to not experience the pain of shame and so represses it. Unarticulated or unexpressed, shame becomes effectively interred in the self. However, regardless of how shame has been confounded, it still powerfully shapes behavior and bodies. Theology participates in this shaping by shame when shame becomes concealed by other affects. Yet, shame's concealment belies its pervasiveness; it is a shared human experience, and when faced, or consciously acknowledged, shame provides significant meaning for the self and for the self in relation to others.

A spotlight on affect fosters an investigation into shame's impact on the Christian self as fully embodied. Focus on the body, promotes analysis that is not only discursive, theoretical, or interested solely on social constructions of the body but that also considers the body as material, as having the capacity—as matter—of being molded and shaped. Mediating social relationships, the body is the affective center of life. Shaped by the stimulation of particular affects, as energy flow where shame plays a central role, the body serves as the site of shame enabling shame's visceral interment. Shame originates in the body, and stimulated by the relational as a component of attachment, shame becomes interred in the body by repeated events that parallel the original shame experience. To deal with the debilitating effects of shame, the body absorbs it, burying it in the self. Yet, thus interred, shame still influences individual behavior. When shame debilitates, it can be considered to be "dysregulated,"[1] a psychological term used to describe when affects increase to a heightened level. In such cases, the experiences of shame do not fall within a normal spectrum of affective experience and are therefore considered hyper-aroused.

The pain that dysregulated shame inspires is often too much to bear. Such an overwhelming experience of shame leads to the experience of ourselves as worthless and inconsequential. As a result, we may consciously or unconsciously attempt to eradicate shame—to the extent that this is possible—by denying it or trading it with other affective phenomena, such as guilt or anger. This conflation of shame with other affects contributes to the difficulty in both identifying and naming shame. But providing markers of shame that point to its physiology, including how it combines with and modulates other affects aids in its identification.[2] Thus, analyzing shame necessitates distilling it from both its stimulus and other affects, especially delineating it from the experience of guilt.[3] Drawing out the biological nature of shame, including its preverbal emergence and visceral interment, clarifies how shame is perpetuated and lived into in affective cycles related to shame itself and anger-rage. These aggregate cycles, exacerbated by trauma, illustrate the distinctive and problematic nature of shame that goes unacknowledged and interred. Repressed, masked, or confused with other affects, shame induces detrimental physiological states and behavior, transforming into additional shame, self-disgust, and violence.[4]

The ranges and cycles of shame along with the capacity of society to shape bodies in shame entails a discussion about how bodies are both affective and affected. Pierre Bourdieu's conception of *habitus* and Silvan Tomkins' script theory offer rich ways to see how shame becomes interred in self-functioning, to shape bodies. Both Bourdieu's and Tomkins' theories elucidate means of bodily learning. Bourdieu's assertions rest on the subtle ways that power is exchanged and manipulated in the hands of social and cultural institutions, while Tomkins' premise rests on his understanding of affect. Both theorists refute the idea that bodies form in isolation or independently from the systems that surround them, thus supporting the assertion that bodies can be shaped in shame.

Affect Theory

Emerging as an accepted theory in the second half of the twentieth century, affect theory has various permutations and multiple disciplinary expressions within psychology and philosophy. Affects gained explicit attention in Silvan Tomkins' 1962 four-volume series *Affect Imagery Consciousness.* Laying out the groundwork for the many interpretations of affect that have emerged more recently, Tomkins' precision and expansion of the idea of affect into an approach also established the foundation for critical theorists who wanted to respond to crisis, suffering, trauma, and violence using more than the lens of Freudian analysis and Freud's theory of the drive mechanisms. Looking for a psychological approach that both acknowledged and grounded the body, these scholars integrated Tomkins' work into their own.

Contemporary research around affect illustrates that affects are both necessary for human connection and often unfortunately ignominious. The stimulation of affects reflects how these comingle the internal and external experiences of an individual. Subsequently, affects influence the interpretation of what is perceived through vision and the body, influencing both short- and long-term behavior.[5] Scholarship focused on affects refutes hard distinctions between stimulus and response, between the world "out there" and the body, acknowledging the malleable relationship between the external and internal. Supported by less definite boundaries between the internality of the self and the externality of the environment, we can understand the body as integrated with mental processes.

The immediacy of affects further negates differentiation between the self and the world. The events of the external environment stimulate bodily affects, usually initially without our conscious awareness, connecting us to that which lies outside of us. In the moment of the affective charge, we are, at best, temporarily seized by that which lies outside of us. Our physiology altered leaves us wondering whether the provocation came from outside stimuli or internal forces. Part of this confusion arises because in affective experience the connections between body and mind happen rapidly.

In affect, the social and biological converge. Most recently, research in affective neuroscience further supports the resistance to the dichotomization of body and mind, demanding that the two comprise a system which is intimately connected to the external world. This destabilization of the hard categories represented by the body and its external environment also materializes in research projects in the humanities. Thus, a characteristic thematic and goal shared by affect theorists is to shift the Enlightenment's epistemological legacy of dissociating body from mind. By merging body and mind, affect theory offers a concept that aids analysis of the body as integrated with and integral to the brain. As a result, the individual can be perceived as unified, not as having separate mental and visceral systems.[6] This construction of the self stresses the importance of the relationship between the brain and the body, or the self and the environment. Thus, the primordial, biological experiences of affects intertwine with the social stimulation of affect.

Affects are spontaneous muscular glandular responses located throughout the body and triggered at the subcortical centers involved in muscle control, emotions, fear, aggression, eating, sex, and other basic functions. These centers are specialized structures that lie beneath the cortex, the part of the brain involved in consciousness.[7] So affects can be said to lie beneath consciousness. Instead of being rational, the experience of affect is more biological and physiological. This also accounts for affects' fractiousness. Affects, like shame, emerge viscerally as a result of triggers or stimuli, and, at least initially, are difficult to control. Arising through the body, from beneath consciousness, they grasp the body and demand attention.

Facial expressions of affects precede bodily behavior, evidencing an affect's spontaneity and intractability.[8] Tomkins's interest in the face emerges from two sources: French neurologist G.B. Duchenne's work in *Mécanisme de la Physionomie Humaine* and Charles Darwin's discoveries in *The Expression of the Emotions in Man and Animals.* In line with Duchenne, Tomkins argues that affects, despite their inherent individual particularity, emerge publicly in the muscles and motor nerves of the face.[9] As evidence for the biological and evolutionary inheritance of affect according to Darwin, Tomkins recorded images of the face using a camera designed to take 10,000 frames per second. He employed this data in his explication of each affect where he uses such images to illustrate the facial expressions affiliated with a particular affect.

The analytical elaboration of how the face displays affect distinguishes affect theory from Freud's drive theory. Thus, the interpretation of affect cannot be explained by drive theory alone which holds that negative affect or tension emerges when an organism's particular needs fail to be met. Indicated primarily through hunger and libido—the appetite for food and sex—drives like affects have a strongly biological component but demand an object to alleviate or to satisfy the need and reduce the drive. For instance, a person feels hungry, and the object of food satisfies the need, eliminating hunger. Theoretically, once the object of a drive is provided, the drive diminishes in strength. Alternatively, if a drive remains unsatisfied, such as physical hunger for food, the lack likely leads to death. In the case of affects however, no "innate, easily identifiable consummatory activity" that will likely reduce the said affect exists, and no affect is cause of natural death.[10] For instance, if a person feels fear, nothing like food or water can be consumed or ingested to reduce fear. Instead, fear's modification occurs through some instrumental activity that will moderate or offset the negative affect with a positive one. Simple examples include taking a walk, managing affairs, and meditation; however, the more deeply ingrained the fear (as with interred shame), the more challenging it is to increase positive affect. Active management does not succeed all of the time or for all of the affects. In particular, the modification of shame does not eradicate the shame experience. Rather as a result of empathic connection, shame's intensity decreases, and the bonds that shame disturbs are restored.

Shame's physiological nature raises a question about how to identify affects apart from feelings and emotions. A first and distinct difference between these states relates to the primitive, preverbal nature of affect.

Affects, before they are perceived, provoke internal physical reactions that precede an affect's emergence on the face. Even so the subsequent facial expressions manifest regardless of whether or not we recognize them. In anger, the brow lowers and the nose flares. In shame, vasodilation and an intense blood flow to the area on the face manifests at the blush. These physiological manifestations of affect occur before we can articulate them, rendering affects preverbal.

Thus, affective experience precedes language. The detachment from language demarcates affects from feelings and emotions. Once we are aware of the presence of an affect, and we attach a word to it, the affect transforms. We "feel" it. A feeling indicates conscious discernment of an affect and the recognition of a trigger. Feelings thus associate with cognitive processing and subsequent verbal expression of an affect. We express feeling shame by using particular vocabulary: embarrassment, humiliation, and mortification. We express the affect of joy by saying we are happy, delighted, and glad.

Feelings grow into emotions when they, along with the affect that inspires them, align with a narrative. Usually this narrative has roots in previous experiences. "Emotion" indicates the combination of the triggered affect with memory or past experiences of a particular affect. Emotions represent "the sociolinguistic fixing of the quality of an experience,"[11] which gives meaning to affects. Attached to cognitive processes, emotions take shape when affects congeal to create a "script," also understood as "sets of rules by which an individual predicts, interprets, responds to, and controls life's events."[12] Scripts are not directly related to performance or roles but rather are variable, internal, attached to affect, and never stop "seizing" an individual. Affects are biological and lack the narrative cohesion of emotions. Furthermore, emotions rely on language development and memory, while affects' nature as preverbal evince what happens to bodies. Feelings attach language to bodily affects pulling them from the primarily visceral, interpreting and communicating affective experience.

Affects' corporeality makes them radically present; words used as feelings constitute attempts to capture affect and require higher order brain mechanisms necessary for discernment, while emotions are the complex constructions that associate affects with memories and the stimuli that trigger them.[13] Affects then serve as a bridge that brings the body's experiences into consciousness, while emotions tell a story about what circumstances or events have inspired feeling. An affect cannot be used as a synonym for emotion or feeling; instead, an affect display, first appearing on the face, emanates from the body prior to the verbal construction of emotion.[14]

The visceral experiences of affect, while fundamental to emotions, are more than emotions in that they seize the body in a way that challenges comprehension. What is this seizing? Tomkins identifies nine discrete biological affects that capture our bodies before consciousness can interfere: interest-excitement, enjoyment-joy, surprise-startle, distress-anguish, anger-rage, fear-terror, shame-humiliation, dissmell, and disgust. The affect pairs signal a range of intensity. For instance, interest peaks at excitement; distress disintegrates into anguish, while shame degenerates into humiliation. Of all the affects, Tomkins writes that "[S]hame strikes deepest into the heart of man."[15] When Tomkins asserts this and later calls shame a "sickness of the soul," he locates shame at the core of the self.[16] His psychological assertion about shame's centrality and its capacity to indicate injury of the self can function to inform understandings of the self in theological anthropology.

Yet, a comprehensive theological anthropology cannot develop if it focuses on the self alone, because the self does not exist in isolation. The self depends on and lives in communion with the other. And as a part of the external world, the other is implicated in the mobilization of affect. We feel joy when we see someone we love approach us, fear when they are threatened, and shame when we have betrayed them. Highly implicated in social relationships, shame emerges and fluctuates within dyads. In fact, shame hinges on the presence of the other, even though it can be experienced in isolation. We need only to imagine a situation in which we feel shamed before the other in order to experience the affect. Philosophically, this can be described as shame in the presence of a real or imagined other in front of whom one feels shame, where shame occurs as a consciousness of a loss or failure of the self to live up to the expectations of an idealized other.[17]

Often this idealized other takes the role of a primary caregiver. Discoveries about affect have transformed prior interpretations of the importance of the caregiver-infant dyad, emphasizing the critical role that the caregiver plays in the affect regulation of the infant. A large part of the empirical data that shows the operation of affect within the caregiver-infant dyad has actualized from research in attachment theory. Established by research on primates by John Bowlby and the Strange Situation Protocol developed by Mary Ainsworth, attachment theory argues for the critical nature of at least one primary attachment figure while stressing the influence that this relationship has on later adult relationships. In the optimal caregiver-infant dyad, the caregiver is attuned to and mirrors the child's behavior, maximizing attachment bonds. Human development cannot be understood apart from the transactions between the caregiver-infant dyad, which consists of an "affect-transacting relationship."[18] The self evolves in progressions directly related to (1) affect experienced by the caregiver that is displayed or replicated by the infant and (2) the regulation of that affect.[19] Affects are, thus, a critical aspect of the attachment phenomenon, which rather than diminishing with age continue to inform adult, and Christian, development.

Within the caregiver-infant dyad and later between adults, affects are shared, elicited, and modulated.[20] The initial caregiver-infant dyad serves as a model for affect regulation, especially important in cases of shame. When negative affects become overwhelming, for instance when a child cries and the caregiver fails to respond, the self experiences a state of disarray. Dysregulation, along with the failure of the attunement of the caregiver to the infant, lead to shame. When this failure of attunement occurs repeatedly, as in cases of child abuse and neglect, a corresponding breakdown in attachment develops. These sorts of early attachment failures become significant sources for shame.

Regarding the role that the caregiver plays in the regulation of affect in an infant, a dysregulated nervous system, or a hyper-aroused nervous system, inhibits safety, cognitive processes, and learning, while promoting dissociation.[21] Therefore, the immediate affective experience of shame creates the conditions for the self to fail at the processing of information that would normally be manageable. This leads to repression, denial, and interment; being flooded by shame has serious physiological ramifications, isolating the self through detachment and, by association, prohibiting or precluding learning even in a theological or ecclesial environment.

On even a moderate level, triggered shame coalesces with or becomes concealed by other affects making it difficult to distinguish these from one another over time. Labeled as a process of "blending,"[22] this disenables both the easy identification of a particular affect and our effective ability to deal with the said affect. For instance, shame blended with guilt, rage, or disgust in the dyadic relationship during dysregulation becomes further interred, confused, and maladaptive, or pathological. Shame concealed by other affects does not reduce its potency. In fact, the appearance of negative affect, especially unregulated, challenges us to look deeper, to uncover if interred shame lies at the root of said affect.

The lens of affect theory and affective neuroscience facilitates this unveiling, establishing shame as a biological, physiological affect that emerges immediately even if equally as rapidly disguised as another affect. Its immediacy gives rise to urgency enhanced and exacerbated by its evasion of language and conscious control: shame as preverbal is often also confused with other affective states especially when words are used to describe shame. In the latter case, affects become imbricated with memory and external stimuli. Further, although affects are biological, their regulation transpires in the social world. Even though affects also emerge in physical isolation, they often require a real or perceived other in relation, both to transpire and to repair. This is especially the case for shame. Therefore, shame, as an affect, stimulated and modulated in relationship must also be repaired in relationship.

Shaping Bodies

In 1995, the publication of two influential essays indicated a move toward affect in critical theory. Apart from psychology and neuroscience, these essays emphasize affect as a bodily source of information while promoting the importance of an interdisciplinary study of affect.[23] The first, written by Eve Kosofsky Sedgwick and Adam Frank, entitled "Shame in the Cybernetic Fold," argued in strong support of Tomkins' work on affect. Situated at the beginning of their edited compilation *Shame and Its Sisters*, the essay pays homage to Tomkins and captures some of his most astute theories. Also published the same year was Brian Massumi's "The Autonomy of Affect."[24] In this essay, Massumi does for Spinoza and Deleuze what Sedgwick and Frank do for Tomkins; Massumi carries forward their theories of affect into contemporary critical theory.

These critical theories establish affects apart from their neurological description and also expand affect to include its influence on experience beyond the psychoanalytic or therapeutic environment. In addition, psychology, philosophy, critical theory, and literary studies all intersect within affect theory in ways that undermine discrete disciplinary boundaries. What does this mean? That affects inform multiple disciplinary inquiries. Scholars working outside of psychology and neurology help in the conceptualization of affect as a phenomenon that impacts ontology leading to the conclusion that affects influence the way that the body is shaped. Different theorists' work fosters an understanding of affects' implication in formation.

For instance, Sedgwick's work helps us understand how affects engage individuals in proceeding toward a progressive truth that embraces shifting and performing selves. Affects inform us of who we are and where we are within cultural political struggles. When we consider the imbrication of ourselves as biological beings situated within cultural frameworks, we come to understand that affective life is foundational to that reality. Yet, the complexity inherent in language and in our personal experiences of the world qualifies affects as both particular and ambiguous. As a result, an affect triggered by a particular moment and related to a particular narrative can also be confused with or concealed by other affective experiences. These qualities of particularity and ambiguity, most poignant in relationship to shame, attach affects to singular encounters of exposure, which often subsume shame or lead to its misinterpretation.

Sedgwick's non-dualist approach grounded in affect theory has its roots in Baruch Spinoza's rejection of the mind-body dualism apparent in René Descartes' *The Ethics*. Affect theorists who have challenged the Enlightenment's mind-body split follow Spinoza's philosophical lead, even if indirectly. The guidance that Spinoza provides includes his view of life as full of variation, always mutable, consisting of rapidly altering affects and ideas. These affects "indicate or express a constitution of the body (or some part of it), which the body (or some part of it) has because its power of acting, *or* force of existing, is increased or diminished, aided or restrained."[25] Thus, affects represent a continuing force of existence that also always changes; in physiological terms, affects immediately alter bodies and, in their urgency, are uncontrollable. Affects are indistinguishable from body and, therefore, are autolectic. That is, affects exist for their own sake. Spinoza's work thus aligns not only with the affect psychologists' and neurologists' claim that affects are of the body and make an impact upon the body's capacity, but his ethical treatment of affect also materializes in Tomkins' examination regarding the intensification or diminishment of affects and in Tomkins' locating shame within a frame that situates the self as always in relation.

Shame deeply influences relationships and relationality, having implications for how the self perceives itself and how others perceive the self. Intensification and diminishment of shame, then, occur as a result of such perceptions. For instance, when Sedgwick discusses shame, she recognizes its valuations as biologically useful when it points to interest and fosters attachment. Toxic shame, on the other hand, as repressed or denied shame, ultimately fosters violence. Both psychological and physical violence sever attachment. In either case, shame becomes formative directing and shaping the self according to the way that attachment bonds concretize, either toward or away from others. The affective movement of shame occurs immediately, slipping away from conscious control, and the mind becomes confused by perceptions affirmed by the body to greater or lesser degree that the mind must then process, being lured and swayed by these affects.[26] This is how shame becomes a structuring agent of identity not only physiologically shaping bodies but also conceptually conceived, articulated, and performed.

But this shaping is always in flux. A body is fluid, and affective forces manipulate a body's performance. Affects operate, as Deleuze and Guattari express, as "projectiles," or "weapons," which cause an increase or decrease in the body's capacity to act.[27] Affects, like shame, thus shape bodies; affects *affect* how bodies move, perform, and exist in the social world. This often happens unconsciously. And affects have an original intensity that is both unformed and unstructured but highly organized according to recursion; thus, affects repeat themselves.[28] Recursion relates to the notion that affects triggered by specific stimuli coagulate in emotional constructions and can therefore be retriggered by similar stimuli far after the initial stimulus has taken place.

Affects are thus varied and surging forces that influence our daily lives. In this sense, they are banal. Shame has a claim on banality: it is an everyday experience. Viscerally self-generated, affects occur with a certain spontaneity that directs human action, pulling us into places we may not want to go. We are continually guided by affective pulls; these account for the array of experiences we express as feelings or emotion that we experience in any given day. Affects underlie these. The affective flow itself is mundane and yet simultaneously unpredictable. We cannot perceive the events of any given day nor can we predict our responses. Difficult to foresee, or calculate, the muscular, glandular reflexes of affect capture the attention of reason and thought often with an unexpected immediacy.

The biological immediacy of affect, stimulated often by social phenomena that subsequently provoke particular bodily behaviors, substantiates affects' importance examined through both a psychoanalytical and a philosophical lens. Emphasis on this disciplinary and conceptual conjunction supports the notion of embodiment, by objecting to what Lauren Berlant calls in her work for cultural and political transformation particular, isolated kinds of embodiment. Offering to affect theory the idea of thinking affect epistemologically, she understands affects as a source of information that attended to foster human growth.[29] Furthermore, the physiological immediacy and variability of affect lead Berlant to assert that "… affect management is always belated."[30] Her perspective links the tradition of intellectual activism inherent in post-colonial theory with the sex-radical works of Deleuze, Guattari, and Sedgwick, who in her estimation, through their progressive work on affect and shame, have "countered the malignity of modern national body politics."[31]

From this viewpoint, it becomes clear that affect, alongside rational thought, shapes epistemology. Translating this assumption into theological language fosters the assertion that affects edify cognitive understanding of belief and faith, just as they shape the Christian self. Affects provoke both pleasure and destruction, shaping personal investment in life and relationships with others; this dynamic interweaves with the Christian or religious life. An affect's power to seize the body in the present moment and then to move that body renders affect undeniable, but all the while the affect obscures itself as the primary mover somewhere between a person's cognitive response to act and conditioned behavior. As such, behavioral responses to the emergence of affect, themselves nearly immediate, call into question whether the response is to the affect itself or instead marks a habituated reaction that evades cognitive processing. Stimulated affect can thus become immediately concealed, or obscured, by other affects as they emerge into conscious awareness, making possible the theological elision of guilt and shame.

Shame as Affect

Understanding shame and how it can be concealed by or combined with other affects necessitates a disentangling of shame from other affective experiences. This entanglement can be described as affect blending. Confusion results from "blending" because affects can "combine with, modulate, or suppress other affects."[32] Shame is particularly susceptible to combining with other affects. This is because, of the affect pairs, shame-humiliation is an especially painful affect. Human nature necessarily wants to deny or escape pain, and as a result, regularly attempts to evade shame. In fact, of the nine affects, the negative affect of shame-humiliation possesses some of the most potent properties capable of merging with, restraining, and/or modulating other affects.

The collusion of affects theologically often occurs, at least rhetorically, between shame and guilt. In recent decades, literature in the humanities and social sciences interested in the impact of shame has sought to make distinctions between guilt and shame as affective experiences. Furthermore, while some scholars, like Tomkins, believe that the distinction between shame and guilt at the initial visceral level is subtle,[33] recent research in affect theory, pharmacology, and neuroscience, such as research by Tangney, Dearing, and Schore, has identified guilt and shame as distinct, particular, and unique experiences.[34] Distinguishing shame from guilt clarifies the mechanisms, logic, and impact of each.

Preverbal

Guilt can be distinguished from shame not only according to its perceivable biological, ontogenetic evolution but also according to the accompanying cognitive operations for each affect.[35] Tomkins distinguishes shame from guilt based on conscious processes that produce physiological shifts in intensity and duration. For instance, he considers the developmental trajectory for children in terms of how children process information and subsequently experience shame. Tomkins observes that vulnerability in the child to shame arises as soon as he or she learns to identify the face of the mother, or in the case of multiple caregivers—familiar faces in general. According to Tomkins, this biological response originates when a child is approximately seven months old, prior to language development, and manifests when a child's emotive response is met by displeasure from the primary caregiver.[36] For example, a child smiles, and this physical sign of pleasure or happiness evokes dissatisfaction or contradictory displeasure in the caregivers' gaze, thus evoking a shame response in the child. The observable body posture of the child usually entails one or some combination of the following: a bowed head, an averted gaze, downcast eyes, blushing, slumped shoulders, inhibited movement, and/or other behaviors that signify hiding.[37]

Ontogenetic distinctions between shame and guilt also exist; this means that in child development the genesis of shame and guilt can be differentiated.[38] Shame emerges earlier in the life cycle than guilt does. In Erik Erikson's theory of psychosocial stages, the infant encounters "crises" of shame beginning at the age of approximately 18 months, a time when the child is becoming aware of being observed, but it lacks the cognitive capacities for more advanced speech constructions. The crisis of guilt begins later, at the age of three, when a child is cognitively able to acknowledge and modify behavior.[39] At this stage of development, the child starts to understand his/her capacity to take initiative and to "do" something, but he/she also begins to realize that attached to the thing done is some qualifier; behavior is either good or bad, and the child can articulate this. In addition, the three- to five-year-old child, aware of his/her existence as an autonomous person, confronts issues of what kind of person he/she might be. Freud's work on ego development underlies Erikson's assertions, as Freud associated shame with early narcissistic conflicts, reflected in the bodily loss of the mother, and guilt with later moral ones.[40]

Children begin to experience both shame and guilt after they are able to differentiate themselves and their bodies as other from the caregiver. Self-recognition is therefore a *prerequisite* for experiencing both shame and guilt.[41] Even so, experienced prior to language development, shame represents a more "primitive" experience than guilt.[42] Therefore, while shame and guilt both require that a child be able to identify the self as distinct from the caregiver, shame occurs before the capacity to use words evolves. Guilt emerges only after a child begins to talk.

This aspect of shame as primitive and preverbal persists in the adult self. Preverbal qualities of shame reflect shame's biological nature and substantiate its immediacy; these qualities inspire a body to act before conscious processes have time to intervene. But this trajectory, along with shame as a painful, negative affect, also often results in shame's interment. The immediate sensation of shame that provokes a visceral response becomes buried in the self until the shame is repaired. The severity of the shame experience does not require language and, therefore, language alone cannot repair shame, which interred is more primal, requires more neurobiological processing, and endures longer than guilt.[43]

The Inferior Self

Where shame relates to the self, guilt results from actions. Thus, shame as a negative affect intertwines with a negative self-perception. In fact, perception of the self represents the key difference in the two experiences: in guilt the self remains unified; in shame parts of the self (or the whole self) are renounced or considered "bad" and inferior. For instance, if I commit an egregious wrong to another person, as in the case of violating another's privacy, and my sense of self is intact, I will simply apologize for having betrayed a trust. An apology can eradicate feelings of guilt. If though, in this situation, I feel shamed, I may choose not to apologize and might avoid the person or discontinue the relationship to evade the conditions for more shame.

Thus, shame relates to an individual's perception of the self, instead of, as in the case of guilt, relating to behavior. Guilt, while experienced internally, emerges when an action or behavior falls outside of what the "I" perceives as good, moral, or accepted. Thus, the *manner* of conducting oneself is criticized. Where guilt and shame often become confused or conflated is when shame underlies feelings of guilt about behavior. Thus, guilt as the result of a wrong action, as an emotional response to an apparent mistake or wrongdoing, distinguishes itself from shame, which implies no standard of comparison as distinct from having done something wrong or right. Instead, shame points to some wrong inherent and inescapable in the self.

Shame's incommensurability is met with guilt's predictability. Moreover, the experience of shame precipitates a lowered sense of self-worth, while an act of apparent wrongdoing precipitates a feeling of remorse. In essence then, shame relates to value placed upon the self, while guilt relates to value placed upon behavior. This distinction becomes more apparent and needed as the guilt-ethic continues to be a source for pedagogy within the Christian tradition.

Tomkins asserts a primary difference between shame and guilt when he relates guilt to morality and choices about moral matters unidentifiable by the infant.[44] Guilt about morality or directives about behavior require more advanced cognitive processes which exceed an infant's capacities. For instance, a child in guilt cognitively associates wrong action with behavior; however, in shame, a child responds even before he/she acquires the ability to reason between right and wrong. Furthermore, guilt provokes the disparagement of behavior that must be perceived as transgressing an established and understood norm. Thus, developmentally and since it stems from more complex cognitive processes, guilt emerges later than shame.

Like guilt, shame can also be aroused by apparent failures or defects that appear to deviate from the norm, but these generally elicit contempt, derision, or avoidance, even if imagined; guilt, while eliciting disapproval, can be appeased by remorse.[45] Furthermore, the physiological symptoms experienced in shame occur less intensely in guilt. For instance, Darwin associated morality and the idea of God with guilt, asserting that the elicitation of guilt from an individual reflecting on a wrong action committed before an all-powerful God did not induce the physiological expressions of shame emitted through the constriction of blood vessels manifesting as blushing.[46] The acuteness of shame, along with its earlier emergence, intertwines with a particular logic, if a somewhat tragic one: "If I disappear, then no one will see me, and my shame will go away."[47] This is the logic developed even in some interpretations of Genesis. Adam and Eve experience shame for their nakedness and run to hide from God.

This biblical description of the response in shame to hide, along with the notion that shame implies an experience of the inferior self in the eyes of another, locates shame's transpiration in what can be called a logic of exposure. Being seen when we perceive ourselves as inferior—or in shame—magnifies the shame experience. Being exposed we are vulnerable, and, thus, we are vulnerable to shame.

The idea that one disappears in shame, escaping the sight of the other, emerges in Tangney and Dearing's research, which distinguishes guilt-prone individuals from those who are shame-prone based on stable or unstable self-attributions related to behavior. In the case of guilt, individuals concentrate on some kind of committed act involving more "internal, specific, and fairly unstable attributions."[48] To illustrate the point, Tangney and Dearing use the example of a guilt-prone woman who cheats on her boyfriend, a specific behavior about which she takes responsibility. She discerns the causes of her cheating and lack of truthfulness as variable and internally processes these in a way that considers her behavior as context specific. She does not perceive herself as promiscuous or disloyal. Alternatively, shame focuses on a global, enduring, inferior self and thus involves "internal, stable, and global attributions."[49] Tangney and Dearing explain the shame-prone individual response to the same indiscretion: cheating.

> A young man in similar circumstances (cheating on his girlfriend) may feel an acute sense of shame – feeling disgraceful and small, wanting to hide, even disappear. Focusing on *himself*, he knows he is responsible (an internal attribution). Moreover, he views the causes of this transgression as likely to affect many aspects of his life, as characteristic of the type of person he is – disloyal, untrustworthy, immoral, even reprehensible! In short, he makes attributions to quote fundamental features of himself that have much broader implications beyond the specific transgression at hand (global attributions). Finally, he views these factors as persisting across time (stable attributions); he'll be facing the same character flaws tomorrow, and the next day and the next.[50]

The shame-prone individual experiences a diminished sense of self in relation to another that is pervasive and long lasting. Instead of being focused on a contingent and dependent act, the shame-prone individual internalizes and overgeneralizes an act that defines his/her state as deficient. Deficiency is understood first through the body; shame "turns itself inside out"[51] exposing the self, eliciting the desire to hide, back away, or isolate. The distinction between shame-prone verses guilt-prone individuals also raises questions about the usefulness of the guilt-ethic in the Christian tradition to prohibit violence, the root of which is shame.[52]

Since guilt does not have the same quality of defining self-worth as shame does, it compels more constructive behavior instead of leading to destructive judgmental behaviors toward the self and others.[53] However, guilt that masks shame, or is misidentified as shame, poses the same problems as shame does. Guilt not conflated with shame can generally be repaired through restitution; often a simple apology can discharge and heal guilt. However, if guilt is left to fester without repair and remuneration, it intensifies and turns into shame, which cannot be resolved or treated through penance.[54]

Thus, shame requires an intervention that involves dissolution of the perception of the inferior self, the restoration of dignity or self-worth, and the repair of broken attachment bonds. If the encounter with shame occurs at the moment of its emergence as a form of immediate intervention, in the form of empathetic connection, shame diminishes. However, unaddressed and dysregulated shame becomes interred in the body and ultimately deleterious. As a result, unlike guilt assuaged by restitution, or a simple "I am sorry," the amelioration of shame requires reattachment, or the promise of a "return to interest, joy, and connection."[55]

Attachment

The narcissistic conflict related to a child's efforts to distinguish him/herself from others, such as the mother or another caregiver, requires what recent researchers of affect theory and developmental psychology call "attachment."[56] Attachment constitutes the instinctual and reflexive behavior of the infant to connect to the caregiver. Attachment manifests in the experience of the shame affect through interest-excitement. The infant cannot experience shame without the presence of interest-excitement and the instinctual urge to connect. The initial shock of shame occurs, according to Tomkins, when the affect of interest-excitement is interrupted but not completely terminated.[57] In other words, the infant pursues attachment to the caregiver, and somehow connection is truncated. Therefore, a general attachment to, or interest in, an object or event is a necessary precondition for the shame experience.[58] The partial curtailing of attachment or interest evokes shame, but attachment to the object, and in this case the caregiver, remains.

Shame is thus predicated upon a relationship to the other where the self (the child), as Helen Block Lewis asserts, "cares" about the other's (the caregiver's) opinion.[59] Here, she presents the nature of most human exchanges, including those within the therapeutic encounter or that occur on theological stages between the believer and God, or between the congregant and the minister/priest. Within these, shame emerges as the "self's vicarious experience of the other's real or imagined negative evaluation," which is more viscerally potent than guilt.[60] Lewis emphasizes the self as a target of attack in shame, in both the "visual and verbal imaging of the 'I' from the other's imagined point of view,"[61] locating shame again within a logic of exposure.

The imagined disapproval of the other provokes the shame affect marking shame's "transition from a preexisting positive state to a negative state."[62] Mediated by the parasympathetic nervous system, shame functions like a "brake" to excited arousal states. Shame floods the body and transforms excited joy into something sober, or completely shuts down the body's capacity to act. Any threat to the self can trigger shame. For survivors of trauma such triggers are numerous and extremely detrimental. In general though, just as fear and its physiological correlates are integral components of the response when the physical self is threatened, shame and its accompanying physiology are constituent components of a coordinated psychobiological response triggered when the social self is threatened.[63]

To believe that the self is threatened can evoke multiple affective phenomena. The shame affect marks the experience as distinctly oppositional to joy, but it does not erase joy, or any other positive affect. Instead, shame lets us know that the possibility of joy, or connection to another that brings joy, is still a possibility, even if the social situation communicates otherwise. Thus, we can interpret shame as it related to the fear of annihilation. This fear or dread accompanies the unbearable pain of shame often experienced in situations of trauma, surfacing when the self experiences abandonment or the threat of abandonment. Actual or anticipated loss of the other, imagined other, or even part of the self instigates the terror of death. A deep sense of shame arises as a result of perceiving oneself as vulnerable, helpless, and powerless in the face of this potential, even if imagined, permanent destruction.

Fear of annihilation ultimately indicates the existence of a perceived or real threat. The amygdala moderates the biological feedback loop that relates to self-preservation in the face of such threat. When it recognizes danger, even psychic danger, the amygdala activates arousal systems.[64] The amygdala is also "involved in the regulation of cortisol arousal, and it controls bodily responses (behavioral, autonomic, endocrine), which then provide feedback that can influence cortisol processing indirectly."[65] Research has shown that shame increases the stress hormones cortisol and ACTH (adrenocorticotropic hormone), while inhibiting the health of the immune system through pro-inflammatory cytokine activity.[66] The result—a body in shame is not only poised for the flight, fight, freeze response of intolerable fear and stress, but it also is susceptible to greater incidences of physical illness.[67] Such evidence points to another distinction between shame and guilt: neural activity in both hemispheres of the brain is greater in real or imagined conditions of shame.[68] The body works assiduously interring the experience of shame.

Part of the body's diligence at avoiding shame includes its ambivalence in attachment situations. While shame impartially truncates the interest-excitement of connection, thus leaving the residue of desired connection, it also provokes a rejection of connection. In this state of turmoil, the self becomes flooded and overwhelmed by affect. Connection to another, or attachment, facilitates affective regulation, or at least within a modeling dyad, teaches an individual how to regulate him/herself. Thus, in part, success in shame's regulation occurs due to the presence of a safe and secure place for a shamed person to attach. This can happen within the therapeutic environment, where part of the therapeutic endeavor entails revealing the relationship between shame and threatened attachment. Intense shame responses point to a lack of healthy or what is called secure attachment in the caregiver-infant dyad. In order to regulate such shame, understanding that the caregiver's response or lack of response to shame in early childhood contributes to its interment is critical to recovery and the development of an embodied process to regulate shame stress states.[69] The role of the therapist is often to teach the individual to regulate shame that has become so interred in the body.

Although this sounds simple, addressing shame, especially that which emerges as a result of a failure of a caregiver to respond to the child in shame, that is to convey empathy, is an exceedingly onerous task. The child as a result of interring shame experiences psychopathological development.[70] In addition, lack of empathy in a caregiver perpetuates shame in the child, and this experienced shame further inhibits the child's capacity for empathy thus contributing to the manifestation of aggressive or violent impulses.[71] According to Gilligan, all drives toward self-preservation, including attachment to others, disappear "when one approaches the point of being so overwhelmed by shame that one can only preserve one's self (as a psychological entity) by sacrificing one's body (or those of others)."[72] As a result, where guilt can lead to the amelioration of a situation, shame can worsen a situation primarily because of its inhibitory qualities; in a way, shame handicaps the functioning (Christian) self and returns him/her to the state of the preverbal infant, interring shame. These complications lead Gilligan to refute the role of shame as producing positive changes in behavior; in fact, he sees shame as foundational for all violence. Other research on shame supports its link to violent behavior manifested in outward violence, self-mutilation, drug addiction, eating disorders, and suicide.[73] The shame experience that Gilligan addresses is the interred shame of self-worthlessness that fears the turn toward the other in vulnerability, which Léon Wurmser expresses as the feeling in shame of "not worth being loved and respected."[74] The feeling of not being loved elicits shame that cannot be tolerated, and so the process of interment begins if it has not already done so.

The diminishment of self-worth and lack of love in shame engenders a physiological response that signals, at least initially, withdrawal from others; yet, the amelioration of shame actually requires attachment to others.[75] Thus, a dynamic within the shame structure includes the inhibition of empathy and hiding from exposure. Shame interrupts what Schulte-Rüther et al. establish as the three core aspects involved in maintaining empathy, "(i) an intuitive feeling of having something in common with the other person which relies on socially shared emotional experiences; (ii) cognitive mechanisms of perspective-taking; and (iii) the ability to maintain a self—other distinction during interpersonal interaction."[76]

While shame disturbs this empathetic connection, which includes exposure, the connection itself counteracts shame. Based on the psychological inferences one person makes about another person's mental and emotional states "occurring within a specific social context," empathetic connection provides opportunity for repair.[77] Shame inhibits empathy and empathetic connection because the inferior self does not feel worthy of connection with the other. People prone to guilt do not share this experience; in guilt, no low sense of self-worth inhibits connection to others.[78] In fact, whereas shame impairs empathy and negatively influences social skills, guilt facilitates empathic responses.[79]

Thus, shame severs the ability to form social connections, disenabling cognitive processes that allow for perspective and interfering with the maintenance of boundaries between the self and the other. The crucial component illustrative of the physiological havoc that shame plays on the body is that shame arrests empathy, both self and other directed.[80]

The Severing

The affect of contempt-disgust that Tomkins identifies closely associates, as guilt does, with shame. Disgust and shame-humiliation correspond so intimately that teasing them apart proves difficult, especially in the experience of self-contempt, evoked by the perception of a lack of self-worth. Distinguishing disgust from shame and defining the biological nature of disgust highlights the dynamism between the two affects and shows how disgust modulates and amplifies shame. From this interchange, an example of the severing of attachment that constitutes shame emerges.

Disgust has been shown to play an important evolutionary role in human existence. As an affect closely associated with the hunger drive, contempt-disgust signals to the brain the presence of some object that could be harmful to life.[81] Shared with the lower animals, those with more primitive characteristics than humans or other mammals, the affect communicates a warning, a signal, of danger and potential harm in the consummation of a specific object. The message of contempt-disgust is one of restraint followed by rejection. Transformed from its evolutionary role to protect an organism from consuming something dangerous, contempt-disgust relates to the human experience of shame.

Disgust for things that are not taken into the mouth is more complex than those inspired by consumption. When we feel disgusted by something that we are not ingesting, we are alerted to the presence of shame. Disgust of this sort surfaces when a stimulus characteristic of an object is similar to what we associate with other disgusting objects or is similar to other disgusting objects produced by similar associations related to an underlying paradoxical wish. This wish comprises a dual desire to incorporate a certain object and also to maximize the distance from the said object.[82] When an unfamiliar object seems similar to something considered disgusting, that object provokes nausea generally because it shares characteristics with an evolutionarily dangerous object, and the body responds with rejection.

The desire for an object perceived as disgusting produces fear, or a wish to maximize nearness that solicits unease; when the fear surpasses desire, disgust results. In either case, disgust constitutes the rejection of something that has the potential to cause pleasure.

Not limited to its function as a defensive response, disgust is also learned. Initially, in the case of a child, learning takes place in the presence of a caregiver, who typically uses disgust to direct the behavior of the infant. Tomkins calls the caregiver who expresses disgust "the controller," or the one who attempts to reduce the affect of another.[83] Disgust manifests in a facial expression of the caregiver with the mouth turned down and the lip drawn up.[84] This physiological response to what a person finds disgusting communicates dislike and rejection; socially, as a means of distancing the self from an object, it operates to sever attachments. Damaging disgust from a caregiver toward a child creates distance between them, eliciting in the child behaviors of withdrawal and hiding indicative of shame.[85] The sequence proceeds as the child responds in shame to a caregiver's disgust, internalizing this disgust and directing it inward toward the self or outward to others. The initial signals from a caregiver indicating the child is to be regarded as disgusting transfers to the child's behavior manifesting socially as the rejection of something or someone.[86]

The caregiver-infant dyad illustrates the initial relationship between contempt-disgust and shame. Each member of the dyad relates to the other through affect, and they rely on each other for affective feedback. The caregiver expressing contempt or disgust at the child elicits shame in the child. The communication is that proper people—those who fall within the norm—do not touch, eat, drink, or behave in a particular way. The internalization of disgust provokes shame and lowered self-worth, severing attachment. But disgust can also be projected outward. If the object remains desirable, but the child has learned that it is taboo, often the fear of acquisition will trump desire and provoke disgust. The rejected object, stigmatized, also represents something shameful.

Beyond the caregiver-infant dyad, stigmas that elicit disgust and subsequent shame also exist. The model of the infant perpetuates itself in adulthood, in any systems of learning that mean to inculcate particular selves formed by culture and society. Understanding where stigmas are evidence of cultural formation lies at the heart of Erving Goffman's work. Goffman observes two kinds of stigma, those that are "abominations of the body" and those that are of "race, nation, and religion."[87] What is considered disgusting is prompted by an awareness of difference, where the norm, as universal or positive attributes, is set up against what is not the norm, particular or negative attributes. Initially, the caregiver establishes norms. Secondarily, culture, society, and religion determine the normal and the not normal, disgusting, shameful. Martha Nussbaum addresses the propensity of society through the law, and other organizing systems, to establish what lies outside of the norm and therefore constitutes disgust: "We use the idea of disgust of the 'reasonable man' to identify acts that may be (or should be) legally regulated."[88]

Social ordinances and religious prescriptions established by the "reasonable man" often merge in systems that reflect power, hierarchy, and domination. These stratified structures establish and identify the disgusting in order to arouse shame. The systems harmonize in a unique way, functioning as caregivers do when they assume the role of "controllers" of affect. Modulating affect through signaling disgust succeeds and is sustained socially because humans share similar visceral, affective, precognitive responses to stimuli. The shared factor exists in the body, specifically the biological experiences of shame and disgust.[89] When shame results provoked by disgust, it inhibits an individual's agency, severs his/her attachments, and enables hegemonic structures to exert control. This kind of social control makes an impact on every level of society dictating the disgusting and evoking shame. As with other kinds of affects, disgust assists in the formation of a certain way of being in the world, one that is both dispositional, or internalized, and manifest.[90] Culturally and socially, disgust helps to concretize shame.

Shame is a complicated experience evoked when we conclude that we are misperceived and treated as something or someone disgusting. We understand this perception as representing something antithetical to us, or representing someone that we believe is antithetical to us but that may also signify some part of self that we find disgusting, what Julia Kristeva calls the "abject" in ourselves.[91] This abjection rests in the image of a foreigner, a criminal, a particular personality type, even a dying person. Defining shame as a reaction to the meeting of the personal "I" with the misperception of that "I" through the eyes of another complicates shame. Shame distinguished from a subjective emotional experience like feeling fear or satisfaction resists the logic of symptomatology.[92] In the experience of shame, a person has difficulty knowing and differentiating cause from effect and feels ashamed for feeling shame. As Timothy Bewes states, "shame seeks to hide itself, and yet it is nothing if not manifest."[93]

Shame seeks to hide itself, to sever attachments, because shame itself presents as disgusting. In addition, the perception of being disgusting elicits shame. Disgust, thus, indicates precisely what must be hidden or cut off. Disgust communicates and classifies the shameful, which transpires because it comes into view. As disgust evades its evolutionary role to assume a social function, it ultimately interferes with and prohibits relationship building because it serves, in part, to sever attachments to people and objects. The person in shame and disgusting (to him/herself and others), thus isolated, finds no avenue for repair, and shame becomes subsequently interred in the body.

The Interminable Spirals of Shame

Shame can be best expressed as the body's physiological and embodied response to stimuli, frequently but not always related to trauma, in what Thomas J. Scheff calls an "interminable spiral."[94] The spiral of shame indicates how the body's response to internal shame reinforces the brain's experience of shame whether through additional shame or through rage. The shame response compounds in layers; it is stratified so much so that the originary shame becomes eclipsed and concealed, interred and denied. For Tomkins, shame—as do all affects—operates on the principle of contagion.[95] The language of affect as "contagion" implies that shame spreads until it is arrested, interfering with and dis-easing internal processes engendering the interminable spiral of shame and other similarly deleterious effects. This quality of shame inspires us to deny it or run from it, but paradoxically this actually increases the tendency of shame while often deteriorating into violence.

The shame experience thus has several progressions. Shame leads to more shame. To protect ourselves we deny connection and perpetuate shame as we deny the possibility of alleviating shame. Often this denial takes the form of violence, a radical attempt to restore self-worth, shame's opposite. These cycles are made worse by the failure to address guilt. Often guilt precedes the shame experience, which, when unaddressed, transforms into shame.

Envisioning shame in terms of two cycles, shame for shame and shame for rage preceded by guilt, Gerhart Piers and Milton B. Singer describe patterned shame behavior as falling within either the realm of sexuality or the realm of hostility; these repetitious sequences show how shame influences the most essential levels of being,[96] figuring into the discussion of Augustine and Niebuhr in later chapters. The first cycle begins with a sexual impulse that contrasts with modes of expected behavior, engages with guilt, and often becomes labeled as "sin." Social norms, laws, and religious doctrine determine the sexually normative and, as mentioned, the disgusting or shame-faced. So when we engage in an act that exceeds the normative, whatever that might be, we might experience guilt, but if this guilt perpetuates itself, shame results. Transgression of boundaries set up by institutions leads to guilt, and then finally, to inhibition or regression. If the guilt of transgression goes unaddressed, it becomes internalized as shame. The sense of having committed a violation or wrongdoing in guilt becomes part of self-definition when it goes unrepaired or ameliorated by remorse or apology. Festering and transmuting into shame, guilt for wrongdoing assimilated into the self invokes the depraved, unworthy self. Feeling sorry for the original infraction turns into disparagement of the self in shame, which fails to inhibit the behavior,[97] but rather leads to more acting out, and the guilt-shame cycle repeats itself.

Cycles of hostility include a similar progression: aggression leads to guilt then the subsequent inhibition of aggression. The resulting passivity morphs into shame, which manifests as over-compensatory aggression and then further guilt.[98] Gilligan's work with incarcerated men who express that they use violence to denounce their own shame illustrates and dramatizes this cycle. As he explains, the aim for these men is to restore what they see as shame's opposite: pride.[99] Like Gilligan, Scheff sees that shame and rage relate, stating, "at the core of this issue is the phenomenon of having emotional reactions to one's emotional reactions."[100] For Scheff, this includes feeling shame, rage, and subsequently experiencing shame for feeling rage. Shame and rage become intertwined, and the person in shame and rage feels further shame for having the feeling. Wurmser calls this the "the well-known endless sequence of shame about shame."[101] These cycles manifest dysregulated shame, and shame that is evoked but not repaired increases or maintains levels of symptomatic behavior.[102] Thus, shame has a propensity to emerge in some context or another, if intervention fails to occur.

Interred Shame

Because of affects' nature as energy from the body, the surge or submergence of affects like shame can cause deleterious effects especially if they remain in the body unconsciously processed. Shame's positive nature of signifying attachment morphs into destructivity when shame goes unacknowledged. Failing to address shame leads to shame's interment in the self. As physiological and visceral, the management of shame proves challenging, especially because, as a painful affect, people tend to want to will shame away, ignoring it or attempting to conceal it with other affects or pride. As mentioned, repressed, disregarded shame, shame interred in the body, can be expected to cause a rift or a problem, especially an internal problem.

Avoidance of shame precipitates its interment in the form of cycles or spirals. As mentioned, the unpleasant experience of shame often elicits more shame, especially when preceded by guilt or perpetuated by rage. The cyclical nature of shame, that shame induces more shame whether of itself or first perambulating through guilt or rage, manifests in trauma survivors as disturbing forms of repetition compulsion.[103] Understood generally as a psychological phenomenon, repetition compulsion comprises the repetition of a traumatic experience by a survivor of trauma, at least symbolically. Characterized by denial, concealment, and isolation, and part of a dialectical system ensconced with corruption and malevolence, repetition compulsion assumes the role of what Sue Grand terms a "malignant dissociative contagion."[104] Whoever represents the initial corruption claims domination and makes "claims to the truth" that confuse reality and seduce the person harmed into a complicated association that repeats trauma and perpetuates shame.[105]

The voice that claims truth represents the voice of the perpetrator or dominator, but the initial role of destruction lies in persons and systems that both deny and reinforce shame promoting its interment. Silence emerging from the embroilment between the person being harmed and the perpetrator supports this process. Unnamed, unarticulated shame inters itself in bodies, and silence thus becomes a weapon of destruction. Silence around shame inculcated in systems of dominance and control leaves survivors splitting themselves, hiding their shame, and at the same time incapable of escaping its deleterious physical effects.

While shame is a part of all of us, in some, shame is very damaging. For instance, when trauma happens in childhood, especially in the family of origin, when violence disrupts relationships based on trust and love, a child is left shamed, helpless, and often silenced. His/her deep shame at the impartial disconnection from the caregiver lays the foundation for interred shame. Pathologies centered on acquiring safety replace empathetic modes of being, and shame inhabits the body, truncating the possibility for further empathic connection. More trauma correlates with more repetition of that trauma, just as interred shame contributes to more shame. Furthermore, traumatic situations in the family of origin disrupt healthy attachment necessary for the regulation of shame. To be unconnected, or vulnerable, equates to being weak, mortal, and shamed; this is the perpetual place of the targeted victim in many kinds of trauma; vulnerable, ostracized, and potentially stigmatized or shamed, the survivor confronts feelings of inferiority and shame. The sense of wholeness, or ability to tolerate vulnerability, that emerges in situations of successful attachment fails to evolve. Shame becomes a multilayered state of existence, too painful to face, and therefore, shame becomes interred.

The interment of shame constitutes an almost natural phenomenon, even outside of situations of trauma. The affective experience of shame marks vulnerability and self-exposure that, instead of exploring to facilitate attachment, people often deny or evade. Nussbaum confirms this when she aligns shame with the "primitive," what is connected to infantile demands for omnipotence, encapsulated in the idea of a "general neediness and vulnerability."[106] Her sense of primitive shame emerges from the defeat of the narcissistic infant in Tomkins' work, whose shame at rejection lies in the reality of his/her body as vulnerable but craving connection with the caregiver.[107] Shame situates itself at this juncture between the self and the other as it implicates attachment and severs attachment. Shame emerges when one experiences the self as not whole and connects "to the more primitive longing for wholeness" a longing that is fulfilled in attuned relationships.[108] The reality of shame emergence and interplay in attunement provokes this exploration of a more nuanced understanding and interpretation of shame within theological anthropologies.

Shaped in Shame

Rhetoric has the power to shape not only speech and self-expression but also bodies. Affects shape bodies but how does this shaping become such a powerful mode of formation? Drawing on Pierre Bourdieu's work on *habitus* and Tomkins' script architecture in affect theory helps to clarify what it means to shape bodies in shame. Further, Tomkins' interpretation of scripts elucidates the concept of embodied self-formation through his particular way of inflecting *habitus*.

Habitus

At the center of Pierre Bourdieu's philosophical work lies the assumption that individuals learn bodily. To explain this concept, Bourdieu developed the notion of *habitus*. In his view, *habitus* creates, "what has to be called an *esprit de corps*."[109] Situated between a discourse of particularity and communality, *habitus* stresses that the principle of individual action is based on the social conditions that form and exercise behavior. Thus, situated within the concept of *habitus* rests the notion that the body absorbs the social world, internalizes that world, and then reflects it. The social world in this sense shapes the body in particular way. Shaping in shame is one of these. Culturally, theologically, and socially, shame is inscribed on the body as *habitus*; it is not only an indelible mark, but once the mark is made, shame is lived into, perpetuated, and interred.[110] As a *habitus*, shame constitutes an internal state formed by the external environment the interchange through which shapes and is always shaping bodies.

Inscribed on the body, shame as a *habitus* constitutes a system of dispositions related to a person's being and doing in the world. It "seeks to create the conditions of its fulfillment," despite the specifics of the environment.[111] As such, a person will, unconsciously or outside of rational thought, repeatedly attempt to find situations that accommodate shame as a specific *habitus*. This manifests in the trauma survivor as repetition compulsion and in the various cycles or spirals of shame.

In addition, shame *habitus* is historically acquired—in families of origin or as a result of insecure attachment patterns in the child-caregiver dyad; these experiences make an impact on later adult experiences marking the body.[112] Moreover, as a *habitus* inscribed on the body by kinship and social relations, shame can "survive long after the disappearance of [its] social conditions of production."[113] Social situations and environments (familial, educational, theological) inscribe *habitus* on a body, shaping bodies, and enacting what Bourdieu calls a form of "symbolic violence."[114] More powerful than physical violence or power because of its more covert operation within social fields, symbolic violence works because it attracts the participation of both the dominant and the dominated. Symbolic violence is "gentle," "imperceptible," and often invisible, supporting the pernicious interment of shame.[115] Shaping the body is equally as imperceptible; it happens gradually related to the rhetoric and practices of the traditions people inhabit.

The rational social world represents the supreme force of symbolic violence, which Bourdieu critiques and which is made up of systems of domination illustrated by the elite. These social groups often determine what is disgusting and therefore what constitutes shame. As an internalized structure and the physical embodiment of an objective structure, shame denotes what has been communicated as disgusting in the social world.[116] Thus, the strength of a *habitus* of shame is that it merges what is spatially outside (social structures) with what is inside, erasing distinctions between the unconscious and the conscious. Bourdieu refers to art, religion, law, and politics as imposing universal categories where the dominant way of being is "tacitly," and thus unconsciously, "turned into a norm."[117] Presently, social media, including religious sources, exacerbates this phenomenon becoming part of the elite that Bourdieu critiques. For instance, when doctrine established by any elite institution constitute norms, they "brand" the not normal, and consequently the "not normal" converts to be stigmatized, disgusting, and, therefore, full of shame. Not being normal, or exceeding any functional norm, thus constitutes being in shame and thus shaped by shame.

For instance, cultural perceptions and conceptions about social and gender hierarchies that create sexual order result in "a matrix of inferiorization [that] happens in those bodies and minds that contravene the norms."[118] External stimuli shape bodies into the perceived norm. In such a process, confused awareness leads to a disregard of the intuitive affective reactions of the body itself. In such a way, affects subvert consciousness and systems of symbolic violence capitalize on this. The strength of such systems lies in how they become embedded in biology, within bodies, according to affects and gender, respectively. Lodged this way in the body makes systems of violence nearly invulnerable. When symbolic power shapes bodies, a loss ensues: a loss of autonomy, self-hood, and individuality. This loss manifests as shame: perceiving oneself as something other than he/she knows him/herself to be.

Being shaped in shame also constitutes, according to the idea of *habitus*, interring shame in the body. In his work on Christian formation and Christian speech, Mark D. Jordan articulates this enigma stating that what is more difficult for Christian homosexuals than their being stigmatized by society is their having "absorbed into themselves the shame of the old traditions."[119] Thus, Jordan argues that changing the criminal laws will not erase shame, especially because religious teaching takes place both near home and at home, and not just in removed councils and church committees.[120] Inscribed on the body as a powerful *habitus*, Christian tradition and accompanying practices function as powerful mechanisms in the shaping of the Christian self.[121]

Thus, shame as interred and cyclical within the body can be perceived as a disposition of the body, a *habitus*. Shame not only perpetuates itself in the body as further shame from feeling of shame, but it is also, as Jordan mentions, absorbed into the body and lives into and is perpetuated within families, groups, and societies. The concept of *habitus* facilitates an understanding of the absorption of shame and its subsequent interment in the body. Once buried and perpetuated, shame becomes an affective means of orientating individuals to the world.

Developing a *habitus* requires repetition that not necessarily be intentional. The recurrence of the action that inscribes *habitus* on the body can be conceptualized affectively through the notion of scripts. A heading displayed on the website for the Tomkins Institute reads, "What we learn from affects becomes programmed as scripts which govern our behavior."[122] The concept of "scripts" typically refers to a set of ordering principles that translate, evaluate, anticipate, and manage scenes, the smallest unit of life experience. Scenes, for Tomkins, resemble photographs or images of past experiences. Either habitual or transient, scenes connect to each other, resulting in magnification into scripts and then into the plot of one's life.[123] The script does not deal with every scene but solidifies according to the power affect affords it. Scripts are thus reinforced by affect despite whether or not they constellate around every specific scene. Shame as a script that governs behavior is highly problematic.

In accordance with Tomkins' nine innate affect pairs, scripts are continually shaped, modulated, confirmed, or reworked by each other and according to particular stimuli. Like *habitus* written on the body, scripts illustrate a particular story composed by affects such as shame that dramatize particular sequences and organizations of affect. Further, scripts are both learned and shaped according to conditioning over time. For example, initially a baby's crying and flailing in distress resulting from hunger represents behavior inspired by a basic urge; however, after learning that crying results in being fed, a child will cry to solicit food to appease hunger.

Shame can also be reinforced by scripts according to how the caregiver responds to the child in shame. Take for instance the toddler attracted to an electric wall outlet. The child cannot resist the temptation to insert a finger into the open space. The caregiver yells to stop the child, and the response might be slumped shoulders and an immediate lack of muscle tension. The child falls to the ground and cries. How the caregiver responds to this reaction of the child can alleviate or reinforce shame scripts. What is important to note is that this scene, whether or not it is shaming for the child, does not itself inter shame. At this point the effect is *indeterminate*.[124] Determinacy results when the future happens, either magnifying or attenuating such experience. Does the caregiver proceed toward the child and engage in affect regulation and soothing? Or is there additional shaming, such as a demand not to cry? Either response begins to lay a foundation for a script; the latter is inherently more shame ridden.

Also important to note is that any experience that reinforces shame is not singular but plural. Script theory accounts for what Tomkins calls "the principle of *plurideterminancy*" accounting for not one effect but for many that change with time.[125] The effect of an experience perpetuates future experience, expanding into scripts related to repeated behavior that coagulate according to memory, language, or culturally derived scripts. This leads to Tomkins' third principle; "Scenes are magnified not by repetition, but by repetition with a *difference*."[126] The same scene repeated becomes assimilated, regulated, integrated, and attenuated, for good or for ill. A similar scene rather than the same scene reinforces a particular script. Thus, scripts are incomplete and rely on auxiliary information to form them. In addition, repeated and perpetuated scripts in a person's life generally confirm rather than disaffirm experience.

Shame can be conceptualized as including a set of four alternative scripts, creating what Nathanson calls a "compass of shame."[127] A different script is located at each directional point on the compass. The oppositional points on the compass constitute what he terms the "poles of shame." There are four poles, which serve as information centers for our behavior cumulating the most potent affect management scripts from which we draw.[128] The first pole includes withdrawal or avoidance scripts; the second pole includes "attack other" and "attack self" scripts. All points of the compass interrelate in a kind of grand narrative. The withdrawal and avoidance scripts manifest in two kinds of behavior: violence directed inward, toward the self, or violence directed outward, toward another.[129]

The compass of shame accounts for violence, sexuality, and shame itself. For instance, shame not only leads to withdrawal from a specific behavior, but shame can also lead to an intensification of that behavior. Violence in general relates to shame varying only in direction—toward the self or toward other. The deterioration of shame into other-directed violence has garnered attention from scholarly research, yet the critical aspect of self-directed violence as a result of shame should also be highlighted. Violence toward the self manifests as submission, docility, condescension, and self-flagellation, or self-defeating behaviors.

The compass construction of shame illustrates how we store the response mechanism to a particular scene or script. The repeated stimulation of affect by similar scenes further strengthens these scripts. Stimulated or triggered by the environment, affects motivate the return to stored behaviors and words to access and then express the response to a particular trigger. Serving like a bridge that connects the body to the mind in a biological feedback loop, affects become dependable.[130] Through repetition, affects strengthen and then dependably appear when triggered. Affects solidify scenes, key components of the feedback loop that constructs scripts. The figuration of particular scripts mirrors *habitus* in that each consists of constellated affects modulated, reinforced, and inscribed as dispositions onto bodies. In order to escape from distinct scripts or a particular shame *habitus*, relearning or reprogramming must occur. For Bourdieu, altering an ingrained *habitus* requires practice of something contraindicative of that *habitus*. For Tomkins, scripts must be altered, and transformation takes place first at the level of affect.

This consideration of *habitus* and scripts provides a means for understanding how the affect of shame operates to shape the self. In addition, this elucidation of the how habitus and scripts generated by families, institutions, organizations, and external stimuli shapes bodies introduces a lens through which theological rhetoric and practice accomplish similar shaping, contributing to the formation of the Christian self in shame.

Conclusion

Addressed and explored at the intersection of psychology, neuroscience, and critical theory through affect theory, shame emerges as an influential and potent affect. Characterized by its unpredictability and immediacy, shame influences a body's capacity to act and its capacity to function fully in the unconscious unrecognized by conscious processes. But, first, shame presents itself as a natural, physiological experience.

As an affect, shame makes its initial impact on the body in several ways through scenes, scripts, and as a *habitus*. Preverbal and primal, shame's biological influence on the body ratifies it as a powerful and intimidating modulator of behavior. Shame motivates the body to hide or go inward, to seek some shelter from what is perceived as dangerous, or conversely to explode in anger, to lash out, to violate another body. Shame, masked by guilt, also inhibits empathy, blocking the human experience that enables the development of compassion. Critical in forming interpersonal, familial, and cultural bonds, empathy fosters shame's reparation while it also relates to self-care. When it is nullified by shame, empathy wavers and cannot be accessed to facilitate repair.

The difficulty this chapter and subsequent chapters address relates to the ability to see how shame emerges in the body according to how society, culture, and Christianity have constructed it. It is from this theoretical terrain that the exploration of Christian texts and practice proceeds. The challenge to address shame increases because shame embedded in other affective experiences easily eludes comprehension. Modulated by disgust, preverbal shame, often concealed by other affects including guilt, lies beneath perceptions of the self as humble, vulnerable, and weak. As a result of the inherent difficulties in identifying shame, in distinguishing shame from guilt, and in understanding disgust's function in shame's development, the body continues to be shaped and profoundly influenced by shame.

To summarize, shame, while inherent and present for all, manifests in the belief that the self or parts of the self are inferior. Shame thus not only has deleterious effects on the body, but it also interferes with empathic connections. When other affects conceal shame, it becomes interred in the body, inhibiting the potential for repair through attachment and instead becoming a self-perpetuating *habitus*. Ruptured by shame spirals and trauma-induced cycles, attuned attachment fails to form. When shame operates without amelioration, it interferes with both connections to the other and to God. The Christian self in shame turns away from these connections, which paradoxically operate to ameliorate shame.

Theology as a socially relevant practice has a responsibility to those of us who experience shame, who are vulnerable to dysregulation, and who live in dysregulated states, alternating between maladaptive behaviors of withdrawal, avoidance, and violence. This responsibility includes thinking about and naming shame with the aim of engaging in practices that facilitate the acknowledgement that shame operates innately in the body pointing toward that to which people are most connected. Attention to innate shame's function would begin to disinter shame, fostering love, and attuned attachment rather than perpetuating cycles of toxic shame, domination, and violence. In this way, instead of the perpetuation of shame or trauma, something radically different could result. The more attention theology devotes to understanding shame's role in fostering or severing attachment to others and to God as well as to comprehending its function in contributing to motivational structures of violence, the more capable tradition and practice will be at nurturing the whole self, in whom shame plays a natural part.

Notes

1. "Dysregulation" is generally a psychological term used to describe emotions or affects that do not fall within a specific range, but it has become more recently employed by Alan Schore in *Affect Regulation and the Origin of the Self.* Much scholarship is currently being conducted in the area of attachment, within and outside of affect theory, although Nathanson argues that since attachment involves affect regulation, the two cannot be separated, see *Pride and Shame*, 217–235. Research has also been conducted by Janina Fisher on attachment, affect regulation and dysregulation, and attunement, see "Sensorimotor Approaches to Trauma Treatment," *Advances in Psychiatric Treatment* vol. 17, no. 3 (2011).
2. Nathanson, *Shame and Pride*, 61 and 73.
3. Work on distinguishing guilt from shame has been done extensively through various analytic or theoretical approaches. Since I am viewing guilt and shame through affect theory, I draw from Tomkins, who does not distinctly call guilt an affect, although he includes it under the umbrella of the shame-humiliation affect, stating that each marks different experiences, aligning guilt with morality, see *Affect, Imagery, Consciousness*, 351. Nathanson follows Tomkins, aligning guilt with morality and distinguishing it from an affect per se in that it is released by a confessional system, see *Pride and Shame*, 19; Schore asserts that more research tracing the ontogenetic course of shame needs to be conducted, but that shame and guilt can be distinguished presently ontogenetically, see *Affect Regulation and Repair of the Self*, 151. I will continually distinguish them throughout this project based on somatic consequence of each, aligned cognitive process, ontogeny, and repair.
4. Lewis, "Introduction: Shame," 21–26; Scheff, "The Shame-Rage Spiral," 109; Herman, *Trauma and Recovery*, 64–70, 105, and 189; and Gilligan, *Violence: Reflections on a National Epidemic*, 110–114.
5. Sedgwick and Frank, *Shame and Its Sisters*, 11.
6. See Adrian Johnston and Catherine Malabou, *Self and Emotional Life: Philosophy, Psychoanalysis, and Neuroscience* (New York: Columbia University Press, 2013) and their use of the word "organism," 30.
7. Tomkins, *Affect, Imagery, Consciousness*, 135.
8. Tomkins, *Affect, Imagery, Consciousness*, 115.
9. Tomkins, *Affect, Imagery, Consciousness*, 123–133.
10. Tomkins, *Affect, Imagery, Consciousness*, 97.
11. Brian Massumi, *Parables of the Virtual: Movement, Affect, Sensation* (Durham, Duke University Press, 2002), 28.
12. Donald Nathanson, prologue to *Affect, Imagery, Consciousness*, vols. 3 and 4, by Silvan Tomkins (New York: Springer Publishing Company, 2008), xxii; see also Sedgwick and Frank, *Shame and Its Sisters*, 179–188.

13. Tomkins, *Affect, Imagery, Consciousness,* 49–50.
14. Antonio Damasio, *The Feeling of What Happens: Body and Emotion in the Making of Consciousness* (Orlando: Harcourt, 1999), 342.
15. Tomkins, *Affect, Imagery, Consciousness,* 351.
16. Tomkins, *Affect, Imagery, Consciousness,* 387.
17. See Paul Sartre's, *Being and Nothingness,* trans. Hazel E. Barnes (New York: Washington Square Press, 1993) and Bernard William's *Shame and Necessity,* 219–220.
18. Allan Schore, *Affect Regulation and the Origin of the Self* (Hillsdale, New Jersey: Lawrence Erlbaum Associates, Publishers, 1994), 7.
19. Schore, *Affect Regulation and the Origin of the Self,* 26 and 178–9.
20. Schore, *Affect Regulation and the Origin of the Self,* 281.
21. Schore, *Affect Regulation and the Origin of the Self,* 192, and 243–44.
22. Schore, *Affect Regulation and the Origin of the Self,* 32–33.
23. Clough and Halley, *The Affective Turn*, 232, and Gregg and Seigworth, *Affect Theory Reader*, 5.
24. Brian Massumi, "Autonomy of Affect," *Cultural Critique,* no. 31 (1995): 83–109.
25. Benedict de Spinoza, *The Ethics,* trans. and ed. Edwin Curley (London: Penguin Books, 1996), 113.
26. Spinoza, *Ethics,* 112.
27. Gilles Deleuze and Félix Guattari, *A Thousand Plateaus: Capitalism and Schizophrenia*, trans. Brian Massumi (Minneapolis: University of Minnesota Press, 1987), xvii.
28. Massumi, *Parables of the Virtual,* 28.
29. Lauren Berlant, "Eve Sedgwick, Once More," *Critical Inquiry* vol. 35, no. 4 (2009): 1090.
30. Lauren Berlant, *Sex, or the Unbearable,* (Durham: Duke University Press, 2013), 41.
31. Lauren Berlant, *The Queen of America,* (Durham: Duke University Press, 2013), 102.
32. Tomkins, *Affect, Imagery, Consciousness,* 76.
33. See Kaufman and Raphael, *Coming Out of Shame,* and Elspeth Probyn, *Blush: Faces of Shame* (Minneapolis: University of Minnesota Press, 2005).
34. See Tangney and Dearing, *Shame and Guilt.* Their work has contributed to much of the current understanding of the differences psychologically between shame and guilt evidenced by the Test of Self-Conscious Affect (TOSCA) first developed in 1989. Modified several times after this publication to make adjustments for age, the test measures shame-proneness or guilt-proneness in individuals and is known for its foundation in distinguishing guilt from shame; for a general assumption of this difference see also Herman, *Trauma and Recovery,* Gilligan, *Violence,* and Nathanson, *Shame and Pride,* 147. Nathanson argues that pharmacological remedies for shame

and guilt differ. Even anthropological literature distinguishes the affects from each other; see Ruth Benedict, *The Chrysanthemum and the Sword.*

35. Tomkins, *Affect, Imagery, Consciousness*, 350.
36. Sedgwick and Frank, *Shame and Its Sisters*, 6; Tomkins, *Affect, Imagery, Consciousness*, 120–135.
37. Tangney and Dearing, *Shame and Guilt*, 141. See also Nathanson, *Shame and Pride*, 141; Block Lewis, "Introduction: Shame," 17; Herman, "Shattered Shame States and Their Repair," 5.
38. Tomkins, *Affect, Imagery, Consciousness*, 368; Erik Erikson, *Childhood and Society* (1950; reprint, New York: W. W. Norton and Company, 1993), 255–258; Erik Erikson, *Identity and the Life Cycle* (1959; reprint, New York: W. W. Norton and Company, 1980), 71–80.
39. Erikson, *Childhood and Society*, 255–258, and *Identity and the Life Cycle*, 71–80. See also Schore, *Affect Regulation and the Repair of the Self*, 153.
40. Freud, *Civilization and Its Discontents*, 30–34.
41. Tangney and Dearing, *Shame and Guilt*, 141.
42. Schore, *Affect Regulation and the Repair of the Self*, 153.
43. Michl et al., "Neurobiological Underpinnings of Shame and Guilt," 5.
44. Tomkins, *Affect, Imagery*, Consciousness, 351.
45. Williams, *Shame and Necessity*, 90.
46. Charles Darwin, *The Expression of Emotions in Man and Animals*, eds. Joe Cain and Sharon Messenger, (1872; reprint, London: Penguin Books, 2009), 306.
47. Williams, *Shame and Necessity*, 90.
48. Tangney and Dearing, *Shame and Guilt*, 53.
49. Tangney and Dearing, *Shame and Guilt*, 53.
50. Tangney and Dearing, *Shame and Guilt*, 53–54.
51. Sedgwick and Frank, *Touching Feeling*, 38.
52. Gilligan, *Violence*, 235–36.
53. Tangney and Dearing, *Shame and Guilt*, 137.
54. Spinoza, *Ethics*, 112.
55. Probyn, *Blush*, xiii; Block Lewis, "Introduction," 23–25.
56. Schore, *Affect Regulation and the Repair of the Self*, 165. Carol Magai and Susan H. McFadden, *The Role of Emotions in Social Personality Development: History, Theory, Research* (New York, Plenum, 1995), 40 and 41.
57. Tomkins, *Affect, Imagery, Consciousness*, 188 and 212.
58. Tomkins, *Affect, Imagery, Consciousness*, 160.
59. Block Lewis, "Introduction: Shame," 16.
60. Helen Block Lewis, "Shame and the Narcissistic Personality," in *The Many Faces of Shame*, ed. Donald L. Nathanson (New York: Guilford, 1987), 108.
61. Block Lewis, "Introduction: Shame," 17.
62. Herman, "*Shattered Shame States*," 6.

63. Dickerson, Gruenewald, and Kemeny, "When the Social Self Is Threatened," 1194.
64. Joseph E. LeDoux, "Emotional Circuits in the Brain," *Annual Review of Neuroscience* vol. 23 (March 2000): 175.
65. LeDoux, "Emotional Circuits," 177.
66. Dickerson, Gruenewald, Kemeny, "When the Social Self Is Threatened," 1194.
67. Anda van Stegeren, Oliver Wolf, Walter Everaerd, Philip Scheltens, Frederik Barkhof, and Serge Rombouts "Endogenous Cortisol Level Interacts with Noradrenergic Activation in the Human Amygdala," *Neurobiology of Learning and Memory* vol. 87 (2007): 63.
68. Petra Michl, Thomas Meindl, Franziska Meister, Christine Born, Rolf Engel, Maximilian Reiser, and Kristina Hennig-Fast, "Neurobiological Underpinnings of Shame and Guilt: A Pilot fMRI Study," *Social Cognitive and Affective Neuroscience* (2012): 6. Their research has shown that guilt also activates the amygdala, more in men than in women. The explanation for the gender difference lies in two hypotheses: (1) that women modulate shameful memories more than guilt memories and are capable of imagining reparation more easily than men, (2) that men perceive a significance in guilt related to guilt-specific emotional consequences or strategies designed to modulate emotion. Michl et al. recognize that these differences could be provoked by socialization, gender-based upbringing, and phylogenic differences.
69. Schore, *Affect Regulation and the Repair of the Self*, 165.
70. Gilligan, *Violence*, 64 and 110. See also Bruce D. Perry and Maia Szalavitz, *The Boy Who Was Raised as a Dog* (New York: Basic Books, 2006), 99 and 204.
71. Gilligan, *Violence*, 64 and 110; Perry and Szalavitz, *The Boy Who Was Raised as a Dog*, 96–100.
72. Gilligan, *Violence*, 110.
73. Tangney and Dearing, *Shame and Guilt*, 7.
74. Wurmser, *Torment Me, but Don't Abandon Me*, 179.
75. Mary Ayers, *Mother-Infant Attachment and Psychoanalysis: The Eyes of Shame* (New York: Brunner-Routledge, 2003) 81 and 224.
76. Martin Schulte-Rüther, Hans J. Markowitsch, Gereon R. Fink, and Martina Piefke, "Mirror Neuron and Theory of Mind Mechanisms Involved in Face-to-Face Interactions: A Functional Magnetic Resonance Imaging Approach to Empathy," *Journal of Cognitive Neuroscience* vol. 19, no. 8 (2007): 1354.
77. Schulte-Rüther, Markowitsch, Fink, and Piefke, "Mirror Neuron and Theory of Mind Mechanisms," 1354.
78. Tangney and Dearing, *Shame and Guilt*, 5.
79. Tangney and Dearing, *Shame and Guilt*, 88 and 112.
80. Nathanson, *Shame and Pride*, 143.

81. Tomkins, *Affect, Imagery, Consciousness,* 28 and 357.
82. Tomkins, *Affect, Imagery, Consciousness,* 357.
83. Tomkins, *Affect, Imagery, Consciousness,* 22, 56, and 57.
84. Tomkins, *Affect, Imagery, Consciousness,* 367.
85. Tomkins, *Affect, Imagery, Consciousness,* 357.
86. Gerhart Piers and Milton B. Singer, *Shame and Guilt: A Psychoanalytic and Cultural Study* (New York: W.W. Norton and Company, 1971), 29.
87. Erving Goffman, *Stigma: Notes on the Management of Spoiled Identity* (1963; reprint, New York: Simon and Schuster, 1986), 4.
88. Martha Nussbaum, *Hiding from Humanity: Disgust, Shame and the Law* (Princeton, NJ: Princeton University Press, 2004), 86.
89. See Paul Ekman, Wallace Friesen, Maureen O'Sullivan, Anthony Chan, Irene Diacoyanni-Tarlatzis, Karl Heider, Rainer Krause, William Ayhan LeCompte, Tom Pitcairn, Pio E Ricci-Bitti, Klaus Scherer, Masatoshi Tomita, and Athanase Tzavaras. "Universals and Cultural Differences in the Judgments of Facial Expressions of Emotion," *Journal of Personality and Social Psychology* vol. 53, no. 4 (1987). This article shows that social mores determining what or who is stigmatized or disgusting changes across cultures, although facial expressions exhibited in response to disgust are similar across cultures.
90. Roy Nash, "Bourdieu on Education and Social and Cultural Reproduction," *British Journal of Sociology of Education* vol. 11 (1990), 433.
91. See Julia Kristeva, *Powers of Horror: An Essay of Abjection*, trans. Leon S. Roudiez (New York: Columbia University Press, 1982).
92. Timothy Bewes, *The Event of Postcolonial Shame* (Princeton: Princeton University Press, 2011), 23.
93. Bewes, *The Event of Postcolonial Shame,* 22.
94. Scheff, "The Shame-Rage Spiral," 109–149.
95. Tomkins, *Affect, Imagery, Consciousness,* 163.
96. Piers and Singer, *Shame and Guilt*, 31–33.
97. Tangney and Dearing, *Shame and Guilt,* 138.
98. Piers and Singer, *Shame and Guilt*, 32.
99. Gilligan, *Violence*, 47.
100. Scheff, "The Shame-Rage Spiral," 112.
101. Léon Wurmser, "Shame: The Veiled Companion of Narcissism" in *The Many Faces of Shame*, ed. Donald Nathanson (New York: Guilford, 1987), 80.
102. Scheff, "The Shame-Rage Spiral," 109.
103. Trauma can be understood as some event so catastrophic that speaking and communicating appears to be insurmountable. Often trauma creates indelible memories, which are not integrated into a person's conscious life experiences. See Cathy Caruth, ed., *Trauma: Explorations in Memory* (Baltimore: Johns Hopkins University Press, 1995), 256.

104. Sue Grand, *The Reproduction of Evil: A Clinical and Cultural Perspective* (New York: Taylor and Francis, 2002), 16–17.
105. Grand, *The Reproduction of Evil*, 16–17.
106. Nussbaum, *Hiding from Humanity*, 183.
107. Nussbaum, *Hiding from Humanity*, 15.
108. Nussbaum, *Hiding from Humanity*, 186.
109. Bourdieu, *Pascalian Meditations*, 37.
110. Pierre Bourdieu, *Masculine Domination*, trans. Richard Nice (Stanford: Stanford University Press, 1998), 61. Pierre Bourdieu, *The Logic of Practice*, trans. Richard Nice (Stanford: Stanford University Press, 1992), 69–71.
111. Bourdieu, *Pascalian Meditations*, 150.
112. Didier Eribon, *Insult and the Making of the Gay Self*, trans. Michael Lucy (Durham: Duke University Press, 2004), 354.
113. Bourdieu, *Pascalian Meditations*, 180.
114. The idea of "symbolic violence" is a central term in Bourdieu's *Masculine Domination* defined on page 1 and expanded on throughout the text.
115. Bourdieu, *Masculine Domination*, 1.
116. Nash, "Bourdieu on Education and Social and Cultural Reproduction," 433.
117. Bourdieu, *Pascalian Meditations*, 72.
118. Bourdieu, *Pascalian Meditations*, xxi.
119. Jordan, *Recruiting Young Love*, 58.
120. Jordan, *Recruiting Young Love*, 58.
121. Bourdieu, *Pascalian Meditations*, 141.
122. "What we learn through affects becomes programmed as scripts which govern our behavior," "What Tomkins Said," The Tomkins Institute, accessed August 15, 2014, http://www.tomkins.org/what-tomkins-said/introduction/what-we-learn-through-affects-becomes-programmed-as-scripts-which-govern-our-behavior/
123. Silvan Tomkins, *Exploring Affect* (Cambridge, UK: Cambridge University Press, 1995), 58 and 318–319.
124. Tomkins, *Exploring Affect*, 325.
125. Tomkins, *Exploring Affect*, 325.
126. Tomkins, *Exploring Affect*, 325.
127. Nathanson, *Shame and Pride*, 30 and 313–315.
128. Nathanson, *Shame and Pride*, 314.
129. Nathanson, *Shame and Pride*, 314. See also Gilligan, *Violence*, 110–114; Tangney and Dearing, *Shame and Guilt*, 3, 5, and 163–165.
130. Damasio, *Descartes Error*, 128.

CHAPTER 3

The Cover-Up

Shame affects us at our core; we bury it, interring it. Elided or covered over by other terms—"interred in rhetoric"—shame fades from view. Thus, shame is covered over, or covered up. Scenes of shame and its concealment emerge theologically in the Edenic drama recounted in the Bible. Theologians interested in understanding the human condition often revisit this foundational Christian narrative. Augustine pays particularly close attention to Adam and Eve, interpreting their situation as an originary drama where shame and covering-up play a central organizing function in their character development. Adam and Eve clothe themselves to cover their nakedness; this begins a trajectory into shame.

An exploration of this multilayered concept of covering-up in shame locates the body as central to Augustine's theological anthropology. This body exudes affectivity and, set within a dynamic of shame, contains an internal stigma of sin that manifests externally as shamed body parts, or as uncontrollable *pudenda*. Augustine's conception of shame simultaneously acknowledges and diminishes the body and affectivity. His theology not only establishes shame on and in the body but also situates shame as integral to the human self. Rereading Augustine via affect theory offers, in relation to his own intellectual inheritance, a way of imagining the formation of the Christian self, including how that self emerges in shame and attaches to God.

Augustine's seminal text *City of God* comprises his attempt to defend Christianity against the pagans while persuading Christians to maintain their faith and seek connection to God. In his defense of both Christianity

S.N. Arel, *Affect Theory, Shame, and Christian Formation*,
DOI 10.1007/978-3-319-42592-4_3

and the Christian's primary relationship with God, he seeks to understand human suffering, a preoccupation that leads him to examine humanity's condition after the biblical fall from Eden. His interpretation of the Fall, along with the precarious position of Christianity at the time, deeply influences his conceptions of the ideal Christian self.[1] Viewing this conception through an affective lens facilitates the uncovering of shame as an affect fundamental to Augustine's perception of Christian anthropology.

Augustine locates a tension between the city of God and the earthly city, between the divine and the human, in the embodied effect of shame. Shame, as a central affect in *City of God*, is also the source of suffering and the primary symbol of the Fall. The core trope that Augustine employs to convey the fall into suffering and earthly life is a shamed body, concretized in Adam and Eve's bodily act of responding to the knowledge of their own nakedness by covering up their *pudenda* with fig leaves. This pivotal scene images both shame, as ashamedness at nudity, and the initial stage of covering up and interring shame.

In paradise, or the city of God, the effect of shame exists as part of nature but remains covered by grace. Grace thus attends to shame, regulating it. This is not the case in the earthly city where affective forces like shame seize bodies. This presence of fractious, uncontrollable affects in the earthly city often renders these bodies dysregulated. To reduce the affective intensity of earthly existence and restore some of the equilibrium disrupted by the Fall, Augustine appeals to humanity to reach for connection with the divine. In Augustine's construction, formidable in the shaping of the Christian self, shame motivates connection to God: although they initially hide, Adam and Eve must turn to God after they find themselves in shame with shamed parts if there is to be any hope for them. Seeking God in lieu of hiding from God would bring the human state of shame out into the open, fully exposed. Yet shame remains hidden or obscured from view in the Edenic narrative Augustine interprets.

Identifying shame and shame's function in attachment begins to uncover in Augustine's theology what Virginia Burrus describes as shame's "productively transformative as well as destructively inhibiting effects."[2] Contemporary work in affect theory, especially regarding shame and patterns of attachment, frames and undergirds the exploration of shame and attachment in Augustine's theology, where the primary attachment figure is God. In theories of attachment, affects, particularly shame, are regulated in what is called psychobiological or neurological attunement with this primary figure.[3] Shame results when attunement fails, or when interest-excitement is partially truncated. Thus, attachment must exist and then be disrupted in order for shame to occur. Dysregulated shame results, and the inability to tolerate shame leads to shame's interment marking shame's "destructively inhibiting" effects. To begin to disinter shame requires recognizing its presence and aliveness in the self and seeking repair of the interpersonal bridge that shame initially severed thus eliciting its "transformative" effects. It seems contradictory to link shame to pleasure, joy, and connection, but shame surfaces in front of a real or imagined other. The experience of the self as unlovable or unloved floods the self with shame. Restoring a love bond, then, has the capacity to reduce the overwhelming shame affect.

The story of the Fall, as Augustine interprets it, formulates a fall out of relation with God and into the knowledge of shame, embodied by the act of covering-up. A deeper look at Book XIV, chapters 11–17 in *City of God*, reveals that Augustine's understanding of the Edenic narrative unmasks two kinds of shame. The first, a kind of natural or true shame, articulated as an innate shame in affect theory, attends to attuned attachment and fosters the original most primal connection, to God for Augustine, to the other in affect theory. Augustine's interpretation of the Fall leads him to identify shame and the shamed body as a bridge between the two cities, personified by Christ, who offers the human imagination a vision of prelapsarian life. Augustine tells a crucial story about this transmuted shame,[4] locating it *in* the body as an affect related to the knowledge of nakedness and *on* the body as *pudenda* or shamed parts.

The second shame occurs as a result of knowledge; Adam and Eve know that they are naked and feel shamed. This toxic shame, for Augustine, perverts human life and contributes to diminished self-worth. In affect theory, this shame assumes a different physiological intensity than true shame and acquires a more pernicious role in the human self. When Augustine consigns to the practice of covering the body a transmuted sense of shame prior to the "lust" for knowledge that both Adam and Eve experienced, he marks shame as the central affect that distinguishes the material world, the city of humanity, from the spiritual world, the city of God.[5]

Edenic Attunement

The Edenic narrative assumes a key role in Augustine's diagnosis of the human condition, and consideration of it through an affective lens illuminates shame.[6] For Augustine, the drama of the Fall serves as a founding narrative of the etiology of human sin. Augustine begins with a prelapsarian description of Adam and Eve's affectively attuned condition in Eden, a condition of unsullied love for God and each other. At the outset, Adam and Eve exist in pure bliss, in a state characterized by affect regulation and, thus, a lack of pain and suffering. In Eden, the love that Adam and Eve feel for each other expresses itself fully including sexual intimacy, which occurs free from conflicting desires, the burden of sin, and toxic shame. Pleasure and interest, in God and each other, abound. In paradise, the material and the spiritual harmonize as one. Both outward or material and inward or spiritual needs are fulfilled.

In this place, where the material and spiritual function in unison, humanity possesses only good will.[7] In Augustine's terms, God made "man upright" and capable of good at God's bequest.[8] Furthermore, for Augustine, all affects including desire[9] are ultimately directed by and toward God. Augustine believes that Adam and Eve initially obey God's demand not to eat from the forbidden tree as a result of their connection with and attunement to God. Therefore, at the earliest roots of human existence, affects did not oppose human will as they were aligned with God's will.[10] Adam and Eve existed as "one flesh;" both were naked, and neither was ashamed.

Interrupting this harmonious balance in Eden, the devil, whom Augustine labels an "arrogant angel," refuses to subject himself to God and, motivated by hubristic pride, rejects God initiating detachment.[11] In Augustine's narration, "envious" of Adam and Eve, the devil ventures to destroy their harmonious state.[12] The devil's "ambition was to worm his way, by seductive craftiness, into the consciousness of man," selecting as his "mouthpiece" a serpent.[13] Serving as a material representation of evil, according to Augustine, the serpent "with his slippery body, moving along in tortuous twists and turns" has a "deceitful conversation with the woman."[14] The devil seduces Eve to eat from the tree, and she in turn encourages Adam, who also eats from the tree. Subsequently, both, "taken captive by their sin and entangled in the snares of the Devil," effectively detach from God.[15]

Augustine portrays this ensnarement dimensionally and sequentially. First, an act of evil will takes place. This act of evil will is the original evil, or secret sin, demarcating the fatal "falling away" from the good will that God created. The Fall articulated by Augustine can be read according to theories of attachment. Adam and Eve's connection to God is severed.[16] Giving meaning to the original evil, Augustine writes that "man regards himself in his own light and turns away from that light which would have made himself a light if he had set his heart on it. The evil came first, in secret, and the result was the other evil, which was committed in the open."[17] In other words, the other evil or subsequently open and more obvious sin ensues as a substantive act: the more overt behavior of eating from the tree. Thus, detachment from God leads to the struggle with all such subsequent acts. These acts have the inevitable potential to entangle with evil, a condition implicated by Adam and Eve's having fallen away from God's will.

The transpiring acts of the evil parallel a loss of personal control. Such circumstances magnify the intractability of affect. The prelapsarian attunement Adam and Eve enjoy subsequently transpires into affective and somatic dysregulation. From this point forward, Adam and Eve, along with their progeny, succumb to desire, fractious affects, and uncontrollable evil will. Their dysregulation marks the moving away from God reflected first when Adam and Eve deflect and deny responsibility for their sin. Adam blames Eve; Eve blames the serpent. Neither seeks God's pardon, nor turns to God to reclaim the lost bond, and so each abandons grace. According to Augustine, in pride and self-love, they deny "any entreaty for healing,"[18] a healing which Augustine interprets as mediated by God. Stated in terms of attachment this would be a connection with and reattachment to God.

In his construction of the Christian self, Augustine designates concupiscence as the motivating force which restricts healing. In his diagnosis, concupiscence overpowers mental alertness, overwhelms the "intellectual sentries," and disturbs the whole self.[19] Thus, claiming power over the body, externally and internally, concupiscence interferes with the intellect and, as unbounded desire, refuses to "be a servant" of the will.[20] Concupiscence as desire illustrates the uncontrollability of the will and is a factor in the will's *turn away* from God. At the mercy of concupiscence, flesh, Augustine asserts, which had been subject to the will, "now gives us trouble through its non-compliance," and our perception that "we need the service of our body" leads to "punishment for ourselves."[21] Concupiscence relates directly to incitement and stimulation of the sexual organs, specifically to the arousal of the *pudenda*.[22] Augustine believes firmly that this arousal—concupiscence flowing through the body inciting the *pudenda*—needs to be tempered through submission to God, and all desire directed rather toward God as an object. [23] For Augustine, desire not directed toward God is desire wrongly directed. The resulting concupiscence manifests as the uncontrollable *pudenda* or shamed body parts, for which one should feel ashamed. Thus, the body bears the burden and the consequences of the soul's disobedience.

This disobedience materializes in pride. Modeled by the devil, pride engenders Adam and Eve's voluntary desertion of God along with their self-reliance and self-complacency in regard to God. Pride spurs the evil will, "darkened and chilled," which motivates the evil act, or the refusal to connect to God.[24] Augustine asserts that pride "is a longing for a perverse kind of exaltation," the root of every form of sin.[25] In fact, for Augustine, the will itself is "the evil tree which bore evil fruit."[26] Augustine further asserts that it is the "man himself who was that tree, in so far as his will was evil."[27] The evil will is thus an unnatural (not of God) "defect," existing only in nature, created out of nothing, not out of that which the "creator begot out of himself."[28] And the generated evil erupts in all subsequent evil deeds. When this evil will engenders the evil act, the will has fallen away from its true being related to and attuned with God. However, Augustine accounts for this Fall due to the self's original creation out of nothing, thus attributing nothing evil to God.[29] Preceded by a turn toward the self in pride and detaching the self from God, discontent brings humanity nearer to its original nothingness.

The severed attachment to God occurs after Adam and Eve succumb to misdirected desire: "The eyes of both of them were opened, and they realized they were naked," and subsequently they hide.[30] This newfound realization of their nakedness materializes at the same time as they are overwhelmed by affect, which manifests as an acquisition of an uncontrollable will and a spiritual loss of grace. This does not mean, as Augustine recounts, that before the evil will they were blind, but part of their prelapsarian existence included their being cloaked in a "garment of grace," which they failed to "recognize" as a blessing that disenabled "their members" or sexual organs from knowing how to rebel against God.[31] Grace did not simply veil shame but inhibited the body from even knowing how to disconnect from God and from experiencing shame as toxic.

After Adam and Eve rebel by eating from the forbidden tree, God tries to find them. Adam answers regarding his whereabouts in Genesis 3:10: "I was afraid, because I was naked; and I hid myself." The combined acts of turning away from God and hiding after they know that they are naked reveal their shame. With knowledge of their newfound shamed nature,

Adam and Eve "[sew] together fig leaves and [make] aprons for themselves."[32] The sewing of the fig leaves memorializes the loss of the garment of grace. Grace alone had "prevented their bodily nakedness from causing them any embarrassment."[33] Grace prevented embarrassment in Eden because grace initially immobilizes evil will, or misdirected desire. Grace does not prevent shame. Insofar as shame is a natural state, grace accommodates shame and directs shame to God. In this way, the cloak of grace signifies attunement with God, evidencing a primal attachment and ensuring a harmonious somatic balance. The impulse to hide their bodies, detaching from instead of turning to God, conveys the loss of grace, expressed as Adam and Eve's being "stripped" of grace. So stripped, they feel an amplified sense of shame instigated by the severed connection to God.

Adam and Eve respond to the loss of grace and their newly realized uncontrollable *pudenda* by feeling more shame at being exposed. The opening of the eyes, Augustine explains, indicates not enablement to see, but an enablement to *know* what they relinquished: primarily grace and the innocence of the secure attachment. Both ensured continuity and stability in Eden. Further, the possession of knowledge becomes for Augustine a curse, since he prefers nescience and obedience to God over consciousness, primarily because innocence as simplicity frees humanity from evil will and ensures the prelapsarian attachment.

Augustine diagnoses this newfound knowledge of shame, concretized by detachment from God, as pride and guilt, which receive particular punishments. Then he establishes the Christian self that derives from the Edenic narrative. First, he writes that "there appeared in the movements of their body a certain indecent novelty, which made nakedness shameful."[34] This punishment tragically communicates that the Christian can no longer "become spiritual even in [the] flesh" but becomes instead "carnal" even in the mind.[35] This carnality, tantamount to a lack of control over the self, or being "at odds" with oneself, emerges as non-compliant, dysregulated flesh, taking on the properties of a lust that surges uncontrollably as affect through the body. Second, they suffer death, the mortal signification of the break in unity between the body and soul that Augustine mourns. As a result, hope for the self of any return to paradise evolves only in reunification and reattachment through the resurrection, which restores unity and subsumes shame in a reconnection with God.

Augustine thus exposes the capacity of pride and evil will longing to redirect Adam and Eve's interest (and his own) toward God. Their sin, which refutes God's order of obedience, ushers in all subsequent sin and alters human nature incommensurably. From this point onward, Adam and Eve, along with their progeny, engage in a perpetual effort to regulate affect. Thus, the effect of the first sin contributes to the "violent and conflicting emotions" that plague human life and subject human nature to lust, pride, and variations of shame, as they move toward "the process of decay" and eventual death.[36] Augustine concludes Book 17 by conveying a similar message: "Thus modesty, from a sense of shame, covered what was excited to disobedience by lust, in defiance of a will which had been condemned for the guilt of disobedience; and from then onwards the practice of concealing the pudenda has become a deep-rooted habit in all peoples."[37]

Thus, Augustine labels the body as shamed, and this perception of the body as shameful has been, until recently, a theological legacy. Yet the true significance of shame in Augustine's conclusion parallels the assertion that shame rests internal to the human person. Augustine names shame, consigning guilt to its most appropriate role as a response to behavior; he does not confuse the two affects, as we will see Niebuhr do later. As a result, Augustine locates shame as central to the self, always existing, but emerging with negative force when the prelapsarian bond with God breaks in the Edenic narrative. No longer attuned with God, shame contributes to the suffering in human life, and Augustine's conception of life as a process of healing can only be fulfilled in realization that in shame the individual must return to God.

Falling Out of Relation

Augustine is preoccupied in *City of God*, as he is in *On Genesis* and the *Confessions*, with making sense of the Fall. He struggles with the fall out of relationship with God and seeks passionately to restore this connection. Adam and Eve experience a loss; deprived of the innocence and harmony characteristic of the city of God, they plummet to the earthly city where, in contrast, conflict marks existence. Fractious affects, enticement from evil, pride, concupiscence, and shame contribute to the conflict. Ultimately, the fall into the human, worldly condition of the earthly city represents a fall into shame that severs attachment.

Attachment, according to Augustine, is wrongly directed in the earthly city. As Augustine asserts, "In one city love of God has been given first place, in the other, love of the self."[38] Additionally, the fall out of proper attachment incurs pain. This suffering, theoretically constructed as concupiscence, can also be understood as the knowledge of shame. Assuming greater intensity than the natural state of shame in grace, this knowledge of shame further shames Adam and Eve, contributing to pathologies, articulated by Augustine in his construction of the Christian self as a subjection to guilt, sin, pride, and lust.

Exposed and with open eyes, Adam and Eve's story patterns the trajectory for the Christian self, naked and bereft of prelapsarian grace and innocence. This self is situated in sin as a result of the originary turn from the secure paradisiacal immutability dependent on God toward the insecure capricious relationships of the human world. In this world, bodies, vulnerable to desire, suffering, and death, seek connection and intimacy, but they fail if God ceases to be the object of attachment. This uncontrollable, material body, lured away from God by insuppressible affects, expresses both a desire to know (or eat from the forbidden tree) and a desire for self-importance or power manifested in pride. Misdirected desire pronounces concupiscence, pulsing through the *pudenda*, the visible parts of shame, overwhelming this self's rationality.

The fall out of innocence thus marks a fall into affective experience, the essential state of the Christian self, "distracted and tossed about by violent and conflicting emotions."[39] For Augustine, this state of affectivity is "less real,"[40] less fixed, and more impermanent than the state of grace and attunement characteristic of paradise. Here, forces erupt from the body, as contingent, unpredictable, and overflowing affects, signifying dysregulation. These forces direct the human body toward an object, often unconsciously. For instance, it is affectivity in the form of interest in the devil that blindsides Eve, then Adam's subsequent interest in Eve that does the same to him. Misdirected desire provokes their attachment to that which God has forbidden, and they consent to the wiles of the devil almost without resistance. Both emerge and arrive at a new state of reality when their "desires become mediated through attachments to modes of life to which they rarely remember consenting, at least initially."[41]

Bewildered, Adam and Eve enter this this newfound state unconsciously, a transition Augustine blames on the individual's devotion to him/herself rather than to God: "When [man] had turned toward himself, his being was less real than when he adhered to Him who exists in a supreme degree."[42] This self-absorption constitutes a distortion of the original attachment to God, and the distortion relates directly to the knowledge and toxicity of shame.

In Augustine's interpretation of the Edenic narrative, the fall into affective experience constitutes a fall into shame, because "shame marks the break in connection" to the primal and prelapsarian existence in relationship with God and with the other, while also disrupting harmony within the self.[43] Further, as an act of body prostration, falling reflects shame. The prelapsarian sexual, regulated body Adam and Eve enjoyed in Eden becomes an earthly body, full of shame and covered by shame as a result of refuting God. It is this body that the Christian self inhabits: dysregulated by affect, distressed by the knowledge of shame, and finally susceptible to death.

Thus, shame comprises the central affect that distinguishes the city of God from the earthly city. In fact, the primary difference in the two cities is not simply shame or the body, but the body *in* shame. This body in shame emerges from Augustine's conceptualizations highlighted by the Fall. The fall away from God thus constitutes a fall out of relation that elicits shame. It is not that shame did not exist before the Fall, but after the connection with God is severed, Adam and Eve know they have shame because they experience it bodily. This shame is carried forward as a result of the stripping of grace, the garment that regulated shame. The Christian self thus struggles to achieve grace, evidenced by the maladaptive qualities of shame *in* and *on* the body which assemble and thrive.

Shame Emerges

Augustine's reading of the Edenic story inters shame in the body, marking the body with shame and constructing a Christian self, who struggles to securely attach. This body cannot share in the assured, attuned prelapsarian attachment to God. Instead, it appears insecure, disorganized, and avoidant.[44] To explain this situation, Augustine describes a Christian self with an internal mark of affectivity, what he labels concupiscence. But this is not enough. For Augustine, pulsing through the body internally, concupiscence also appears externally as the exposed *pudenda* or visible sexual organs on the body. The uncontrollable *pudenda* signify lust that precipitates shame.

At least, Augustine names shame and inherent in his theological anthropology is a recognition of shame's intensity; he knows how detrimental shame can be. He also understands how shame manifests as bodily behaviors and describes gestures of shame which, first enacted in the Edenic drama, replicate themselves in human existence. Augustine's recognition of shame as a powerful element in human life, along with the role that it plays in how we connect with others, offers a pathway to the consciousness of shame as an operative affect in our own lives.

The Internal Mark: Uncontrollable Will

In shame, the self perceives itself as corrupt, immoral, and depraved. Marked by the stigma of evil will, the self understands its position as being observed as deficient. The will caused the sin and a turn away from God, marking the body, internally and externally with concupiscence. As is the case for affective shame, this observation takes place within the logic of exposure. For Augustine, deficiency evolves when Adam and Eve come to understand themselves in a particular way; they know (and see) that they have shame. Their knowledge initiates shame. The incumbent evolution into shame is marked by a rapid descent from high positive arousal into a negative state.[45] Adam and Eve's prelapsarian innocence emulates infants who, according to affect theory, experience pleasure with the interested caregiver but with the detached caregiver perceive something wrong in the self.

The internal mark of shame that validates this perceived wrong is marked by affectivity—the struggle to attune or regulate oneself. In Augustine's rhetoric, this state manifests as "concupiscence."[46] Having movement and capacity to excite the body,[47] concupiscence taints from the inside. As an internal, repugnant imprint on the soul, it spreads from generation to generation, defining the affectivity of human life. Concupiscence shares qualities of shame in more contemporary shame literature, which delineates shame as a "soul wound,"[48] a "sickness of the soul,"[49] or as a "sleeper" in psychopathology.[50] Deeply internal, defining a state of being, concupiscence and shame function as intense forces that motivate and direct human behavior.

Fractious affectivity in the self leads to shame, suffering, and isolation. For Augustine, all negative affective phenomena confirm detachment from God. Humanity experiences the truncation of interest in God through two forms of punishment: shame which acts as a brake to arousal, disrupting interest and severing connections,[51] and death, the severest method of severing attachments in human life. From this severing, at least for Augustine, lies the hope of bodily resurrection, where the self is to be "with the Lord forever" in a renewal of attachment.[52] The alternative, for Augustine, leaves "the ungodly" walking around "in circles."[53] Read alongside affect theory, these circles represent the pernicious cycles of unaddressed shame.

In resurrection, Augustine believes that the entire body is preserved, including presumably innate shame. He asserts of this bodily resurrection that "even if a body is incorruptible, such as a body as is promised to the saints at the resurrection...the body is not identical with this incorruptibility, since the corporeal substance remains."[54] Thus, shame remains, yet in the resurrected body, it does not impede attachment.

While shame acts as a "brake" to arousal, it also evokes the inner experience of pain. The human responds, according to Augustine, seeking amelioration or eradiation of pain through means not generally associated with God. The earthly objects of desire act as "pseudo-nourishment," taking God's place and forming attachments perpetuated through compulsive, repeated behavior.[55] After Adam and Eve, humanity tries repeatedly to eradicate shame by affiliating with worldly and other external things. In Augustinian terms, they attempt to direct desire but fail to do so—as a result of concupiscence—correctly.

Augustine generalizes both "concupiscence" and "lust" as terms for desire, although they are not precisely the same thing. Concupiscence includes lust and desire but describes more of a state of being than an action. As "an agenda perpetuated on the body rather than instigated by the body," concupiscence "includes all the debilitating forms of anxious grasping – whether it pursues the objects of power, possessions or sex."[56] When Augustine uses the word "lust," he uses it almost always unfavorably: "we have the lust for vengeance, called anger; the lust for possession of money, called greed; the lust for victory at any price, called obstinacy; the lust for boasting, called vanity."[57] Further, lust "of any kind" manifests in humanity's search for pleasure in hopes that such pleasure will eradicate pain.[58] However, desire can be constructive when it is directed toward God; this sense of desire corresponds to the interest-excitement of Tomkins's nine affects, constructing and maintaining connections, drawing the self toward an object, and leaving the self open to experiencing shame.

External Mark: The **Pudenda**

For Augustine, the internal mark of concupiscence manifests externally through the *pudenda*.[59] *Pudenda* reveal and signify sensual desire pulsing through the body. The involuntary movement of the body actualized in the *pudenda* is the punishment for desire wrongly directed. Augustine insists, "It is right, therefore, to be ashamed of this lust."[60] But this is not enough for Augustine. Not only does the internal mark of desire as concupiscence incur shame, but the external manifestation of that mark in *pudenda* also constitutes a corporeal extension of that shame. Augustine continues, "it is right that the members which [lust] moves or fails to move by its own right, so to speak, and not in complete conformity to our decision, should be called *pudenda* ('parts of shame'), which they were not called before man's sin."[61]

Thus, the uncontrolled and uncontrollable movement of the *pudenda*, or shameful member, signifies the disease humanity carries, the etiology of which is concupiscence.[62]

Amplifying shame, Augustine talks about a "sense of shame" embodied in covering the *pudenda*, the impugned parts provoked by lust. Body parts represent shame and should be covered as they precipitate a sense of shame. In either case, for Augustine, shame both is covered, as the *pudenda* are covered, and covers up, as the fig leaves cover the *pudenda*. The dynamic instituted in Augustine's text posits what is secret against what is exposed. Between the covering and uncovering belongs the body shaped in shame.

Intensity

Augustine articulates shame as intertwined with the internal mark of concupiscence imbricated with the evil will, which inspires knowledge of shame, creating an intensity of affect that defines human life and which perpetuates the possibility of toxic shame. The multidimensional condition Augustine diagnoses correlates with three major types of shame affects as they are understood in contemporary thinking.[63] In the first type, the affect of shame evokes anxiety, which manifests in the fear of punishment, or the severing of attachments. The first affective experience of Adam and Eve reflects this shame as they hide from God naked, afraid, and ashamed of their disobedient act. However, this simple shame anxiety evolves into a more intense, complex affective structure in the second type of shame, which requires two parts: (1) that some expectation of self (conscious or unconscious) fails to be fulfilled and (2) that "the inner wishful *image* of the self be 'betrayed' setting in motion a self-critical, self-punishing, and reparative process."[64] Adam and Eve both fail to meet expectations set forth by God, and their self-punishing and reparative process entails covering-up the *pudenda* and hiding. Aware of being exposed, this second type of shame plays a dominant role in the character of Adam and Eve since shame situates itself both on and in their bodies. In the third case, the behavior preventing dangerous exposure entails a refusal, even a fear to attach. This represents the deepest most serious problem of shame.

Entrapped, the self creates further isolation, and shame intensifies in the forms of cycles. Continually dysregulated, shame becomes toxic and plays a prominent role the "etiology of all primitive psychopathologies and psychosomatic diseases."[65]

The Gestures of Shame

When Augustine conveys the story of the Fall, and more specifically, when he details Adam and Eve's response to the *pudenda*, he depicts their behavior in terms of the gestures of shame. Adam and Eve, following the devil, "turn away" from God; they hide, and they cover up. These bodily gestures that Augustine describes correlate with the corporeal responses to shame established in affect theory. Shame reduces facial communication: the eyes turn down; the head and sometimes the upper torso drop or turn away from observing eyes; and blushing often occurs.[66] As kinesthetic articulations of the body, gestures reflect interior life, and in this case, the gestures indicate interred shame. Augustine astutely identifies these gestures.

Turning and covering are gestures that not only signify an inner experience but also inspire particular visceral and affective states working to shape the Christian self in shame. Taking place within the logic of self-exposure, the gestures Augustine describes can be seen as constituting the impulse to hide inherent in shame's logic. Functioning within a logic of exposure, the gestures demonstrate how humanity turns toward its own light and "turns away from that light" which is God's.[67] The result is a hiding and covering-up, which secondarily signifies that sexual actions are "accompanied by a feeling of shame."[68] Before the Fall, this "right action" of promulgation was not concerned with escaping "the light of the eye's vision," presumably in shame.[69] Augustine's diagnosis of the self in shame leads him to advise how humanity should behave, suggesting gestures of shame, as covering-up, to address concupiscence. So while he admonishes the turning-away from God, he finds covering-up a necessity in the trajectory back to God.

Turning Away, Hiding, and Covering Up

In the Edenic narrative, shame emerges initially in the turning-away from God. While Augustine does not tie shame directly to this gesture, but rather describes it as a result of pride, it cannot be dissociated from shame. In affect theory, one corporeal embodiment of shame is to turn away. Augustine labels this turn as one conducted in pride or in self-absorption.

Turning from God toward the self to please the self represents the "evil" that happens for Augustine "in secret." The "other evil, which was committed in the open," results in the act of disobedience of God emblematized in the disconnection with God.[70] For Augustine, pride is a kind of *a priori* condition that enables the enticement by the serpent toward materiality. But pride also happens in secret. As Augustine does with shame, he also sets pride within the field of vision. The turning away is an effort to escape sight, to disappear from view. In addition, privacy and secrecy sought in the turning away are perpetuated by the sexual act. Augustine writes the sexual act performed with lust "seeks privacy."[71] Only after a realization of shame does any effort to hide sex from God exist. In fact, in bodily resurrection, Augustine concludes that sex is restored as a natural part of attachment, to God and to others. Only in detachment from God, in shame, does sex become hidden, secret.

Secrecy and isolation perpetuate shame. In fact, in Augustine, from the first, secret sin or turning away from God in pride, shame emerges. Augustine writes, "It was in secret that the first human beings began to be evil."[72] In secret, their bodies are also implicated. Adam and Eve turn from the light provided by God and attempt to escape God's field of vision.[73] Adam's turn from the light, as if hiding, evidences shame, the shame that truncates interest and severs attachment. Bodies diagnosed in shame turn away, blush, and hide from exposure. Such bodies seek, as Adam and Eve did, to perform in secret, and then to, upon exposure, hide, avoiding reattachment.

Once they have eaten from the forbidden tree, Adam and Eve hide because, Adam states, they are "naked and afraid." Their newly understood nakedness provokes fear and a desire to hide, a classic indicator of shame. Now when they see their bodies, they feel shame. However, the gesture of hiding fails to prevent the experience of shame or to hinder it; instead, hiding, like secrecy and isolation, amplifies shame.[74]

Reactions to shame that include hiding can be compared to the behavior of withdrawal, a "learned defense against intense and enduring shame affect."[75] Like shame, withdrawal happens on a spectrum. Temporarily withdrawing allows for reparation and recovery from shame, but if acknowledging shame fails to occur, withdrawal permits it to be further aggrandized and ultimately interred. In fact, "unacknowledged shame creates a form of self-perpetuating entrapment in one's own isolation."[76] Whether through hiding or withdrawing, reducing shame requires that it come into view, just as amelioration requires attachment and attunement. Hidden shame grows, while shame exposed diminishes.

However, Augustine observes that hiding shame becomes the norm, aligning it with guilt and pride. For instance, for Augustine, after the Fall, sexual intercourse, which provokes the internal "natural sense of shame," requires secret hiding places. The right action of sex as procreation has become sullied and though "it longs to become known, it blushes to be seen."[77] The feeling of shame that accompanies sexuality is, for Augustine, simply a "punishment."[78] His construction here illuminates what can be interpreted in Christianity as the interplay of the normal feeling of sexual impulses with the projected norms of the tradition: hide it and cover up the shamed parts. This living in shame, illustrated by "covering-up," develops into the natural state of humanity after the Fall.

In summary, after having located shame in the body, Augustine asserts that shame is also on the body as the *pudenda*, or shamed parts. Covering-up the *pudenda*, or "visible" shame, serves as the keystone to Augustine's explication of shame. The *pudenda* prove and ratify the internal stigma. Shame is a mark on and in the flesh; covering-up the flesh and hiding are the first steps in a habituation process that serves to counteract the evil will which provokes pride and desire. Augustine suggests that gestures of shame modulate pride and desire. So in alignment with the Edenic narrative in Genesis, he observes that Adam and Eve cover the *pudenda* with fig leaves—to conceal and contain shame, but also to protect their *pudenda* from eliciting further shame through sexual acts. The leaves prompt the final visual cue that Adam and Eve reject God and sever the prelapsarian attachment, perpetuating the condition of the Christian self—a highly affected self—grasping and seeking God, but often doing so unsuccessfully. The cover-up of the *pudenda* signifies the whole turning away from God. Put another way, the cover-up signals the punishment that humanity has incurred by rejecting God, revealing the body and the newfound state of the body in shame. But the cover-up also conceals something critical, achieving an aim that Augustine does not intend: it veils the self that seeks the primal attachment, interfering with the connection to God.

Pride and Humility

When Augustine addresses pride, he is usually understood as meaning *hubris* and self-aggrandizement, defined as pathological in affect theory. Thus, a pathologized notion of pride rests at the core of Augustine's critique. Quoting from Ecclesiastes, he asserts that pride, as sin's root, constitutes "a longing for a perverse kind of exaltation" and a person's rejection of an immutable God to please him/herself.[79] In pride "man regards himself in his own light."[80]

Augustine defines pride as a force manifested in the "arrogant angel," which aligns pride not only with nothing but also with evil. Thus, the affective structure of pride includes its motivation by envy of and desire to be God. Pride serves as the affective impulse, or impetus, that motivates Adam and Eve to turn from God. Pride falsely permits the belief that the self can exist and subsist in isolation without dependence on others, and for Augustine, this means dependence on God. As *hubris*, pride scoffs at the other as an object of attachment and attunement, seeking instead power adumbrated in self-reliance. In the *Confessions*, he admits to succumbing to pride himself and thus detaching from God. He directs his angst and own suffering toward Satan, blaming Satan's pride. This pride rejects subjection to God and provokes an individual to desire to be followed rather than to follow God.

This sinful state, a stigma for which one should be ashamed, precedes the next or subsequent sinful act of disobedience for which one experiences guilt. The shame Augustine says should be felt of pride precedes guilt and should not be confused with guilt. Guilt signifies a result of wrongdoing throughout the *City of God* linked to specific acts of sin, murder, criminal activity, and eating forbidden fruit. Guilt is thus compartmentalized and addressed rightly as a response to wrongdoing.[81] The evolution of shame, though, occurs sequentially. First, pride provokes an initial layer of shame, increasing the possibility of temptation and lust, provoking an additional layer of shame, not guilt. The prescription for this pride, for Augustine, is humility. Humility tempers the secondary evils of temptation and lust. Again, humility as the cure for pride is, in one sense, a final layer of generated shame.

As the first sin, pride engenders a postlapsarian shame and provokes a disobedient act, which, in turn, engenders guilt. The resulting knowledge of nakedness and lack of control of bodily movement engenders additional shame. As a result of Adam and Eve's actions, individuals are bound to privilege the self over God to address shame. Augustine's cure: more shame, in the form of modesty embodied in covering-up. Thus, Augustine describes and suggests a shame cycle as shame felt for some behavior perceived as shameful, each of which eventually leads to gross withdrawal, or anger and rage as an amelioration of such shame.[82] In addition, shame as an outcome of the shame cycles serves as a "mediator of identity."[83] Although cycles of shame differ among individuals, cultures, and time, such shame modulates character. The Christian self is shaped to feel shame for feeling pride, which has a retriggering effect. Thus, the Christian tradition ushers the self into the cycle or spiral of shame.

In Augustine's shame cycle, pride contrasts with humility; pride, as evil should, according to Augustine, elicit shame, while it simultaneously humiliates or shames the self. Augustine asserts that pride as "exaltation abases" whereas "humility exalts."[84] Furthermore, pride brings humanity nearer to nothing. As unnatural or not of God, pride serves as a rejection of God and obedience, where obedience is "the mother and guardian of all the other virtues."[85] As such, pride is perverse and constitutes a turning away from the good in God.

Augustine juxtaposes humility and pride, but as discussed earlier, he addresses two types of pride: pride as self-exaltation, related to shame, and pride as esteem garnered from God. Self-worship constitutes the pride that humanity suffers which results in shame—as a punishment and because, for Augustine, this pride hides shame in the first place. Pride as esteem from God is better expressed as grace and desire rightly directed toward God. This is the pride of self-compassion and human dignity necessary to flourishing. Augustine prescribes humility to alleviate the former sense of pride, urging Christians to turn back to God. But in Augustine, another sense of humility persists, and it relates to the innate sense of shame that points to relationality. Therefore, at least two manifestations of pride emerge: (1) pride as *hubris*, which affectively masks shame, along with the subsequent response of humility, and (2) a true humility that relates to self-worth and attachment, linking with the true, prelapsarian shame that bonds individuals to each other and to God.

In the first sense, humility is a state that Augustine suggests humanity assume in response to pride, but to his relief, it also counteracts the compulsive habit provoked by lust, manifested in *pudenda*.[86] This humility has the potential to assuage both pride (the exaltation of the self over God) and lust (desire for something/someone other than God). Augustine asserts that the individual feels toxic shame as a result of pride, the secret sin, and should practice humility, also conceived of as modesty, to prevent pride from further soliciting human attention.

To prevent pride, Augustine suggests that the will and the self be turned toward God in acts of obedience, which "can belong only to the humble."[87] He details this turn toward God as the opposite of pride as *hubris*. In his view, humility exalts by subjecting the mind to God, and thus thwarting self-exaltation. For Augustine, then, submission to God is the only way to combat pride. Therefore, humility also opposes the devil as the posture assumed in the city of God, where the love of God precedes love of self.[88]

In Augustine, humility that counteracts *hubris* includes modesty and obedience. Like Adam and Eve, humanity's response to anything that distracts from the relationship with God should be a gesture of submission that in effect turns the subject back to God. When Augustine denounces pride and prescribes this particular humility, he extols shame. This shame hovers close to its convergence in Greek literature with humility and modesty encompassed in the term *aidos*, which also conveys a sense of prospection and inhibition.[89] Augustine asserts that this kind of humility be assumed in response to the pride he describes as evil will. Humility, in this sense, engenders obedience and opposes the raucousness of pride as *hubris*. In terms of shame theory, modesty, linked to shame and positioned dangerously close to humility, engenders a sense of lowered self-worth and emerges in the gestures of shame.[90]

However, grace received from the turn to God also intertwines with humility for Augustine, but this sense of humility compels reattachment to God. This humility relates to innate shame, not pathologized by gestures that reinforce subservience, loss, and deficiency. Interpreting Augustine's humility in this way leads to healthy humility; this is not the habituation of embodied shame imaged in covering the *pudenda* but is instead related to what Stephen Pattison calls "true humility."[91] This is the humility that Augustine presents as related to Christ, the manifestation of the humility of God, who combatted evil "in the form of a servant."[92] Godly humility derives from Christ's earthly manifestation in the form of an imperfect, mortal human body. In this case, humility becomes an acceptance of human flesh. Thus, there is a *good* shame, an orientation of life attached to others, embodied and embedded in humanity and becoming apparent *in Christ*.

While Augustine's extolling modesty and shame for shamed parts problematizes humility, his alignment of true humility with *good* shame acknowledges in the human condition a presence of shame that is positive. He corroborates this when he uses Christ as the model of humility when incarnated in the flesh, since humanity, not God, feels humility as linked to shame. This kind of shame is simply a condition of being human; a shame set before God and always visible to God. True humility turns humanity toward God so that the vulnerable, humble, modest, shamed human can connect to God just by turning toward God. Humility marks the path toward God made possible through God's grace. Moreover, in human life, grace liberates and controls nature, that which is good or of God. And God acts as a physician healer administering grace for the cure of human ills. Such ills are never completely eradicated on earth, according to Augustine, but grace, rather than any earthly component, makes pain more bearable and inhibits or contains the evil will. In grace, the affective energy that had been directed by the evil will surges toward God.

The Body as a Bridge

As can be seen through Augustine's writing, the body represents not only the central trope that connects the city of God to the earthly city but also constitutes materiality in paradise. Augustine does not dispute this.[93] Bodies are sexually intact in either realm, which further elucidates the blurring between the two worlds, and sexual proclivity persists in both. In opposition to early Church fathers, Augustine developed a sexual ethic that included sexual intercourse for reproduction in heaven.[94] If Adam and Eve had not sinned or detached from God, they would have continued to enjoy this state of supported reproduction without concupiscence for eternity. As evidence of Augustine's inconsistencies, some scholars identify an "unbridgeable gap" between the two cities despite how intermingled they are.[95] As a result, the cities emerge as two distinct entities. However, this decisive division fails to account for the body. The gap between the two cities is filled with body.

As Augustine envisions Christian existence, the primary difference between the body in paradise and the body on earth relates to the object of attachment. The Christian body develops in relation to God, always at the mercy of fractious affects and desire. The concept of the body full of desire connects the two cities. However, in paradise, the body's desire surges toward God. Freed from fractious affectivity in the city of God, bodies do not succumb to desire for anything but God. Desire for God subsumes shame that is inspired by the uncontrolled movement of sexual parts.

According to Augustine, having fallen victim to the sins of the first parents, the unadulterated condition of prelapsarian bodies can only be recaptured in the resurrection.[96] These bodies are radical, in that through resurrection "bodies and souls will achieve control beyond control and submission beyond submission: as the difference between control and submission disappears, they will discover a freedom beyond freedom. They will perform acts of lust now deemed shameful with shameless abandon."[97] This city is also that to which humanity must reach. This reaching constitutes the sense of intermingling of the two cities. Body is the model, in Christ.

Body is the bridge between the two cities; body is the link, through Christ, between the human and the divine. In paradise, Augustine celebrates bodies and directs their affectivity toward God in affective desire, interest-excitement, and joy. On earth, this shamed body is a body covered and the *pudenda* concealed. The affective experience that marks this cover-up is shame. Where does the shame go? Augustine tells readers that it goes into the body, as a deeply rooted habit that is transmitted from generation to generation through procreation.

Toxic shame, thus, marks the end of innocence, the loss of the prelapsarian body that engenders a sense of loss in all bodies. Shame evolves into a habitual, affective state, signified as a wound, a mark, a stigma, whose amelioration comes about by covering up in modesty. Shame is the affect that Augustine uses to capture the way that humanity encounters the world. Interred in body as a stigma related to pride and concupiscence, shame is "deeply discrediting."[98] This attribute, inherent in Augustine's notion of the Christian self, is something that can induce aversion and transform into more shame, and even further shame, in a cyclical sense, for feeling shame.[99]

Conclusion

Evil, sin, and, as a result, shame are not things to be removed from the Christian self for Augustine, but rather they require "healing and restoration of the original [self] which had been corrupted and debased."[100] Augustine envisions this healing as humanity's reaching toward God in life, achieving resurrection after death. His vision of a perfect being is resurrected in body, without sin, but theoretically still with shame as the binding agent to God. So although Augustine names shame rightly as an inherent aspect of affective human life, his prescription of shame as *habitus* contributes to cycles of shame, misinterpretations of pride, and shame for and of bodies in Christian theology.

Augustine's assertions translate into a few key assertions vital to the formation of the Christian self. The first of these is that shame is a part of us. This claim is consistent with affect theory, which argues that shame is not only inherent in the self but also indicative of secure human attachment. In this view, the experience of shame occurs when a condition of love toward another is present. In such a way, shame before God indicates an attachment to God.[101] However, shame can go too far, when not named, or when interred in the Christian self. When Augustine reveals something "contaminated" about the Christian self in shame, he effectively inters shame. Toxic, postlapsarian shame punishes the self in the form of a pulsing desire manifested by *pudenda*. The *pudenda* underscore shame interred in and about body, carried through the Christian tradition—that is, that bodies need to be covered up and hidden from exposure.

Second, Augustine presages shame theorists who argue that guilt is related to an act of wrongdoing, while shame is an intrinsic sense of some wrong associated with the self. He associates guilt directly with enacted behaviors associated with free will, set free by God but threatened by evil will. The act of disobedience itself provokes guilt, but guilt can be easily assuaged with repentance, repaired, and treated by grace. Conversely, shame as Augustine conceives of it cannot be assuaged, eradicated, or easily repaired. However, for Augustine, shame functions as a primary motivator in the human desire for God's healing grace. Therefore, according to Augustine, a full relationship with God presupposes shame. Paradoxically, shame, as a corporeal affect, in its innate social function draws Christians closer to each other and God. Deeply interred shame buried by other affects and maladaptive behaviors must be disinterred for shame to emerge and so to allow for attachment. Affect theorists point out how shame is only possible in the presence of a positive affect, generally love or interest. We feel shame when we have something to lose, namely another's interest. We protect ourselves from experiencing the pain of rejection, of love sought and refused, by feigning indifference, by steeling ourselves against affects of interest and guarding ourselves, even to the extent of refusing love and shaming the other.[102] In this sense then, shame points to love, and for Augustine that love is for God.

Augustine's theological anthropology which emerges out of the two cities is a treatise built on the idea of a shamed body. The body with its *pudenda* should assume a shamed posture in order to reach out to God and avoid concupiscence and pride. Augustine is remarkable in his ability to name shame, to see shame, and to distinguish it from guilt. It is not guilt that lies for him at the center of the Christian self but rather shame. This is not altogether bad news though because of attachment and affect. The prelapsarian shame, the innate shame of affect theorists that underlies human bonding, emerges in Augustine through the body of Christ. It is not shame or humility, as Augustine interprets it, but is rather proper attachment. It *is* and *is not* shame. This formation of the Christian self, then, includes a primal shame that does not diminish into toxic shame which disrupts instead of facilitates the Christian connection to God.

Notes

1. See Margaret R. Miles, *Reading Historical Theology: Before, During, and After Augustine* (Eugene, Oregon: Cascade Books, 2008), and Peter Brown, *Augustine of Hippo* (Berkeley: University of California Press, 1967), 299–312.
2. Burrus, *Saving Shame*, 4.
3. Schore, *Affect Regulation and the Origin of the Self*, 79.
4. Work on shame in the *Confessions* has been conducted by Virginia Burrus; see "Bodies, Desires, Confessions: Shame in Plotinus, Antony, and Augustine," in *Shame between Punishment and Penance: The Social Usages of Shame in the Middle Ages and Early Modern Times*, ed. Bénédicte Sère and Jörg Wettlaufer (Firenze: Sismel, 2013), 23–48. In "Bodies, Desires, Confessions," 45, Burrus posits that in *Confessions* Augustine is not "ashamed to be in a body," but is instead "ashamed to will his own voice, to lay claim to the power of words to do what they say: 'Put on the Lord Jesus Christ.'" Her work on shame in this piece is read with affect theory, especially through the work of Eve Kofosky Sedgwick. A more thorough analysis of shame occurs in her text *Saving Shame: Martyrs, Saints, and Other Abject Subjects*, where Burrus argues that the early Christian tradition has something to teach contemporary society about shame. I concur with her argument about shame that extends from a reading of *Confessions* to the *City of God*.
5. See Augustine, "The Literal Meaning of Genesis," in *On Genesis*, ed. John E. Rotelle, O.S.A., trans. Edmund Hill, O.P. (Hyde Park, NY: New York City Press, 2002), 9.10:16, "However it would be better, more becoming to believe that the 'ensouled' bodies of those two established in Paradise, not yet having been condemned by the law of death, were such that they did

not have the same lust for carnal pleasure as these bodies of ours do now, derived as they are from the propagation of death."

6. Augustine's reading of Genesis in the *City of God* (c. 416) proceeds from a large body of his own writing on the creation story, including, most prominently, *On Genesis: A Refutation of the Manichees* and *Unfinished Literary Commentary on Genesis,* both in *On Genesis,* ed. John E. Rotelle, O.S.A., trans. Edmund Hill, O.P. (Hyde Park, NY: New York City Press, 2002); *Confessions* (397–401), where he most clearly relates the story to his own becoming and conversion; and *The Literal Meaning of Genesis* (401–416), a literal interpretation to complement his earlier figurative interpretations in response to the Manichees. For this history, see Peter Brown and Michael Fiedrowicz, "General Introduction," in *On Genesis,* ed. John E. Rotelle, O.S.A., trans. Edmund Hill, O.P. (Hyde Park, NY: New York City Press, 2002). Every effort at exegesis of this story illustrates maturation in Augustine's thought and further development of his theological anthropology.
7. Augustine, *City of God*, 14.11: 568.
8. Augustine, *City of God*, 14.11: 568.
9. Teresa Brennan discusses the separation of "desire" from "affects" in the twentieth century, a division that would not have held for Augustine; see *Transmission of Affect* (New York: Cornell University Press, 2004), 4. My usage of the word "desire" often conveys it as an affect, which I think relates to interest-excitement.
10. Augustine, *City of God,* 14.12: 571.
11. Augustine, *City of God,* 14:11: 569.
12. Augustine does not locate the devil as directly oppositional to God, and herein lies his argument against the Manicheans. He articulates this clearly in Book 11:13, where he says that the devil fell from the "truth" related to God. It was not that the devil was originally unconnected from that truth. Augustine, *City of God,* 14.11: 569.
13. Augustine, *City of God,* 14.11: 569.
14. Augustine, *City of God,* 569–570.
15. Augustine, *City of God,* 14.12: 571.
16. Augustine, *City of God,* 14.11: 568.
17. Augustine, *City of God,* 14.13: 573.
18. Augustine, *City of God,* 14.14: 574.
19. Augustine, *City of God,* 14.16: 577.
20. Augustine, *City of God,* 14.16: 577.
21. Augustine, *City of God,* 14.15: 576.
22. Augustine, *City of God,* 577.
23. Burrus, Jordan, and MacKendrick, *Seducing Augustine*, 101.
24. Augustine, *City of God,* 14.13: 572.
25. Augustine, *City of God,* 571.

26. Augustine, *City of God,* 572.
27. Augustine, *City of God,* 14.11: 568.
28. Augustine, *City of God,* 14.11: 568.
29. Augustine, *City of God,* 14.13: 572.
30. Augustine quoting Genesis 3:9, *City of God,* 14.17: 579.
31. Augustine, *City of God,* 14.17: 578.
32. Augustine, *City of God,* 579.
33. Augustine, *City of God,* 578.
34. Augustine, *City of God,* 578.
35. Augustine, *City of God,* 14.15: 574–575.
36. Augustine, *City of God,* 14.12: 571.
37. Augustine, *City of God,* 14.17: 579.
38. Augustine, *City of God,* 14.13: 573.
39. Augustine, *City of God,* 14.12: 571.
40. Augustine, *City of God,* 14.13: 572.
41. Berlant, *Cruel Optimism*, 52.
42. Augustine, *City of God,* 14.13: 572.
43. Probyn, *Blush*, 13.
44. See Peter Fonagy, *Affect Theory and Psychoanalysis* (London: Karnac, 2004) for an in-depth analysis of the idea of attunement, along with the integration of affect theory, attachment theory, and psychoanalysis.
45. Schore, *Affect Regulation and the Origin of the Self*, 203.
46. Peter Burnell, "Concupiscence and Moral Freedom in Augustine and Before Augustine," *Augustinian Studies* vol. 26 (1995): 50.
47. Timo Nisula, *Augustine and the Function of Concupiscence* (Boston: Brill, 2012), 44 and 97.
48. Gershen Kaufman, *The Psychology of Shame,* 2nd ed. (New York: Springer, 1996), 5 and 24.
49. Tomkins, *Affect, Imagery, Consciousness*, 387.
50. Block Lewis, "Introduction," 1.
51. Schore, *Affect Regulation and Repair of the Self*, 162.
52. Augustine, *City of God,* 12.14: 489.
53. Augustine, *City of God,* 12.14: 489.
54. Augustine, *City of God,* 10.10: 441.
55. Miles, *Reading Historical Theology*, 97–98.
56. Miles, *Reading Historical Theology*, 101.
57. Augustine, *City of God,* 14.15: 576.
58. Augustine, *City of God,* 14.15: 576.
59. Rosemary Radford Reuther, "Augustine: Sexuality, Gender, and Women," in *Feminist Interpretations of Augustine*, ed. Judith Stark (University Park, PA: Pennsylvania State University Press, 2007), 56. According to Reuther, concupiscence is a state especially projected onto women, whose bodies are responsible for stimulating the sin of concupiscence in the male.

60. Augustine, *City of God*, 14.17: 578.
61. Augustine, *City of God*, 14.17: 578.
62. Tianyue Wu, "Shame in the Context of Sin: Augustine on the Feeling of Shame in the De Civitate Dei," *Recherches de Théologie et Philosophie Médiévales* vol. 74, no. 1 (2007): 23.
63. See Wurmser, "Shame: The Veiled Companion of Narcissism," 68, where he states these as "simple shame anxiety; shame as a complex affective and cognitive reaction pattern; and shame as a character attitude preventing dangerous exposure."
64. Wurmser, "Shame," 72.
65. Schore, *Affect Regulation and the Origin of the Self*, 248.
66. Tomkins, *Affect, Imagery, Consciousness,* 352.
67. Augustine, *City of God*, 14.13: 573.
68. Augustine, *City of God*, 14.18: 580.
69. Augustine, *City of God*, 14.18: 580.
70. Augustine, *City of God*, 14.18: 580.
71. Augustine, *City of God*, 14.18: 579.
72. Augustine, *City of God*, 14.13: 573.
73. See Marjorie Suchocki, "The Symbolic Structure of Augustine's 'Confessions,'" *Journal of the American Academy of Religion* vol. 50, no. 3 (September 1982): 367. Suchocki analyzes Augustine's development in *City of God* of Adam's fall as both a secret sin and an open sin.
74. Tomkins, *Affect, Imagery, Consciousness*, 454 and 480. Here Tomkins asserts that requiring shame to be hidden makes shame even worse. Conversely, allowing a child to feel shame within the field of exposure allows for shame to be reduced.
75. Nathanson, *Shame and Pride*, 321. Nathanson also asserts that an adaptive response to shame is withdrawal to reflect on the shame experience in order to learn something from it, or in order to "not be overwhelmed" by an experience; see page 318.
76. S.M. Retzinger, "A Theory of Mental Illness: Integrating Social and Emotional Aspects," *Psychiatry* vol. 152, no. 3 (1989): 5.
77. Augustine, *City of God*, 14.18: 580.
78. Augustine, *City of God*, 14.12: 571.
79. Augustine, *City of God*, 14.13: 571.
80. Augustine, *City of God*, 14.13: 573.
81. Further, in Book 13.4, Augustine frees humankind from the guilt of the first act of disobedience by showing that it is shame, not guilt, that is carried forward. Then, in Book 14, he mentions guilt only in relation to disobedience, an action provoked by what Augustine thinks is a much greater sin: pride. Augustine writes, "The pride of the transgressor was worse than the sin itself," 14.14: 574.

82. See Scheff, "The Shame Rage Spiral;" Kaufman, *The Psychology of Shame*, 128, 129, and 239. See also Sedgwick, *Touching Feeling*, 64, where she calls this cycle a "chain reaction of shame dynamics."
83. Sedgwick, *Touching Feeling*, 63.
84. Augustine, *City of God,* 14.13: 572.
85. Augustine, *City of God,* 14.12: 571.
86. There are several places in *City of God* and *Confessions* where Augustine talks about habit. In his biography of Augustine, Peter Brown discusses the saint's interpretation of habit as a "compulsive force" derived from memory, especially the experience of pleasure so "inflicted" on memory; this pleasure is amplified, remembered, and repeated and thus becomes a compulsive habit; see Brown, *Augustine*, 149.
87. Augustine, *City of God*, 14.13: 573.
88. Augustine, *City of God*, 14.13: 573.
89. See David Konstan, "Shame in Ancient Greece," where Konstan discusses this extensively.
90. Bourdieu discusses humility embodied and patterned as a female quality the gestures of which replicate shame and modesty, see *The Logic of Practice*, 72; and Tomkins cites Freud, as aligning modesty with the covering up of deficient female genitals, see *Affect Imagery Consciousness*, 566. These examples point to the social association of shame or something shameful with modesty and humility.
91. Stephen Pattison, *Shame: Theory, Therapy, Theology*, 220 and 252.
92. Augustine, *City of God*, 9:20: 366 and 10:20: 400.
93. Augustine's conversion to Christianity brought about an anti-Manichean stance that is illustrated in his linking the two worlds with bodies and in his rejection of the body as passive. Further, Augustine, in contrast to the Manicheans, believed that bodies were not a product of an evil power, which relegated reproduction to the power of darkness.
94. Elizabeth Clark, ed., *St. Augustine on Marriage and Sexuality* (Washington, D.C.: The Catholic University of America Press, 1996), 32 and 72.
95. See, for instance, Johannes Van Oort, *Jerusalem and Babylon: A Study into Augustine's City of God and the Sources of his Doctrines of the Two Cities* (New York: Brill, 1991), 115.
96. Miles, "Sex and the City," 321.
97. Burrus, *Saving Shame*, 133.
98. Goffman, *Stigma*, 3.
99. Goffman, *Stigma*, 4 and 108.
100. Augustine, *City of God*, 14.11: 569.
101. Helen Merrell Lynd, *On Shame and the Search for Identity* (New York: Harcourt, Brace &World, 1958), 27.
102. Nathanson, *Shame and Pride*, 251.

CHAPTER 4

Masked Shame

Some of Reinhold Niebuhr's most prominent theological concepts regarding human life emerge in his uncompromising commitment to moral progress, which he asserts begins with the individual. His rejection of the "tender-minded" bent of liberal theology[1] accompanies his commitment to the formation of the Christian self according to the "deep mythical meanings of Christian teaching" in the face of growing abusive, coercive world power.[2] Niebuhr claims that an individual Christian's commission includes "understanding the reality of evil within himself," while escaping "the error of attributing that evil to any one but himself."[3] Thus, Niebuhr's theology promotes radical honesty, challenging the Christian to look within to confront whatever inhibits or interferes with a connection to God. His perception that the world needs the guidance of the Christian story to access grace emerges in his delivery of the Gifford Lectures, The Nature and Destiny of Man.

Pragmatic and utilitarian in his use of sources in this text, Niebuhr returns to the Edenic myth to illustrate his opposition to an utopian vision of humanity. He concludes that only a Christian theology with a concept of sin can offer redemption from pride and the desire for power. Niebuhr's development of a theological anthropology in *The Nature and Destiny of Man* establishes his role in the Christian tradition as a master diagnostician of the human condition. His influence on Christianity and Christian formation is far reaching. From the Gifford Lectures to the widespread popularity of the Serenity Prayer, Niebuhr's words have come to shape

S.N. Arel, *Affect Theory, Shame, and Christian Formation*,
DOI 10.1007/978-3-319-42592-4_4

Christian consciousness. Dedicated to the growth of the Christian self, Niebuhr theorized about human motivation and psychology always in pursuit of the faithful relationship with God. However, in his diagnosis of the guilty, prideful Christian self, Niebuhr neglects to name shame.

Shame is an inherent part of human life. It can neither be dismissed nor be completely eradicated. Only by being faced and disinterred can shame's maladaptive effects be mitigated. How does Niebuhr's diagnosis of the guilty, prideful self relate to shame while also being committed to the amelioration of the human condition plagued by suffering? How does Niebuhr's diagnosis effect the formation of the Christian self? What new understandings of Niebuhr's theological anthropology emerge once shame is shown to be present?

Exposing where implicit shame operates in Niebuhr's theological anthropology requires the disentangling of shame from his rhetoric about the Christian self where he discusses pride, guilt, sin, and anxiety. In fact, guilt operates as an objective category for Niebuhr that masks shame. Reading Niebuhr through an affective lens, coupled with the use of psychoanalytic theory, uncovers shame somewhat obscured within Niebuhr's analysis. This unidentified shame within his writing emerges paralleling the nature of shame outlined in affect theory: its complex structure, its capacity to provoke pain, and its expression as a problem of attachment. We need a language of shame to explore the subjective dynamics of the suffering to which a fallen world exposes us. In this way, affect theory helps us get a better sense of how the human being must name, manage, and disinter shame in order to confront guilt in the way that Niebuhr suggests we should. In this way, the insights of affect theory foster moral progress.

Exposing that which masks shame in Niebuhr's diagnosis of the Christian self facilitates an identification of shame in his theological language. Uncovering where shame operates in his text reveals how its concealment in rhetoric produces a *habitus* opposite from the one Niebuhr's theology intends to create. Niebuhr envisions a Christian self repentant and turned to God, but by misinterpreting shame, his work portrays a guilty Christian self who represses shame; this repression leads to maladaptive effects.[4]

Just as uncovering shame in Augustine began with the Edenic narrative, probing Niebuhr's reading of the scene is a starting point for discriminating shame in Niebuhr's theological anthropology. Like Augustine, Niebuhr considers the Edenic drama indicative of the human situation in sin. However, Niebuhr's position is rooted in his interpretation of the

Fall as a myth that founds human life. In his analysis of the Edenic drama, he uses key terms to define and delineate the human situation: "original sin," "anxiety," "guilt," "pride," and "sensuality." Niebuhr's descriptions of these terms intertwine with, relate to, and contribute to the production of shame. Niebuhr's slippage in languaging shame allows this affect to be interred both figuratively in his language and practically in the Christian self. Finally, despite Niebuhr's lack of articulation of shame, something akin to shame clearly emerges in his theological anthropology and is central to each self-identifying Christian.

The Drama of the Fall as a Human Drama

Identifying the shame that underlies Niebuhr's theology requires a look at his view of the Fall. Augustine articulated the Edenic narrative as foundational to understanding shame in the formation of the Christian self. And while Niebuhr's language elides shame, something like shame emerges in his understanding of Christian development. In *Nature and Destiny of Man*, Niebuhr does not read the Eden scene quite as literally or systematically as Augustine does. Instead, he rereads Augustine and resists prior historical interpretations of the drama of the Fall, understanding the narrative and other biblical narratives purely as myths symbolic of the human condition.[5] Yet, for Niebuhr, the Edenic narrative signifies a foundation for Christian life.

The central character in Niebuhr's interpretation of the Fall is the devil. Originally a fallen angel, the devil symbolizes evil which "arises from his effort to transgress the bounds set for his life" by God.[6] As the original "rebel" against God, the devil is a figurative foil to God. Symbolizing the self full of pride and resentful of the limitations set upon him, the devil rejects God, who is boundless and free. As a result of this transgression in pride against God, "sin posits itself" within the devil.[7] Consequentially, original sin, manifested in the devil's pride, becomes a "force of evil" and a source of temptation that will subsequently surge through Adam.[8] However, Niebuhr neither locates Adam as the actual source of the first sin, nor does he believe, as Augustine does, that Adam and Eve initiate the passing of sin from person to person. Sin, for Niebuhr, is neither inherited nor intrinsic because as the devil does, Adam functions figuratively as a representative, who symbolizes the condition of humankind. Thus, Adam epitomizes or serves as a personification of a Christian person.

Niebuhr addresses the sin of Adam, stating that "the sin of each individual is preceded by Adam's sin: but even this first sin of history is not the first sin."[9] Niebuhr wants to assert that the source of sin in Adam is not biological. It is a spiritual force, represented by the devil, "the principle or force of evil antecedent to any evil human action."[10] Niebuhr locates sin situationally, rejecting Augustine's notion that sin endures as an "inherited corruption."[11] Sin is, thus, not intrinsic. However, for Niebuhr, original sin resides internal to Adam's being and creates the conditions for the sinful act, a manifestation of the temptation brought about by the devil. The sinful act thus emerges out of the sinful condition or the desire to be God.

Sinful action, then, reveals internal sin. Adam's refusal of God, made in a rejection of God's rule not to eat from the tree of knowledge, authenticates his imperfection, internal sin. Niebuhr states that "Adam was sinless before he acted and sinful in his first recorded action. This is a symbol for the whole of human history."[12] According to Niebuhr's statement here, because of the devil, Adam's nature includes this "bias toward sin."[13] If Adam had not acted and if Adam had remained under God's control fully attached, surrendering his own will and urges to God, his sinfulness would not have come to light. Niebuhr writes further that "Adam is a representative, not of our freedom to choose either good or evil, but rather of our falling through unbelief [in God] and pride into a state of *sin* that renders us unable to choose the good we would choose."[14] Unable to choose between good and evil, the Christian self, caught between a pull from both the devil and God, can only achieve freedom by submitting his/her will to God. Paradoxically, disempowered will, or individual will turned over to God, is free.

Retaining Augustine's emphasis on sin as a consequence of freedom, where sin illustrates humanity's desire to embrace the will to be powerful, Niebuhr's notion of sin as self-love, or pride, illustrated by the devil's descent into imperfection, is secondarily reflected in sensuality. Niebuhr writes that although the account of the Fall in Genesis "describes sin as primarily disobedience to God through the temptation of pride and not sensual passion, [it] understands that guilt becomes involved in sensual passion after the Fall, for man becomes suddenly conscious of his sexuality."[15]

Like Augustine, Niebuhr asserts that human will and human action are subject to what could be considered affective forces, that push the individual to be more self-concerned. Augustine views these forces as urges that rise from the *pudenda*, while Niebuhr locates these forces in the bias toward sin, which blinds individuals, or disenables them from being fully conscious.[16] Both Niebuhr and Augustine describe a self that comes into consciousness, or into its full potential, only through attachment to God. In fact, Niebuhr calls himself an Augustinian when he locates will at the center of his discourse, over and above reason, noting that the strength of will trumps the intellect.[17] According to Niebuhr, human will subjected to God's will connects humanity to God; independent human will disrupts the connection to God.

Having established Adam as a representative of the Christian individual and asserting that human will must be subjected to God, Niebuhr uses the Edenic narrative to connect Adam's internal sin to both the rejection of God and pride, or the desire to be God. Niebuhr states that "the anxiety of unbelief" motivates this desire, or temptation.[18] Inspired by the devil, the anxiety of unbelief undermines human agency (to turn toward God) and signifies this key deficiency as original sin.[19] Thus, the predilection for sin is rooted in humanity's anxious, animal nature, connecting humanity to the devil, temptation, and unconsciousness, which results in humanity's wrong interpretation that its condition of finiteness is escapable. Instead of accepting the condition of the paradox, that life is situated between finiteness and freedom, humanity falsely grasps the idea that freedom will help with an escape from finiteness. This possibility of transmuting a "mutable good into infinity,"[20] as Niebuhr puts it, does not exist. Niebuhr posits that Adam fails to bear finiteness and vulnerability, succumbing to the anxiety that results from both. Such anxiety transmutes into temptation to sin, which is precisely where Adam discovers the inevitability of original sin—in his own freedom and detachment from God.

Along with anxiety, Niebuhr identifies guilt and remorse following sinful acts. Before God sees him, Adam is confused by the devil and commits an act of disobedience which Niebuhr also calls a deception of God. In Niebuhr's terms, the choice to disobey God stems from "a general state of confusion" or a lack of consciousness.[21] But an awaking to consciousness of sinfulness occurs, accompanied by a lack of understanding that God's grace can help in overcoming the confusion, which evokes "the despair of remorse," or guilt.[22] To explain guilt, Niebuhr quotes Genesis 3:7, "And the eyes of them both were opened, and they knew that they were naked; and they sewed fig leaves together, and made themselves aprons."[23] He asserts that this account "understands that guilt becomes involved in sensual passion after the Fall."[24] Niebuhr's interpretation of the Edenic narrative contrasts with Augustine's, who quotes Genesis 3 to indicate shame.

Niebuhr relates Adam and Eve's covering up of their newly perceived nakedness to "consciousness of sexuality," which he aligns directly with guilt. Thus, he implies that the proper affective response to body awareness is guilt.[25] Viewed this way, both the act of wrongdoing and the body itself—in nakedness and its sexual function—represent things for which humanity experiences guilt. Furthermore, Niebuhr claims that not only wrongdoing inspires guilt, but Adam's state of confusion, lack of consciousness, and inevitable sin also elicit guilt. The element of consciousness makes Adam responsible for inevitable sin and, thus, guilty. However, represented as a failure within the self to be responsible, guilt assumes qualities of shame.

For Niebuhr, Adam represents the guilty sinner, who should feel guilty for what Niebuhr generalizes as acts of sin. Through Adam, Niebuhr recognizes the Fall as the moment that illustrates preconditioned sin, a situation in which all of humanity finds itself. Sin's ubiquity accounts for the human will that must be subjugated to God.[26]

Thus, for Niebuhr, the Christian self, replicating Adam's situation, exists within a series of paradoxes. The Christian self in sin is situated at the juncture of "imperfect" nature and "holy" or "pure" spirit, with the freedom to be both creative and tempted, while simultaneously restricted by finitude. Sin illustrates a misuse of freedom by the spirit in pride. The situation of tension between freedom, humanity's possibilities, and finiteness, its limitations, emerges once evil resides in the devil. The existence of evil in the devil permits Adam's situation of finiteness and freedom to be "falsely interpreted" by Adam.[27] That is, Adam thinks that on his own, through his freedom, he can ascend from finiteness, while in truth, freedom can only be achieved through attachment to God. But attachment to God is hampered, and he is left in perpetual anxiety. To quell his anxiety, he commits the actual sins of pride and sensuality, but attempts to flee anxiety are made in vain. Adam suffers, as a sinner who seems to be afflicted by guilt, but who actually languishes in shame.

Diagnosis and Original Sin

Niebuhr takes up the drama of the Fall to beseech humanity to change behavior. The narrative analyzed in *The Nature and Destiny of Man* provides a map of the human situation. In order to intensify the lessons of the drama of the Fall, Niebuhr sets forth certain conditions in which humanity finds itself: original sin, guilt, anxiety, pride, and sensuality. These conditions serve as the key components of Niebuhr's complex etiology for human suffering, and they undergird his theological anthropology. He evaluates each category objectively, to offer ways of navigating Christian growth and connection to God. Embedded in these objective categories lies the shame affect, which uncovered, promotes the formation of the Christian self in the way that Niebuhr actually intends.

Original Sin

In *Nature and Destiny of Man*, Niebuhr locates original sin internally as a kind of wound, an inevitable "corruption" illustrative of apathy, the "sloth of nature" born in humanity—in affect theory, what is called the torment of the soul in shame.[28] Niebuhr uses the traditional religious symbols of the Fall to illustrate that evil is not only related to the "ignorance of the mind" and "the passions of the body" but also connected to a principal force antecedent to any human action and embodied *a priori* within the devil.[29] "Man's willful refusal to acknowledge the finite and determinate character of his existence" evidences the operation of evil in the self.[30] Thus, evil persists in the self because of a person's denying the contingency of imperfect, limited human life characterized by ambiguity.

Since human life predisposed to evil radically distinguishes itself from God, it struggles with imperfection, finite existence, and the impossibility of perfection, which psychologically provoke shame. Moreover, sin is inevitable, though unnecessary, and this inevitability presents one part of the paradox Niebuhr puts forth in his theology. Sin is inevitable, but humanity is responsible for sin because it is not necessary. He believes that all individuals must attend to sin and combat the slothful characteristic of a path of sinful actions. Devotion to this end requires an aspiration to subject the self to God through grace. While never completely assuaged, sin can only be ameliorated by "subjection" of the "particular [individual] will" to God's will.[31] Thus, life, while imperfect, can only be improved according to Niebuhr, when the individual surrenders his/her personal desires and sinful temptations to the will of God.

This subjection of the will to God's occurs only through what Niebuhr considers the spiritual practice of consciousness. For Niebuhr, consciousness distinguishes humanity from other forms of life. He articulates a world where consciousness helps humanity not only perceive original sin but also recognize it as a wounded condition necessitating remediation. This amounts to a consciousness of guilt, which belies the shame the wound of sin more effectively represents. Although the inner wound of sin situated in the Christian self cannot be changed, developing human consciousness moderates the extension of original sin into sinful actions for which the self should experience guilt. For Niebuhr, finite humanity, limited by animal nature, has the capacity to change, grow, and modify this nature through an individual spirit of which consciousness is a part. Niebuhr insists that consciousness, the spiritual aspect of humanity, links humanity to God and makes humanity both capable of turning the will toward God and risking attachment. Consciousness is thus both complicit with original sin, since awareness for Niebuhr constitutes sin, and comprises the primary state of being that permits the guilty Christian self to seek a remedy for sin.

Anxiety

While sin's etiology is the fall into imperfection, its proof is an affective life of anxiety, a direct result of original sin, underlying all human experience and defining humanity's state of being. Indeed, for Niebuhr, ontological anxiety constitutes the human condition, which, along with insecurity, comprises the "psychological facts"[32] that support original sin. While different from neurotic or pathological anxiety, which can both be considered abnormal states,[33] ontological anxiety represents the core and consistent state of being in which humanity finds itself.

For Niebuhr, anxiety emerges from two sources: Adam's awareness of being finite, limited, dependent, imperfect, and his inability to see the limits of his freedom. For instance, in the face of his dependency on God, Adam feels anxious. Yet this anxiety also perpetuates his desire to be like God. The presence of desire to be like God evidences the denial of the limitations of human life and experience.

For Niebuhr, awareness or consciousness of anxiety constitutes a spiritual sensitivity to the state of affective anxiety that develops as a result of Adam's knowing that he is caught perpetually between desire and denial. Ultimately, engendered by humanity's awareness of the "caprices and perils" of the natural world, anxiety defines human life. And while consciousness contributes to anxiety because it includes an awareness of human nature's predisposition toward evil, it also enables a cognitive control that Niebuhr recommends. Cognitive control materializes in Adam's dual realization of his mortality and his dependence on God for amelioration. Any such reprieve from anxiety thus results from a connection with God.

While this reprieve from anxiety is never absolute, it can be tamed and at least affectively regulated. Niebuhr understands regulation as always in tension; he conveys in his work how anxiety proceeds as the condition of "man's relation to the temporal process on one hand and to eternity on the other."[34] But this happens unnaturally, so it should be controlled in so far as it contributes to the "boundless character of human desire."[35] Thus, Niebuhr situates anxiety at the fulcrum of a paradox. Anxiety emerges out of the union between the perception of individuals as at once creatures and *imago dei*, where the "vulnerable and insecure creatureliness" meets "the awareness of our temporality and mortality that spirit makes possible."[36] Anxiety entails an individual's rejecting God and endeavoring to transmute "finiteness to infiniteness, weakness into strength, dependence into independence."[37]

Anxiety serves as the precondition or the breeding ground for actual sin;[38] it is not sin. Original sin plus anxiety create the affective conditions from which actual sin "flows."[39] Clearly, for Niebuhr, anxiety is "bound together in human actions and the errors which are made in the search for perfection."[40] Thus, anxiety contributes to a cycle that leads the self to desire more and more of what he/she perceives as perfect. Anxiety "tempts the self to sin; the sin increases insecurity which it was intended to alleviate until some escape from the whole tension of life is sought."[41] This tension of life emerges as humanity's anxious situation caught between the finite world and infinity, a situation Niebuhr asserts that humanity attempts to deny. Importantly, denial emerges because "the ego does not feel secure," and the individual grasps for more power "to make itself secure."[42] This anxious grasping, for Niebuhr, can never result in anything but more anxiety, and power cannot heal the ontological condition of anxiety. Yet, humanity, according to Niebuhr believes otherwise, and anxiety, along with insecurity and the search for greater security, leads either to the actual sin of "egoistic" pride (self-deification) or to "egotistic" sensuality (the deification of another).[43] In a sense then, Niebuhr's conceptualization of anxiety effectively masks shame.

Actual Sins

Original sin emerges as actual sin when the individual Christian self "lacks the faith and trust to subject itself to God."[44] The primary actual sins that Niebuhr identifies are pride and sensuality precipitated by anxiety. Niebuhr succinctly details the manner of emergence of actual sin: "Man falls into pride, when he seeks to raise his contingent existence to unconditioned significance; he falls into sensuality when he seeks to escape from his unlimited possibilities of freedom."[45] Thus, in Niebuhr's perspective, mitigating anxiety equates to investing in self-aggrandizement, in order to defy mortality, or in avoidance, denying freedom of choice.

The dimensions of sin demonstrated by pride and sensuality allow Niebuhr to account for the idea of sin's "expansion."[46] Significantly for human experience, both pride and sensuality are qualified by their scope. Pride represents excessiveness substantiated in humanity's unbounded desire, self-worship, and effort to defy the limitations of mortal life, while sensuality consists of escaping or losing the self in sensual love and idolization of another person or thing.[47] Actual sins, the further manifestation of original sin, decline into more sin as they inhibit and eventually destroy the possibility for growth. Therefore, they require continual conscious attention and either some form of repentance when the sin is against God, or remorse when the sin is against another.

Pride

Acts of pride, for Niebuhr, operate as the most basic and the basest of actual sins.[48] Pride emerges out of ontology: original sin and anxiety create a toxic mix that produces pride in each individual. Self-love, further aggrandized when love and desire are continually injected back into the self, crystalizes in the visual image of the puffed-up self in pride. Niebuhr depicts this self as having a boundless ego, which he considers sinful.[49] The prideful self aims to "enhance the ego," to experience "a sense of power."[50]

Niebuhr addresses "the boundless and limitless tendencies of human desires,"[51] which manifest as the ego committing sins that emerge in the "lust-for-power" and in pride itself related to "prestige and honour."[52] Rejecting finiteness, the boundless ego seeks infinity, the state of limitlessness and perfection before the Fall, a state that can only be assumed by God. Thus, full of pride, the self attempts to be God rather than to preserve attachment by submitting to God.

The attempt to be God illustrates humanity's attempt to eradicate anxiety. Pride's characterization as the affirmation of self-sufficiency, the denial of contingency, and the refusal to acknowledge insecurity culminate ultimately in a rejection of dependence on God. Pride before God composes the "religious dimension of sin."[53] Pride in the horizontal plane materializes as injustice, or sin against humanity.[54]

The slippery slope that leads to injustice begins for Niebuhr with pride. Setting oneself above all others, including God, the prideful self celebrates personal gain and power. The competition inherent in this position leads the self to express contempt toward others. Opposition toward the other illustrates "the reverse side of pride and its necessary concomitant in a world in which self-esteem is constantly challenged by the achievements of others."[55] Excessive love of the self, as *hubris*, therefore, also comprises hatred toward the other, detracting from the possibility of connection. This love though, not as the love of self-worth, reverberates an insecurity in the self, one that has an affective charge of shame.

Sensuality

In Niebuhr's theology, where boundlessness reflects humanity's pride and signifies a fleeing away from God toward human power, sensuality signifies a fleeing from God toward the other (a thing or a person) in what Niebuhr calls an "escape,"[56] a retreat from consciousness, including a denial of the self and a desire to seek "escape from [this] unlimited freedom."[57] This self cannot bear the anxiety experienced when choosing between surrender to sin and surrender to God's will. Self-denial results, provoking the "fall into sensuality"[58] where self-love becomes invested in another, which Niebuhr equates to rejecting God. Furthermore, as with pride, the act of escaping in sensuality is conducted through a variety of methods—addictive behaviors for Niebuhr—including "sexual license, gluttony, extravagance, drunkenness and abandonment to various forms of physical desire."[59]

In addition to referencing sexual instincts, Niebuhr also notes that alcohol dependence evidences sensuality and claims that both behaviors serve as "anodyne[s]" or "escape[s] from the tensions of life."[60] Moreover, both alcohol and sex serve to repress the actuality of life as finite and the feelings of insecurity, inferiority, and anxiety that finite life evokes.[61] In addition, alcohol and sex expand the ego, muting insecurity.[62] Niebuhr writes that "sex reveals sensuality to be first another and final form of self-love, secondly an effort to escape self-love by the deification of another and finally as an escape from the futilities of both forms of idolatry by a plunge into unconsciousness."[63] Niebuhr's dramatic language presents this plunge as an ultimate state of denial and repression that he wholeheartedly rejects. For Niebuhr, consciousness of finiteness, which provokes anxiety, connects humanity to freedom, while unconsciousness illustrates *dis*-ease, of which sensuality serves as an example.

Relatedly, the desire to remain unconscious emerges when sensuality becomes a tool to avoid anxiety. For Niebuhr, sensuality is precisely "a further sin, which is also a punishment for the more primary sin [of pride]."[64] For Niebuhr, sensuality can be generalized, as lust can be for Augustine. Significant for Niebuhr as well is that society sanctions pride (the worse sin) but generally resists sensuality. To build his position, Niebuhr quotes Augustine from the *City of God* and *On Marriage and Concupiscence* where the latter states that the disobedience of Adam and Eve led to a "rebellion" of the flesh and "vicious desires."[65] Such vicious desires are both impure and ferocious; they evidence internal evil as anxiety, further described as "the internal description of the state of temptation" and sin. Like Augustine's *pudenda*, which he portrays as inspiring uncontrollable bodily urges, Niebuhr identifies the sex impulse, which he says has far exceeded its role as a procreative act. Brandishing it as disorderly and uncontainable, he writes that the sex impulse has frequently become an "instrument of compensation" for humanity's insecurity and fear of freedom, providing an "avenue of escape."[66] Whereas Augustine promotes a redirection of desire, Niebuhr promotes atonement of the inner sin or deficiency that motivates such desire. Thus, Niebuhr characterizes the Christian life as consisting of a continual turning toward God, in what he labels as guilt and repentance.

Guilt

In Niebuhr's analysis "guilt is the objective consequence of sin, the actual corruption of the plan of creation and providence in the historical world," for which, Niebuhr states, "the inner sinner must be held responsible."[67] Guilt necessitates the responsibility of the individual for his/her own imperfection since the self is situated existentially in guilt, related to ontological anxiety. For Niebuhr, guilt both illustrates the existence of sin and serves as the appropriate reaction to original sin, the appropriate affective stance which acts as a regulator of humanity's inner, if variable, layers of corruption.

Just as Niebuhr conceives of layers of sin—first original and then actual—he also perceives layers of guilt. The first layer consists of guilt for sloth related to humanity's lack of resistance to original sin. From that sloth, actual sins emerge for which humanity feels guilty, inspiring regret and a desire to act otherwise. He asserts, "The fact of responsibility is attested by the feeling of remorse or repentance which follows the [inevitable] sinful action."[68] Thus again, humanity exists amid the paradox of inevitability and responsibility.

In Niebuhr's view, self-love fuels much of the suffering in human life, and subsequently, humanity feels guilt. Reflected in Niebuhr's following account, this guilt underlies many societal ills that regularly befall humanity:

> It is the guilt of the sinner that his self-love results in the consequence of broken or unhappy homes, of children made unhappy by the tyranny of their parents, of peoples destroyed by wars which were prompted by the vanity of their rulers, of the poverty of the victims of greed and the unhappiness of the victims of jealousy and envy.[69]

Guilt, with its attendant remorse for self-love, is thus critical to humanity's release from such volatile situations. However, only an aware and reflective self can access guilt and therefore address it. This aware and conscious self both indicates the state of sin and participates in the healing of sin. But the assuaging or ameliorating attention to guilt occurs only when the individual seeks God. Viewed through an affective lens, detached from God and subsequently from others, the self exists in a fractured state of isolation, which perpetuates pride, unhappiness, and greed, all pathologies to Niebuhr. Underneath them though, lies the "sleeper" affect, ubiquitous but often neglected, shame.

Shame Emerges

Throughout *Nature and Destiny of Man*, Niebuhr rarely mentions shame explicitly. However, viewing his work through the lens of affect theory reveals something like shame in Niebuhr's work enmeshed within and/or elided by other terms. This elision of shame in Niebuhr's writing is not dissimilar to the human experience of shame itself. Shame functions primarily in the body under the guise of something else, including anxiety, withdrawal, general guilt (without the possibility of pardon), generalized rage, and violence.[70] The pain of shame, thus, seeks respite in some other affective formulation.

In Niebuhr, original sin, anxiety, pride, sensuality, and guilt all mask shame in some way. Drawing from the work of affect and shame theorists to disentangle these terms from each other helps to delineate "marks of shame" in Niebuhr's writing, extricating shame from his rhetoric and revealing where it lies obscured. In addition, distinguishing shame from other affects clarifies its role as a central affect of human life that when repressed and interred has deleterious effects.

Significantly, the trajectory of original sin can be understood in terms of shame. The stigmatization of original sin and the associated degradation of self-worth, posited internally and establishing the individual as inferior, both relate to shame. While the inner defect of original sin elicits what Niebuhr labels guilt, this guilt looks more like shame when read with reference to affect theory. Further, Niebuhr asserts that pride and sensuality—the outgrowths of original sin—emerge as a result of the individual's failure to manage anxiety. Read through the lens of affect theory, pride and sensuality as Niebuhr defines them illuminate the way that humanity fails to manage shame.

Internal Wound

While Niebuhr's idea of sin as posited sounds much like Tomkins's "sickness of the soul," Niebuhr states that healing or ameliorating this wound, or evil in the self, requires a turn toward God motivated by guilt. In contrast, according to literature on affect, the response to this wound, or experience of the self as lacking, is shame. Whereas guilt is a response to behavior, shame is a response to a perceived inadequacy in the self. Thus, guilt focuses outwardly; shame, inwardly. What Niebuhr diagnoses as guilt, then, reflects a shame response. Thus, Niebuhr's idea of guilt can be seen affectively as shame.

Niebuhr describes the Fall as one from perfection to imperfection. Original sin, resident in the individual as an inner defect, marks this descent.[71] Niebuhr's presentation of original sin as an interior corruption establishes a broken humanity in need of repair. For such reparation, Niebuhr looks to guilt, which exists separately from shame, but affectively the self experiences shame as corrupting or damaging the self. Affective shame surfaces in Niebuhr's work in his conception of the guilty sinner who seeks ways to eradicate inner pain. For Niebuhr, though the origin of such pain is guilt. Although amelioration of guilt and subsequent pain can never be total, remorse and repentance offer some mollification. Humanity can manage sin through reparation and connection to God. However, the sinful state humanity finds itself in, can never, according to Niebuhr, grant us full access to divine grace this side of the eschaton. Access is always partial. But naming shame assists our access to divine assistance because it validates affective life. The turn to God in guilt, without a recognition of or vocabulary for shame, inhibits the connection to God because it allows detrimental shame to operate and sever connection. But when shame is named, that self can turn to God even in shame; connection to God and shame exist simultaneously. Thus, we are connected to God, although partially, even in our shame.

For Niebuhr, original sin, whether individually "conscious or unconscious," marks the beginning of what he calls a "pathetic vicious circle" and "the consequence of blindness," figuratively speaking, to the wound of sin itself, evidenced in humanity's imperfection.[72] On a social level, internalizing this gross human imperfection as a stigma supports shame's centralization in the stigmatized person. Individuals thus experience themselves as inferior, blemished, and sick. Belief in the inferior self makes counteracting a sense of shame difficult, leading to distress "which further activates shame, which thus ends in further defeat and strengthening the image of the self as inferior" or shamed.[73]

Niebuhr suggests that for amelioration one must turn toward God. This turn to God grants respite. Thus, in Niebuhr, to address what appears to be shame requires exposure and meeting God, constituting a contraindication of the shame response of hiding. Bear in mind, although counterintuitive, the repair of shame occurs when shame itself comes into view in the sight of another to be affectively attuned in relation. However, shame masked as other affects or experiences, such as guilt, becomes interred and thus inhibits repair.

In shame literature, generally, shame occurs in response to an attachment, and shame often acts as an affect that connects the person who has experienced the shame to the person in front of whom the shame has been experienced. In Niebuhr's case, "guilt" for sin, or what I see as shame, becomes both obvious and assuaged before God. In this sense, shame and sin progress similarly. Original sin and guilt, in Niebuhr's analysis, connect and bind the Christian self to an idolatrous world and to earthly sin.[74] Niebuhr presses the Christian self to accept grace and turn to God in remorse, using "guilt" as an indicator of sin. But so often in his wording, he implicates shame; he suggests shame. This confusion disables a clear understanding of both shame and guilt, interfering with Niebuhr's intent of motivating the Christian self to accept what grace can be given, even in the face of suffering so as to ameliorate that suffering.

Stigma and the Bad Self

The formation of the Christian self in Niebuhr's work includes the locating of an internal, original sin. This sin rests in bodies and signifies something of a central and injured core. This idea of an internal defect can be understood through the idea of an internalized stigma which sociologist Erving Goffman understands as provoking shame. Goffman describes shame arising "from the individual's perception of one of his own attributes as being a defiling thing to possess."[75] Defilement occurs on an interrelational level, between individuals or small groups, but it also expands when society and culture develop concepts of otherness thereby deciding who lies outside of normative superior or "more pure" categories and, therefore, who is interpreted as impure or defiled.

Such defilement communicated by society and cultural inheritance shapes the body of the stigmatized into something "not quite human."[76] Stigmas create labels and foster the delineation of social groups accordingly. This dynamic emerges, for example, in categorizations based on race, gender, sex, disability, mental illness, physical illnesses, criminal status, or anything perceived by society as aberrant. Furthermore, socialization based on stigmatization contributes to a dilemma where the stigmatized has the pressure to decide either to embrace the group in which he/she "belongs" or to let it go. Shame results from either decision. The stigmatized or labeled person experiences shame from the accepted or rejected group which leads to individual ashamedness either way, followed by feelings of further shame for feeling the first shame—thus illustrating the shame cycle highlighted in affect theory.[77]

The cycle ensues when the interment of whatever is defined as "bad" leads to a subsequent splitting of the self in an effort to repress what is perceived as the stigma. Repression's intent is to quell anxiety and additional shame. This manifests as the social notion of eradicating the stigma. Group alliances facilitate a synthesis that camouflages particular perceived traits labeled as stigmas. Importantly, for Goffman though, releasing such stigmas and considering them "bad objects" equates psychologically to the eradication of the self and/or the eradication of the self's association with a social group. However, relationships with "bad objects" produce anxiety. Both the bad object and the bad self are experienced as shameful. Thus, the individual in shame will often attempt to destroy that part of the self that is perceived as bad, sick, wrong, or wounded.[78] In the effort to dispel the bad object and the bad affect, the individual experiences a kind of self-annihilation. The perceived result manifests as a double-edged sword: either inter shame and find some way to align the self with a group or face the source of shame, the stigma, and risk social or perceived death.

Whatever the bad object is, it also solicits our attention either consciously or unconsciously. In repression, we devote ourselves to these bad objects perhaps because we fear their release from the unconscious, while we also fear these objects might support our own deficiencies.[79] The subjects of repression are bad internalized objects, which may involve the repression of particular impulses and memories because they are concomitant with the bad object.[80]

Viewed affectively, Niebuhr's concept of original sin resembles a stigma that incurs shame and facilitates a component of repression, a splitting or a cutting off parts of the self.[81] He sees repression or splitting as conducted by actual sins. When this happens, individuals see the good and bad as separate aspects of the self but fail to integrate them. For Niebuhr, this manifests metaphorically in the connection of the Christian self to idolatry. This self needs grace, but the turn-away from God toward sin refutes grace. This tension leads to shame, which goes unnamed in Niebuhr. Shame misnamed as guilt explicitly in writing (and in speaking) helps to prevent shame from entering consciousness, thus repressing it. But neither a forgetting nor an excluding, the repression of shame contains an interior representation, depicted in Niebuhr's work as the defect of original sin.[82]

As a general process, repression serves as a human defense mechanism when negative affects become too overwhelming and cannot be sublimated (redirected to a more socially or morally pleasing form) or replaced with positive affects.[83] This kind of psychological process is particularly acute in cases of personal trauma where repression, including the repression of shame, strengthens because any situation that resounds too loudly with the original trauma or stimulus invokes further repression.[84] Repression, then, is precisely the interior mechanism that permits the stimulus of shame to work to obscure it. But repressed shame, contained and represented as something else, often has dire consequences: it emerges in physical symptoms, as other affects (in Niebuhr's lexicon, guilt and anxiety), or it is transmuted into some harm done to others.[85]

The Slippage

A closer review of Niebuhr's ideas alongside the insights of shame theorists further elucidates the problematic nature of shame. In Niebuhr, the Christian self feels anxious about original sin and, therefore, aspires to subject the self to God through grace. The remedy for the internal wound of original sin is repentance and submission. But this is always partial and imperfect. However, if human experience is described and understood in this way, the experience of shame continues to go unaddressed, both theoretically and practically. Niebuhr's understanding of guilt as a response to original sin has more to do with shame than with guilt. For instance, when he suggests we feel guilt for inferiority, he actually intimates shame, and when he suggests that Adam and Eve feel guilt at being seen by God, he refers rather to the phenomenological association of shame with sight. This is neither to say that Adam and Eve do not experience guilt nor that shame and guilt cannot coexist. They do. In fact, unaddressed guilt, guilt not atoned for, turns into shame. Even so, the way that Niebuhr describes Adam and Eve's behavior, and the subsequent internal affects of their behavior, indicates shame. Shame rather than guilt emerges as the affective condition of humanity in response to original sin.

Shame theorists assert that the internal response to the idea of a deficient self is shame, not guilt. This assumption relies on distinguishing guilt as a response to *wrongdoing* from shame as a response to a perceived *wrong in the self*.[86] If this is indeed the case, then the response to original sin is not guilt as Niebuhr describes it but rather shame. When Niebuhr asserts that guilt functions as a necessary response to original sin, he supplants shame with the term "guilt," illustrating guilt's function as a marker of shame. Adam is guilty of wrongdoing, but subsequently and then concomitantly, Adam also experiences shame. Niebuhr recognizes and identifies Adam's sin but fails to identify and articulate his shame. Furthermore, the blemish that Adam carries signifies a wound that cannot be healed, but for which, according to Niebuhr, Adam should feel guilt. However, instead of marking Adam in guilt, original sin marks Adam in shame, which requires covering-up. Accepting Niebuhr's prescription for the self in guilt allows for the repression of shame and its continued interment in the self.

Furthermore, while remorse psychologically heals guilt, it has little to no impact on shame.[87] The ability to tolerate guilt and express remorse presuppose an integrated personality, whereas in shame, the self becomes fragmented as a result of the ontological condition of belief that some part of the self is bad. By extension, ameliorating shame presents a far more complex challenge than the healing required for guilt, in part because shame goes unrecognized so often. Individuals who feel shame often unconsciously substitute guilt for shame because guilt is a "less acute emotion" than shame.[88] Guilt is not as toxic to the body as shame; however, guilt left unaddressed turns into shame.[89] All of this indicates a much deeper problem than Niebuhr presents; reduced to a sense of worthlessness the person experiencing shame disintegrates, and repressed shame morphs into additional shame or violence.

Although Niebuhr does not explicitly articulate or mention shame, the sensory mode in which he sets what we can identify as shame is the fear of being seen. This idea of exposure centers the problem of shame and starts to shed light on how shame can begin to be addressed. Niebuhr's major assertion in *Nature and Destiny of Man* is that sinful humanity lies in full view of an omniscient and omnipotent God: "all men and nations are sinful in the sight of God."[90] Thus, the nature of seeing and being seen lies at the foundation of Niebuhr's doctrine of God; he retains the visual metaphor throughout his work, and it has a direct, if unstated relation to shame.[91] According to Niebuhr, God can see guilt, alluding to the Genesis story where God's seeing that Adam and Eve ate from the tree provokes both the shame experience and the guilt experience. However, he supplants biblical shame with guilt, while eliding shame. In shame literature, shame, rather than guilt, connects phenomenologically to the idea of being exposed.

As in the biblical event of the Fall, physical or psychological personal exposure usually prompts the desire to cover or hide that which lies exposed. Etymologically, and traditionally, shame associates with such "covering," and as an affect, it surges through the body when the self experiences exposure, often eliciting a bodily response of blushing. To be sinful in the sight of God can easily be read as to be ashamed in the sight of God. Shame requires the internalized or externalized other to whom an individual seeks attachment. For example, the Christian self, embodied by Adam, seeks attachment to God. Exposed before God after sinning, the connection to God and all that God represents in paradise is severed. This loss, the loss of secure attachment, and the subsequent interior sin that resembles a diminished self-worth, establishes the foundation for the interment of shame in the self.

Niebuhr applies guilt for sinful action as well as for the sin posited in the individual and experienced as shame. He blends the experiential condition of remorse for wrongdoing—for the sinful action—with the ontological condition of something inherently wrong with the self, identifying both as guilt. Niebuhr misidentifies shame as guilt, embedding it into a tragic cycle of shame. On a broader level, part of this cycle includes the attempt to deny human experiential contingency through behaviors, which for Niebuhr are the sins of sensuality and pride. Interestingly, Niebuhr's images of escape and unboundedness pertaining to sensuality and pride reflect the behaviors of shame identified in shame literature. When we feel as if we cannot bear to be seen by the other, when we want to disappear from view or cannot bear to be vulnerable, we are in shame. Alternately, when we feel as if we are powerful enough to control another's behavior or resort to violence in any form to restore the pride of *hubris*, we may be making an attempt to expunge shame.

Affective Exclusion

In the Edenic narrative, the desire to eradicate the unpleasantness of what Niebuhr calls "guilt" produces anxiety in the Christian self and establishes that self's ontological condition. However, when we isolate and identify shame in this experience, anxiety can be interpreted as pointing to or marking the existence of shame, a persistent precedent to sin that undulates for Niebuhr in the Christian self always as an obstacle to secure attachment to God. Thus, in Niebuhr's theology, references to anxiety along with insecurity eclipse shame, as references to guilt do, but in different ways. As noted earlier, Niebuhr superimposes the term "guilt" for "shame," in effect masking shame with guilt. The affective life that Niebuhr postulates includes a cyclical relationship of anxiety, what I see as shame, and then additional, subsequent anxiety.

Anxiety underlying original sin, comparable to shame, fosters additional debilitating anxiety and insecurity for which humanity feels further shame, thus shaping the Christian self in shame. Shame is a distressing experience spurred by anxiety in three phases: the anxiety of exclusion, the confusion that guards against anxiety, and the feeling of shame itself.[92] In Niebuhr, the anxiety of exclusion emerges in the distance between God and the self that Niebuhr perceives as resulting from original sin. Humanity's effort to deny contingency guards against anxiety but in vain. The realization of insecurity in the world incurs, along with the anxiety of exclusion, further shame. A cycle of shame ensues forming shamed bodies: affective anxiety emerges when additional shame results from the anxiety of the first shame. Shame, having a parallel structure to Niebuhr's ontological anxiety, emerges when the "primitive longing for wholeness and the sense that one ought rightly to be whole" cannot be fulfilled.[93] Individual attempts to find wholeness constitute attempts to eradicate the affective experience of shame, which is often subsumed and obscured by references to anxiety.

Niebuhr's lexicon disenables an identification of shame apart from anxiety. His theological anthropology conceives of the Christian self as feeling anxious for conditions which would innately provoke shame. Socialization in this manner results in the affects' becoming toxic. Toxicity results when shame and anxiety converge or are perceived as analogous to other negative affects. Furthermore, in the case of toxicity, the positive affects of interest and excitement, which encourage attachment and empathy necessarily present in the presence of shame, fail to assemble to transform shame; the strength of shame overpowers them, curtailing attachment and thus preventing any amelioration of shame. Instead, preoccupation with negative affects like anxiety—over and above or at the expense of shame as in Niebuhr's work—promote shame's repression.

As a result, anxiety, especially anxiety as a mask for shame, is toxic.[94] Tomkins addresses this toxicity as follows:

> If shame is so mortifying, [as is anxiety] it is ill adapted to serve as a general broad negative affect. Despite its high toxicity, however, there appear to be a multiplicity of innate sources of shame, since there are innumerable ways in which excitement and enjoyment may be partially blocked and reduced and thereby activate shame. Man is not only an anxious and suffering animal, but he is above all a shy animal, easily caught between longing and despair. When one adds to the innate sources of shame those which are learned, the normal human being is very vulnerable to a generalized shame bind almost as toxic as anxiety neurosis.[95]

When such a level of anxiety becomes a perpetual state, symptoms occur. Affects that go unaddressed inevitably make their presence known through other means, taxing the body through physical symptoms and becoming more detrimental. In fact, both Block Lewis and Tomkins argue that overgeneralized, minimized anxiety central to the human self disguises and represses shame, interring it.[96] Tompkins labels the over usage of the word "anxiety" a kind of "socialization of distress,"[97] articulated as the state of being stressed, that generates repression and not the other way around.[98] In Niebuhr's theology, anxiety becomes a generalized condition that subsumes other affects, including shame, and thus, due to its neglect, shame is repressed.

The Two Poles of Shame

In Niebuhr, from the aggregate of original sin and anxiety flow the actual sins of pride and sensuality. Both sins result in diverting attention from God by investing that attention either into the self or into another person or thing. Niebuhr expresses the human state in these sins as either puffed up, boundless, and expanded, or withdrawn and evasive, seeking a means for escape. While his descriptive imaging does not detail or formulate shame, his articulations of pride and sensuality do mirror the dual behaviors of aggression and withdrawal that, according to shame theorists, are generated by shame. So, again, while Niebuhr does not involve shame explicitly in his analysis, his recognition of pride and sensuality can be read as indicative symptoms of shame, or as markers of where shame operates even though masked, enabling a more robust understanding of his theology.

Significantly, Niebuhr's diagnosis of original sin as resulting in pride and sensuality parallels Goffman's diagnosis that shame leads to the stigmatized person becoming either too aggressive or too shamefaced.[99] Pride correlates with the idea of being too aggressive, while sensuality, in the sense of an escape, relates to a person's being too shamefaced. To expound upon this, Goffman quotes an unemployed German man during the Depression: "When I go out, I cast down my eyes because I feel myself wholly inferior. When I go along the street, it seems to me that I can't be compared with an average citizen, that everybody is pointing at me with his finger. Instinctively I avoid meeting anyone."[100] This posture mirrors the way that humans, according to Niebuhr, avoid contingency and turn away from God. Goffman describes behaviors similar to those inherent in the shame affect: either the stigmatized person bears a posture of "false bravado," or he/she responds with "defensive cowering" and the impetus to hide.[101] Most often, the stigmatized vacillate rapidly between these two poles.

In addition, "false bravado" and "defensive cowering"—which parallel Niebuhr's pride and sensuality—can be developed and understood further in terms of Nathanson's shame compass. Nathanson suggests a range of behaviors in which shame operates. These behaviors constitute attempts of the person in shame to experience an affect perceived as less painful than shame. Patterns of defense include withdrawal (escape), avoidance (repression), attacking the self, and attacking the other.[102] Within each category, an entire behavioral repertoire persists consisting of an aggregate system of affect management or ways that an individual has adapted to manage the shame affect. The function and aim of the strategy is to transmute shame, "to make it feel different."[103] Each defense serves as a means burying shame beneath some other affective experience to greater or lesser degrees. In either case, within the "shame/pride axis," most individuals seek more pride and less shame.[104]

The "attack other" pole relates to Niebuhr's primary diagnosis of the human in pride. For Nathanson, this pole includes the violence-inducing type of pride that disturbs Niebuhr, not the pride that constitutes a good sense of self-worth. Although Niebuhr does not analyze pride in any way that relates it to a positive experience, he does address pride as *hubris*, which affect theorists relate directly to shame.[105] The primary aim of the "attack other" pole of Nathanson's compass is to replace shame through the acquisition of pride as *hubris.* Dangerously, the attempt to restore pride often erupts in violence toward others. James Gilligan sees such violence as the result of a deep desire to eradicate shame from the body and to reinstate pride; thus, violent behavior represents an urge to exchange the painful feeling of shame for a false pride. Gilligan writes that "the basic psychological motive, or cause, of violent behavior is the wish to ward off or eliminate the feeling of shame and humiliation—a feeling that is painful and can even be intolerable and overwhelming—and to replace it with its opposite, the feeling of pride."[106] As with Augustine, this type of pride emulates *hubris*, not self-worth.

What Gilligan's work with violent men has shown is that generally these men strive for the affective opposite of shame, "self-esteem, self-respect, and self-love."[107] Yet violence fails to achieve this aim, and more shame results; eventually a very malignant absence of feeling takes its place. This absence of feeling, what Gilligan calls "cold," "numbness" and "deadness," results when shame has been compounded, repressed, and deeply interred into the body with no outlet.[108]

Violence in Nathanson's theory alternately emanates in the form of "attack self," an approach situated at the opposite pole of "attack other." More surreptitious and harder to identify than attacking another, "attack self" mode appears benign at first and often occurs within attachment relationships. For instance, a person in an abusive partnership continues to stay in the relationship and tolerate abuse as a result of shame. Essentially, forms of violence toward the self, which manifest pathologically, rely on a sentiment that includes diminished self-worth; a person in this posture feels deserving of punishment and perpetuates that procurement through a variety of means.

Niebuhr's theological aim is to provide some guidance for humanity on how to mitigate the cycles of aggressiveness, withdrawal, and violence that lead to an unjust society, and which ultimately distance humanity from God. He seeks to show that the acquisition of pride through violence, through what he would call aggrandizement of the self at the expense of others, always fails. Only through attuned attachment and reciprocity can the repair of shame that motivates violence occur. Humanity "infected by pride" leads to evil behavior,[109] which is often met with humiliation and what I label as additional shame. Niebuhr recognizes shame, even though he does not name shame, in his characterization of the puffed-up or escaping self. Viewing his perception of humanity in original sin through an affective lens reveals that he understands shame, but it also affirms that shame is a more serious problem than is even represented.

Without an outlet, shame is a silent killer. Under the mask of anxiety and guilt, while also attached to the idea of a stigma, shame is too easily disregarded. Unnoticed but not absent, shame transmutes into self-deprecation that leads to withdrawal and further repression. Shame manifesting in "escape, in the language of withdrawal" is "swift and occasionally total," reducing the self to destitution.[110] Shame unaddressed eventually amounts to the loss of the self. Attempts to acquire pride as *hubris* illustrate the effort to combat low feelings of self-worth and to recover the lost self. But all too often, as Gilligan's work shows, this acquisition occurs violently, and attempts at violence to recover the self always fail.

Paradoxical Shaping

In his argument against sensuality and pride, Niebuhr articulates the need for an affective stance of guilt. The way that he articulates guilt also parallels shame. Guilt is the identified affective response for both the sin posited and the rejection of finiteness, leading from the fall into imperfection and subsequently to the perils of pride and sensuality. The only way to counter such a detrimental path is through Christ. And the way through Christ includes remorse, which aligns with guilt but does not touch shame. Adam represents, therefore, the wounded but sinful man; he assumes the *habitus* of a guilty man, according to Niebuhr; however, this *habitus* includes deeply interred shame and all of the ramifications of that state of being. Niebuhr, thus, establishes the grounds from which shame emerges, but he fails to name shame and to bring its aftereffects to light.

In Niebuhr, shame would be both the consequence of sin "the actual corruption of the plan of creation and providence in the historical world" and responsible for bad acting. When this is the case, Niebuhr echoes the assertions of shame and affect theorists: (1) that shame cannot be overcome and (2) that shame motivates harmful action, to the self and to others. Shame, though, plays a central part in human life, and even though it elicits pain and can be maladaptive, especially when related to trauma, it is inherent in the self and in the body. Niebuhr goes awry when he fails to name shame and instead centralizes anxiety and guilt, thus permitting shame to go unnoticed and to be interred in the Christian self.

Yet shame persists churning in the Christian self—potentially regulating social relationships but, if interred, making a negative impact upon these. Shame's function in the self can be compared to the structure of the paradoxical Christian self Niebuhr conceptualizes as suspended between finiteness and freedom in relationship to God. In *On Niebuhr: A Theological Study*, Langdon Gilkey details Niebuhr's conception of human nature as establishing interrelated paradoxes each of which taps into the notion of shame in affect theory.[111] The elements laid out in each paradox fold in upon each other forming "a unity,"[112] not foreign to the paradoxical nature of shame. Niebuhr's analysis of guilt, anxiety, and sensuality overlook shame, even though something like shame undulates beneath these. However, in order to disinter shame, it must be made explicit to be addressed so as to avoid its interment which inhibits attachment. However, recognizing shame permits the affect to be sensed while also permitting connection.

The paradoxes continue. Niebuhr considers humans as animals; even though as a part of nature, humanity can be self-transcendent.[113] Niebuhr does in fact believe that humanity can ascend from the animal/mortal state and affective life where shame plays a part as a result of the self, but only as a result of binding the self to God. What this offers the Christian self is the potential for shame's regulation in a secure attachment to God. According to affect theory, shame is inherently present in the self but emerges affectively only in relationship to another person. Attachment represents the key component to regulating shame, which usually occurs when interest or excitement is also present. The first mark of shame intertwined with the stigma of original sin can only be assuaged through attachment. Applying this to Niebuhr's analysis, the figure to which one would attach to ameliorate but never eradicate shame is God.

Second, although Niebuhr believes that humans are essentially moral and seek to do good works, they are also immoral beings and commit sins.

Niebuhr believes that sin has a way of interfering with humans' ability to do good, distorting such good. Therefore, the choice to do good works necessitates attachment to God. In addition, as noted earlier, Niebuhr does assert that guilt, another mark of shame, represents the unavoidable response for the failure to choose the good insofar as repentance leads individuals back to God. However, by positing original sin in the self and identifying guilt as the appropriate response, Niebuhr thus increases the likelihood of the very condition of humanity that he protests: a boundless ego that rejects God and desires power over the other—in other words, the self in shame.

In the third paradox, humans, as a result of evil, demand "significance" while they feel "obviously insignificant."[114] Guilty of evil, individuals can only become free of such evil through full submission to God. Niebuhr struggles with sensuality in the form of addictive behaviors, escape, and withdrawal, and with pride, as expressed through competition and violence. As shown previously, such behaviors at root indicate shame.

Hovering between insignificance and significance, the human lives both guilty and free. He or she is guilty of original sin and incapable of avoiding actual sin but free to choose and free insofar as humanity is created in God's image. Thus, the Christian self finds himself or herself in another paradox. This final paradox emerges as the overarching guilt-ethic in the Christian tradition. Critiquing this ethic as misdiagnosing shame calls its usefulness into question. Shame emerges as a major component in the discourse around rue and contrition inherent in traditional theology. Shame and two other affects operate within the cycle of remorse and repentance adopted by the Christian tradition from the Edenic narrative. Nathanson expresses this well when he states that "*Shame* triggered by awareness (both of the nature of one's actions and the nature of the self who committed them); *fear* of punishment for what one has done; and *distress* produced by the constancy of one's shame."[115] At the heart of the guilt-ethic lies shame. In this interpretation, shame, not guilt, emerges as the initial and primary affect, but shame also bookends the entire Christian experience.

Too often though, shame is obscured and interred in narratives, in rhetoric, and in Christian selves. The resulting notion of the isolated sinner, the central character of the guilt-ethic, is a Christian in shame, and since shame represents a problem of attachment, this ethic fails. Instead of fostering secure attachment, it provokes shame and shame's interment.

Shame without a place for expression, unnamed and interred, is responsible for a range of problems from individual depression, suicide, and personal violence to larger instances of societal, historical violence. The ideas of rue and contrition that reinforce codes of shame and honor inherent in episodes of genocide, gang activity, organized crime, and religious conflicts, including in the US context, legitimate violence which goes in many ways unsanctioned. Systems that advocate punishment and violence as a means of control, including but not limited to the prison and criminal justice systems, perpetuate shame. Institutions within such systems attempt to assuage bad behaviors with guilt, illustrating the powerful influence of the Christian tradition on such systems. The guilt-ethic's binary, a core component in the formation of the Christian self, cannot solve the problem of violence. It cannot because, as Gilligan recognizes, it "does not dismantle the motivational structure that causes violence in the first place (namely, shame, and the shame-ethics that motivates it)."[116] The perpetual guilt-ethic bind sustains the problem of violence because it directs violence toward the self, which perpetuates shame. Thus, the guilt that Niebuhr commends perpetuates the problems within human nature that his work attempts to mitigate. Instead of turning toward others to seek attunement, the shamed self falls deeper into a sense of isolation and affective humiliation, often resorting to violence to ease the pain.

Conclusion

Niebuhr's conception of original sin, preceded by and evoking anxiety, parallels the interpretation in shame theory that a stigma evokes shame. Ontological anxiety, then, correlates with a conception of ontological shame, both of which logically stem from the idea of "imperfection." Ontological anxiety bound up with original sin can be expressed in terms of shame, inherent, unavoidable, and cause for human angst. To assuage this condition, Niebuhr posits that humanity commits the actual sins of pride and sensuality, behaviors that when viewed through the lens of affect theory both mask shame and signify shame's presence.

Shame theory asserts that attempts to assuage shame by hiding or restoring pride occur as regular phenomena, and shame appears in what Niebuhr calls the sin of hiding, the human response to exposure. In addition, shame, in Niebuhr, manifests as pride in the form of violence, which attempts to eradicate the stigma of sin and anxiety. While embedded in

Niebuhr's theology is a dialect of guilt, shame undulates beneath this dialect. Guilt represents the affective response that he advocates to both the wound of original sin and the behaviors of escape and pride. Although Niebuhr fails to name shame directly, he provides theological anthropology with clear marks of shame.

In Niebuhr, the Christian self feels anxious about original sin and, therefore, should aspire to subject the self to God through grace. Repentance and submission to God serve as remedies for the internal wound of original sin. However, if human experience is described and understood in this way, the experience of shame continues to go unaddressed, both theoretically and practically. If the Christian self is marked by shame, in order to keep this shame from becoming toxic and deleterious, compounded, repressed, and interred in the Christian self, shame must be attended to and named.

Reading Niebuhr through an affective lens reveals shame, including how and when shame surfaces in his rhetoric. Shame emerges in Niebuhr's lexicon as alternative terms of "guilt" and "anxiety," just as it surfaces viscerally altered in the human self in physical symptoms, as other affects, or transmuted into some harm done to others. Attending to the marks of shame that surface as addiction, withdrawal, and hiding—as well as to the pride that emerges like *hubris* which detracts from the human connection and, instead, distances the Christian self—begins to get at the problem of shame in Niebuhr. But the problem is bigger than it seems.

Niebuhr prescribes repentance and connection to God to ameliorate the human problem he identifies as guilt. His theological anthropology determines that suffering, including the affective experience of something like shame, while an unavoidable component of Christian life, does not happen in isolation. However, his impression of the self that seeks God in guilt, alone and in sin, delimits the possibility of the connection with God he professes humanity most needs, because shame lies buried in that self and masked by other affective experiences. Thus concealed, shame is bypassed which leads not to connection but to "humiliated fury" and "depressive ideation" that inhibit social bonding.[117]

According to affect theory, shame is inherently present in the self, but it emerges affectively only in relationship to another. Attachment signals shame. A severed attachment incurs shame; the attachment bond must be repaired to ameliorate shame; however, paradoxically, shame also inhibits attachment, especially shame veiled by other terms or affects. Thus, what Niebuhr professes as a solution cannot be achieved because shame has gone unnamed and interred in self to interfere with bonding and attachment, to others and to God. To do what Niebuhr seeks so adamantly to do, to ameliorate and stop violence in the world, the shame that festers beneath it, motivating it, must be disinterred, recognized, and disempowered.

Notes

1. Gary J. Dorrien, *The Making of American Liberal Theology: Idealism, Realism, and Modernity 1900–1950* (Louisville: Westminster John Knox Press, 2003), 442. Considering Niebuhr's philosophy and rhetoric is especially important due the reengagement of his work and theological contributions by mainstream politics of the twenty-first century. This is evident in President Obama's crediting Niebuhr as contributing to his political philosophy and mission; see R. Ward Holder and Peter B. Josephson, *The Irony of Barack Obama: Barack Obama, Reinhold Niebuhr and the Problem of Christian Statecraft* (Burlington: Ashgate: 2012), 4. It is widely acknowledged that Obama has mentioned in a number of interviews both how he himself has been shaped by Niebuhr's theology and the association of the Obama administration with Niebuhr's philosophy. See David Brooks, "Obama, Gospel, and Verse," *New York Times*, April 26, 2007, accessed August 15, 2014. http://www.nytimes.com/2007/04/26/opinion/26brooks.html?_r=0, and John Blake, "How Obama's Favorite Theologian Shaped His First Year in Office," CNN.com, last modified February 5, 2010, accessed August 15, 2014, http://www.cnn.com/2010/POLITICS/02/05/Obama.theologian/. Most recently, scholarship in theology and political philosophy has recovered Niebuhr and his analysis of the Christian character to further a critique of American exceptionalism and nationalism. Informed by the context of war, Niebuhr's political theology has credence today, see Kenneth Morris Hamilton, *The Doctrine of Humanity in the Theology of Reinhold Niebuhr* (Ontario: Wilfrid Laurier University Press, 2013), where Hamilton traces the impact of Niebuhr's view of human nature. See also Catherine Keller, *God and Power* (Minneapolis: Augsburg Fortress Press, 2005), especially chapter two, "Preemption and Omnipotence: A Niebuhrian Prophecy," 17–34. See also political theorist Andrew Bacevich, "Illusions of Managing History: The Enduring Relevance of Reinhold Niebuhr," *Historically Speaking* vol. 9, no. 3 (2008): 23–25, and *The Limits of Power: The End of American Exceptionalism* (New York: Holt Paperbacks, 2009). For a more theological perspective, see Gary J. Dorrien, *The Obama Question: A Progressive Perspective* (Lanham, MA: Rowman & Littlefield, 2012), and introduction to *The Children of Light and the Children of Darkness: A Vindication of Democracy and a Critique of its Traditional Defense*, by Reinhold Niebuhr (Chicago: University of Chicago Press, 2011), ix–xxvi.

2. Dorrien, *The Making of American Liberal Theology*, 466–467.
3. Niebuhr, *Nature and Destiny of Man*, 17.
4. There is conflicting opinion about repression and affect in Freud's work on the unconscious and in Lacan's on anxiety. The issue relates to whether an affect can actually ever be repressed. Generally, both Freud (at least in his later work, see *The Ego and The Id*, ed. James Strachey (W.W. Norton & Company 1960)) and Lacan assert only the signifiers of affect are repressed; that is, the signs of the affect that appear in a physical form or that secure the affect are repressed. See Jacques Lacan, *Anxiety: The Seminar of Jacques Lacan, Book X*, ed. Jacques-Alain Miller, trans. Joan Riviere (Malden: Polity Press, 2014). However, as Johnston and Malabou point out in *Self and Emotional Life: Philosophy, Psychoanalysis, and Neuroscience*, 75-82, Freud is inconsistent with his assertions along these lines.
5. Cooper, *Reinhold Niebuhr and Psychology*, 13 and 43; Langdon Gilkey, *On Niebuhr: A Theological Study* (Chicago: University of Chicago Press, 2001), 137.
6. Niebuhr, *Nature and Destiny of Man*, 180.
7. Niebuhr, *Nature and Destiny of Man*, 181.
8. Niebuhr, *Nature and Destiny of Man*, 254.
9. Niebuhr, *Nature and Destiny of Man*, 254.
10. Niebuhr, *Nature and Destiny of Man*, 180. This is where Cooper also sees Niebuhr distinguishing himself from Freud, as not locating human destructiveness in biology; see Cooper, *Reinhold Niebuhr and Psychology*, 44.
11. Niebuhr, *Nature and Destiny of Man*, 263.
12. Niebuhr, *Nature and Destiny of Man*, 280.
13. Niebuhr, *Nature and Destiny of Man*, 250.
14. Gilkey, *On Niebuhr*, 136; and Niebuhr, *Nature and Destiny of Man*, 261.
15. Niebuhr, *Nature and Destiny of Man*, 238.
16. Niebuhr, *Nature and Destiny of Man*, 181.
17. Gilkey, *On Niebuhr*, 91.
18. Niebuhr, *Nature and Destiny of Man*, 252.
19. Unbelief, as Gilkey puts it, is presupposed and transforms finitude into a problem; see *On Niebuhr*, 103.
20. Niebuhr, *Nature and Destiny of Man*, 253.
21. Niebuhr, *Nature and Destiny of Man*, 205.
22. Niebuhr, *Nature and Destiny of Man*, 205.
23. Niebuhr, *Nature and Destiny of Man*, 238.
24. Niebuhr, *Nature and Destiny of Man*, 238.
25. Niebuhr, *Nature and Destiny of Man*, 238.
26. Gilkey, *On Niebuhr*, 130–134.
27. Niebuhr, *Nature and Destiny of Man*, 180.

28. Niebuhr, *Nature and Destiny of Man*, 242 and 246. See Tomkins, *Affect, Imagery, Consciousness*, 287, where Tomkins describes shame, as "an inner torment, a sickness of the soul" that "strikes deepest into the heart" of humanity.
29. Niebuhr, *Nature and Destiny of Man*, 188.
30. Niebuhr, *Nature and Destiny of Man*, 174–177.
31. Niebuhr, *Nature and Destiny of Man*, 252.
32. Niebuhr, *Nature and Destiny of Man*, 251.
33. Cooper, *Reinhold Niebuhr and Psychology*, 27–28.
34. Niebuhr, *Nature and Destiny of Man*, 253.
35. Niebuhr, *Nature and Destiny of Man*, 253.
36. Gilkey, *On Niebuhr*, 104.
37. Niebuhr, *Nature and Destiny of Man*, 251.
38. Cooper relates this to Karen Horney's etiology of psychological afflictions, where anxiety itself is not destructive but is the breeding ground for neurosis; *Reinhold Niebuhr and Psychology*, 64.
39. Niebuhr, *Nature and Destiny of Man*, 250–251.
40. Niebuhr, *Nature and Destiny of Man*, 185.
41. Niebuhr, *Nature and Destiny of Man*, 235.
42. Niebuhr, *Nature and Destiny of Man*, 189.
43. Cooper, *Reinhold Niebuhr and Psychology*, 33.
44. Niebuhr, *Nature and Destiny of Man*, 252.
45. Niebuhr, *Nature and Destiny of Man*, 186.
46. Niebuhr, *Nature and Destiny of Man*, 226.
47. Niebuhr, *Nature and Destiny of Man*, 185 and 283.
48. Niebuhr, *Nature and Destiny of Man*, 186.
49. According to Niebuhr, a serious problem related to the boundless ego occurs when this stance is adopted by nations, which aim to defy limits of finiteness and adopt a position of being Godlike. This is his evidence for the pride that hides weakness, which Niebuhr aligns with shame through his analysis of Hitler.
50. Niebuhr, *Nature and Destiny of Man*, 234.
51. Niebuhr, *Nature and Destiny of Man*, 253.
52. Niebuhr, *Nature and Destiny of Man*, 211.
53. Niebuhr, *Nature and Destiny of Man*, 223. This religious dimension is generally associated with moral pride. Niebuhr conceives of three different types of pride: pride of power, pride of knowledge, and pride of virtue. The third type, pride of virtue, grows into a spiritual pride that is aligned with a fourth type or moral pride. All types of pride are prompted for Niebuhr by a sense of insecurity and manifest in various modes of self-deification.
54. Niebuhr, *Nature and Destiny of Man*, 188.
55. Niebuhr, *Nature and Destiny of Man*, 211.

56. Niebuhr, *Nature and Destiny of Man*, 186.
57. Niebuhr, *Nature and Destiny of Man*, 147, 185–186, 235, and 237.
58. Niebuhr, *Nature and Destiny of Man*, 186.
59. Niebuhr, *Nature and Destiny of Man*, 228.
60. Niebuhr, *Nature and Destiny of Man*, 237.
61. He uses the work of mid-century psychiatrist Karl A. Menninger to support his position; see *Whatever Became of Sin?* (New York: Bantam Books, 1988), 234–235.
62. Niebuhr, *Nature and Destiny of Man*, 234–235.
63. Niebuhr, *Nature and Destiny of Man*, 239.
64. Niebuhr, *Nature and Destiny of Man*, 238.
65. Niebuhr, *Nature and Destiny of Man*, 231–233.
66. Niebuhr, *Nature and Destiny of Man*, 236.
67. Niebuhr, *Nature and Destiny of Man*, 222. Gilkey quotes the same selection in his discourse on sin and guilt where he asserts that sin refers to the vertical, religious relationship to God, for which humanity must repent, whereas guilt is the horizontal, social consequence of sin; see *On Niebuhr*, 113.
68. Niebuhr, *Nature and Destiny of Man*, 255.
69. Niebuhr, *Nature and Destiny of Man*, 222.
70. Serge Tisseron, "De La Honte Qui Tue Á La Honte Qui Sauve: De La Catastrophe Á L'Affiliation," in *Shame between Punishment and Penance*, ed. Bénédicte Sère and Jörg Wettlaufer (Firenze: Edizioni del Galluzzo, 2013), 393–396; see also Michael Lewis, *Shame: The Exposed Self*, 119–127.
71. Niebuhr, *Nature and Destiny of Man,* 159, 160, 268, 278, and 290.
72. Niebuhr, *Nature and Destiny of Man*, 250.
73. Tomkins, *Affect, Imagery, Consciousness*, 330.
74. See Susan Nelson, "For Shame, For Shame, The Shame of It All: Postures of Refusal and the Broken Heart," where she says "Shame wounds and binds like sin wounds and binds" in *The Other Side of Sin: Woundedness from the Perspective of the Sinned-Against*, ed. Andrew Sung Park and Susan Nelson (Albany: SUNY Press, 2012), 72.
75. Goffman, *Stigma*, 7.
76. Goffman, *Stigma*, 5.
77. Goffman, *Stigma*, 108.
78. See William Ronald Dodds Fairbairn, *Psychoanalytic Studies of the Personality* (1952; reprint, London: Routledge, 1986), 63.
79. Fairbairn, *Psychoanalytic Studies*, 73.
80. Fairbairn, *Psychoanalytic Studies*, 63.
81. Fairbairn, *Psychoanalytic Studies*, 89–90.
82. This description of repression derives from Jacques Derrida, *Writing and Difference*, trans. Alan Bass (Chicago: The University of Chicago Press, 1978), 197.

83. General repression is a mechanism agreed upon by both psychoanalysis and affect theory, but see note 8 for conflicts of interpretation. See also Tomkins, *Affect, Imagery, Consciousness*, 79, and Sigmund Freud, *New Introductory Lectures on Psychoanalysis*, trans. James Strachey (1933; reprint, New York: W.W. Norton & Company, 1989), 19–23 and 114. Repression indicates a holding down of the unconscious and instinctual impulses.
84. Tomkins, *Affect, Imagery, Consciousness*, 556.
85. Lewis, *Shame: The Exposed Self*, 119–127.
86. See Tangney and Dearing, *Shame and Guilt*, 18–25, where they trace the differences between guilt and shame according to what Helen Block Lewis first presented as the distinction in shame between the self and behavior.
87. June Price Tangney, Jeff Stuewig, and Logaina Hafez, "Shame, Guilt and Remorse: Implications for Offender Populations," *The Journal of Forensic Psychiatry and Psychology* vol. 22, no. 5 (2011), 710.
88. Block Lewis, *The Role of Shame in Symptom Formation*, 23 and 121.
89. James Gilligan, *Violence: Reflections on a National Epidemic*, 110–114; Tangney and Dearing, *Shame and Guilt*, 3, 5, and 163–165.
90. James Gilligan, *Violence: Reflections on a National Epidemic*, 110–114; Tangney and Dearing, *Shame and Guilt*, 3, 5, and 163–165.
91. Niebuhr dramatizes the notion of humanity as sinners under the enduring sight of God. For a more detailed analysis of sight and shame from a theological perspective, see Elizabeth A. Clark, "1990 Presidential Address: Shame, Sex, and Rhetoric: En-Gendering Early Christian Ethics," *Journal of the American Academy of Religion* vol. 59, no. 2 (1991): 221–245. On page 235, Clark considers the early Church Fathers' writing to assert that the primary site where human community experiences shame is under the "All Seeing Eye of God."
92. Tisseron, "De La Honte Qui Tue Á La Honte Qui Sauve," 404.
93. Nussbaum, *Hiding from Humanity*, 186.
94. Tomkins, *Affect, Imagery, Consciousness*, 293.
95. Tomkins, *Affect, Imagery, Consciousness*, 387.
96. Tomkins, *Affect, Imagery, Consciousness*, 931, and Block Lewis, *The Role of Shame*, 23. See also related to this phenomenon Freud, *New Introductory Lectures*, 111.
97. Tomkins, *Affect, Imagery, Consciousness*, 347.
98. Freud, *New Introductory Lectures*, 111.
99. Goffman, *Stigma*, 18.
100. Goffman, *Stigma*, 17.
101. Goffman, *Stigma*, 17.
102. Nathanson, *Shame and Pride*, 250 and 318–319.
103. Nathanson, *Shame and Pride*, 312.
104. Nathanson, *Shame and Pride*, 20.

105. Nathanson, *Shame and Pride*, 213; Lewis, *Shame*, 78. See also where Lynd distinguishes between pride as *hubris* and pride as honor or self-esteem, *On Shame*, 252.
106. Gilligan, *Shame, Guilt, and Violence*, 1153.
107. Gilligan, *Violence: Reflections on a National Epidemic*, 47.
108. Gilligan, *Violence: Reflections on a National Epidemic*, 47–48.
109. Niebuhr, *Nature and Destiny of Man*, 178.
110. Nathanson, *Shame and Pride*, 313.
111. Gilkey, *On Niebuhr*, 80–82.
112. Gilkey, *On Niebuhr*, 81.
113. Gilkey, *On Niebuhr*, 81.
114. Gilkey, *On Niebuhr*, 81.
115. Nathanson, *Shame and Pride*, 327.
116. Gilligan, *Violence: Reflections on a National Epidemic*, 235.
117. Block Lewis, *Shame and the Narcissistic Personality*, 99 and 107.

CHAPTER 5

Touching Shame: A Pathway to Disinterment

People crowd the church at an Ash Wednesday service. Their hushed voices leave barely an echo. Heavily incensed air fills the nave, and all stay attentive to the priest who speaks during the homily of the biblical truth of this day as an entrance into Lent, inviting worshippers into the most affecting and tragic aspects of Jesus's story. On Ash Wednesday, congregants walk with Jesus into the desert commemorating his preparation for death not only to join with him in prayer, fasting, and almsgiving but also in anticipation of renewal and conversion of the heart. The summons to enter into penitence and prayer is also an invitation to enter into mourning, to communally grieve what has been lost in Jesus and what has been suffered. The officiate meditates on this past, blessing the ashes, but no "Alleluia" precedes these words; the absence of this praise, as well as the missing "Gloria," frames the spirit of reflection, which precedes and accompanies the ritual in which flesh meets flesh during the Christian practice of imposing ashes.[1]

Observing this moment of touch provides us with a glimpse of how physicality is both present and influential in religious practice. This brief occasion of human contact provides an indication of the power of touch. The investigation focuses primarily on the Catholic tradition's application of this haptic practice; however, the ceremonies enacted during Ash Wednesday in Catholic services have been and continue to be adapted into the Protestant church.[2] Ash Wednesday serves a point of convergence of shame and Christian praxis, because during the liturgy touch on the

S.N. Arel, *Affect Theory, Shame, and Christian Formation*,
DOI 10.1007/978-3-319-42592-4_5

face occurs, but also because as a day that marks the beginning of Jesus's isolation in the desert before he was crucified, Lent entails a recollection of suffering, humiliation, and shame. This recollection is apart from the personal shame that exists for all participants at a biological level, and for some, more intensely as a result of prior trauma.

Shame comes to the forefront in the affective encounter of touch during the imposition of ashes on the forehead. Despite the complexities inherent in disinterring shame through touch in Christian praxis, consideration of the interplay of shame reveals new meaning for Christian formation. Touch in this chapter widens the lens so that we see this formation as literally a body formation. Drawing attention to the touch of the body in Christian practice illustrates its indispensability to Christian development. Thinking more deeply about how touch leads to an understanding of the Christian as embodied and affected by liturgical practices broadens sensitivity to the visceral impact Christian beliefs have on bodies. Considering shame and touch simultaneously recognizes the potency of Christian practice.

Physical touch possesses remarkable and daunting power in social relationships, in intimate situations, and in everyday experiences. Touch provokes somatic, affective, and neurobiological shifts in the body. Because of the impression touch can impress upon bodies, its use in Christian worship is significant for theological analysis. Shame can emerge within the context of touching the forehead during the imposition of ashes, and instead of being interred, shame can be drawn out, or touched. The practice of touch both recognizes the power to inter and operates to disinter. The question that emerges from this duality relates to how the practice of the imposition of ashes both touches shame (located on the forehead for Augustine) and ameliorates it by making touch in Christian praxis more deliberate. Furthermore, what implications does the connection of shame and touch have for theology?

Emphasizing the theological significance of touch, this chapter explores the theological and affective understanding of shame's emergence on the face, built upon interpretations presented in previous chapters regarding shame as an affect with distinct physiological, psychological, and philosophical manifestations. Drawing especially from Augustine, whose deep understanding of shame aids an exploration regarding how shame functions as part of the Christian self, the inquiry reveals how manifested shame becomes accepted, ameliorated, and less destructive or inhibiting. Investigating the Lenten practice of imposing ashes on the forehead uncovers particular ways in which shame, the face, touch, and the Christian narrative intersect.

Drawing from classical philosophy, Christian tradition, and affect theory elucidates the liturgical convergence of touch and shame, revealing the potential of touch to disinter shame by changing affect; drawing participants into the present moment without neglecting the past; naming, recognizing, and constituting being; and cultivating intimacy, relationships, and empathy. However, touch itself poses a threat in many cases where Christians have experienced trauma. Thus, keeping in mind the traumatic aspects of touch fosters sensitivity to sensual experiences that may actually be unwanted or unhelpful. With this in mind, encountering the imposition of the ashes on the forehead during Ash Wednesday uncovers how, through touch, the practice and the accompanying Christian narrative either inter or disinter shame.

Theological Touch

Touch plays a varied and vital role in the relationship between God and the Christian self. As Teresa Swan Tuite illustrates in *Tactile Engagements in Christian Understanding*, touch emerges in biblical history as one way of "making explicit the ways in which bodies give sense to the theological landscape."[3] Swan Tuite points directly to how Christians are made known through touch, using as one example the disciple's recognition of Jesus through touch in the Gospel of John. She also argues that in Luther's teaching on baptism related to justification by faith, touch "provides a more adequate metaphor for justification imagining union in terms of God's abiding with the sinner and extending an ever open invitation to deeper relating."[4]

Swan Tuite challenges the Christian tradition's focus on the visual and auditory, encouraging the material as both a valuable and essential aspect of Christian praxis. She identifies a tactile landscape in Christian practice and theology. Taking Swan Tuite's lead, discovering where touch emerges biblically and rhetorically in the Christian tradition substantiates the theological significance of touch.

The power of touch is ratified throughout the Bible where it adopts a variety of functions. Biblical touch corroborates the duality of touch, which can serve as a means of connection or punishment, highlighting both the potential usefulness of touch and its inherent danger. For example, in some instances, as in Leviticus 5:3 and 6:18, touch constitutes a transmittal: touching something either unclean or sacred bequeaths the properties of that thing to the flesh it meets. Generally, God's touch substantiates and blesses existence. However, God's touch can also be punitive. In Job 19:21, the hand of God "touches" him and exacerbates his suffering. In Daniel 10, touch has a different effect. When Daniel has a vision in which a messenger from God touches him, he moves from a position of prostration to his hands and knees. The angel then touches his lips so he can speak and touches him once more to strengthen him. In these examples, touch has varied consequences, sometimes transmitting good or bad, sometimes inciting empowerment.

The New Testament continues to emphasize the healing aspects of touch and touch's role as a kind of tactile testimony. In Matthew 8, Jesus touches a leper, cleansing and healing him. In the Gospel of Matthew, several poignant occasions of touch reveal that physical contact with Jesus is transformational. Jesus takes the hand of a dying girl and revives her (9:25). Jesus touches the eyes of two blind men, enabling them to see (9:29). In the same chapter, a woman reaches out to touch Jesus's cloak to be healed from hemorrhages. Jesus senses the energy leaving him and turns to her, declaring that her faith healed her. Touch, in all cases, inspires affective charges and shifts for all those engaged in contact, even in Jesus himself.

The power of touch adjudicated in biblical texts and narratives about Jesus can also be traced in the Christian textual tradition. Augustine's idea of touch corroborates the variety of biblical interpretations of the sense revealing some of his own perceptions of touch's complexity. In his *Confessions*, he uses touch to express the consummation of an experience of devotion to God. Augustine addresses God, "You touched me, and I am set on fire to attain the peace which is yours."[5] Being so touched, he is therefore blessed with grace and capable of sharing in God's light. For Augustine, touch inaugurates cleansing through a confession of sins. Touch in this sense bears grace and heals. However, when Augustine relates touch to prohibitions, he highlights his own perceived tension in touch. In a moment of self-critique, he quotes 1 Corinthians 7:1: "It is not good for a man to touch a woman." Therefore, for Augustine, touch has not only the potential to connect him to God, enlivening his senses, but also, lamentably in his view, the power to confirm him of earthly life. Even so, when Augustine mentions touch, he primarily does so to convey passionate devotion to God; his primary aim is attunement with God.

Viewed through the lens of affect theory, being touched by God's grace constitutes secure attachment and regulated affect.

The saints and mystics also express passionate, intimate relating to God or the divine, where touch serves, either metaphorically or actually, as the affective pathway to deeper spiritual connection with God. For instance, in *The Journey of the Mind to God*, Saint Bonaventure experiences the soul as embracing Christ; divine connection, expressed as a physical act, comes to its greatest apex at the moment of contact.[6] Perhaps the greatest collusion with the divine occurs in the stigmata, as in the case of St. Francis, where the human body bears the wounds of Christ. Through this mirroring of wounding, God enters the body by means of the flesh. The French mystic Marguerite Porete expresses a similar entrance of God into her own soul as being "touched by God."[7] This touch initiates her ascent through the seven stages of grace. These haptic examples reflect that "God is made known to us through touch" as a source of most intimate relating.[8] In such intimacy, God touches the whole self, including the self in shame. These textual examples also mark Christian formation and spiritual growth in connection with God as decidedly and necessarily physical.

Our vulnerability to touch makes individuals radically present in the world but also susceptible to shame. In the imposition of the cross on the forehead, for instance, the Christian practitioner is a passive recipient of the blessing, vulnerable to the touch of the person imposing the cross. Receiving the cross requires a unique posture of relative surrender embodied by the bowing of the head. The bowing of the head is a gesture of shame that connects the Christian with Jesus's shame. Yet the touch brings affect to the fore and draws the practitioner into the present.

The symbolic gesture of the touch in the imposition of the cross on the forehead on Ash Wednesday figures in what Bryan P. Stone calls the "movement and logic" of practice.[9] Intimated in Dirk Lange's work, in the ideas of the iteration of a process and the pedagogy of the catechisms rests the idea of liturgy as practice.[10] To understand practice as forming the Christian self, as Stone and Lange do, is to understand liturgy as movement involving repetitive events, moments, and ruptures, in which touch plays a significant role. Furthermore, liturgical engagement at its best ushers the Christian self into a story that intends not only to remind humanity of its imperfections and vulnerabilities but also to awaken the Christian to the promise through praxis of the possibility of renewal and restoration. This possibility of renewal emerges in the notion of existing in relation as part of a communal body; in ecclesial language, this translates into an understanding of the church as the body of Christ. As community, and body, Christians in practice also share affective experiences, which include the experience of shame. Confronting this shame most effectively begins with a consideration of shame's physical manifestation—on the face.

Shame on the Face

Understanding shame's place in Christian formation requires a concentrated consideration of how shame emerges on the face both in the tradition itself and as an affect. The conjunction of these—shame as a biological blush and shame in Christian theology—occurs in Augustine's commentary on Psalm 141.

> So far am I from blushing at the Cross, that in no secret place do I keep the Cross of Christ, but bear it on my forehead. Many sacraments we receive, one in one way another in another: some as ye know we receive with the mouth, some we receive over the whole body. But because the forehead is the seat of the blush of shame, He who said, 'Whosoever shall be ashamed of Me before men, of him will I be ashamed before My Father which is in heaven,' set, so to speak, that very ignominy which the Pagans mock at, in the seat of our shame. Thou hearest a man assail a shameless man and say, 'He hath no forehead.' What is, 'He hath no forehead?' He hath no shame. Let me not have a bare forehead, let the Cross of my Lord cover it.[11]

Here, Augustine names shame and esteems what it offers to the Christian self. He recognizes shame's ability to connect the self, simultaneously to God and to other Christians. Placing shame on the face, primarily on the forehead, he locates shame within the logic of exposure as something to be both respected and even, cherished, reflecting the true shame that emerges in *City of God*.

With the forehead as the corporeal location of shame, Augustine again focuses on the body. Shame resides both on the body and in the body, here on the face and affectively in terms of blushing. He pays attention to the biological blush, understanding this physiological tendency as both natural and indicative of relationality with God. Further, he prays that he will never have a "bare forehead." Thus, he beseeches God that his shame not go uncovered, but he indicates specifically that this shame be covered by "the Cross." In this way he embraces shame, but he turns his shame to God, requesting that the Lord's cross cover it.

This request reflects Augustine's imploring in the *Confessions* that he be clothed with Christ.

Augustine does not petition then for shame's eradication; metaphorically, that would mean having no forehead, or being shameless. Instead, he exposes his shame to God in an entreaty for healing. Just as he does in *City of God*, Augustine asserts an intrinsic shame. Yet, the imposition of the cross can be interpreted in multiple ways. First, by turning to God and bearing his shame, Augustine models an acceptance of shame. He is not afraid for God to see his shame. However, next, he covers shame with the cross. This covering can be read as Augustine's own interment of shame, or paradoxically, it can also be read as Augustine's avowal that shame constitutes part of the self and, by extension, exists in the Christian community, where the cross binds that community. By covering the forehead as the seat of shame symbolically with the cross, Augustine conjoins his shame with Christ, as if his shame is not only covered in the sense of being veiled but also somehow blessed. For Augustine, this cross envelops shame and even protects it.

Shame emerges affectively on the face. The eyes, along with the skin of the face, function as receptor sites for the affect system. As the center of sensory intake, the face, through the "transmission and reception through the muscles and receptors"[12] manifests shame, demonstrating the most intimate sharing of affects. When the face is central to the processing of information and in communicating affect, what then is the impact of touch on the face?

Among socially acceptable forms of touch, facial touching comprises the most intimate and potentially volatile type of touch.[13] A soft stroke or caress across the cheek is among the most inappropriate and most harassing tactile gesture in work situations, perceived even more inappropriate than putting an arm around someone's waist.[14] This type of touch conveys power relations and control, emerging as "particularly dominant when it is initiated rather than returned."[15] Issues of both intimacy and dominance, whether perceptible and/or actual in tactile encounters, make touch, especially of the face, significant and worthy of attention in theological analysis.

Central to modes of human communication, the face exposes the vestiges of every affect including shame. Hiding the face, turning away, and averting the eyes all function as dominant corporeal attempts to evade the pain of shame. The face serves as the primary locus of shame. Tomkins supports this in his assertion that the "the self lives in the face" and in his notion that shame hovers close to the experience of that self.[16]

Thus, the face represents both the location of shame, as in Augustine's description, and the place where first encountering shame occurs. Eye-to-eye contact is quickly reduced as a result of shame if upon looking at another, one perceives in the other's countenance a look of disgust. Alternatively, recognizing another with an expression of respect affirms self-worth and counteracts the shame affect with interest-excitement, without ever quite obliterating shame. Both experiencing shame and ameliorating shame's detrimental effects take place in relation, in front of a real or imagined other, with the face exposed. Thus, reciprocity between people can be articulated in terms of shame and exposure at the locus of the face.

The Force of Touch

Attachment

Touch is a critical part of human life. Without it, infants die. Even the slightest touch alters biology. Indeed, even before a fetus has eyes and ears it will respond to touch.[17] In Ashley Montagu's *Touching: The Human Significance of the Skin*, she calls skin a "first medium of communication."[18] Significantly, neglecting or not touching a child is understood as precipitating the greatest shame and having the greatest negative impact on brain development.[19] In preverbal children, repairing interpersonal bridges which connect the child to the caregiver requires touching and holding.[20] Without such touch, the child cannot and does not learn what it means to ameliorate a situation with regards to others, or even to regulate his/her own affective experiences.

The lack of physical contact as in cases of gross neglect in childhood leads to failure to thrive: abnormal or thwarted growth and development result from a lack of touch. Bruce Perry and Maia Szalavitz equate this state of the underdeveloped child suffering neglect to the runt of a litter in mammalian species.[21] In their telling chapter titled "Skin Hunger," they detail the lives of neglected children "starving for touch."[22] For children in this predicament, the need for touch to stimulate brain development goes unmet resulting in vacuous affect and deep levels of shame. This perpetual state of neglect indicates to a child that he or she has little to no self-worth, leading throughout adulthood to infant-like behavior, extreme isolation, little to no eye contact with others, and/or violence.[23]

Touch, required for a thriving child, is critical to human development. The tactile necessity of flesh relates both to affectivity and to the field of exposure, where touch serves as an amplification of being seen. To see is to become aware, and when someone feels authentically seen, the potential for a mutual recognition of regard transpires—even amid shame and guilt. In this way, touch takes on the radical aspect of substantiating existence. When it serves to substantiate existence of a vulnerable body, touch performs a function similar to conscious comprehension conducted through sight. Thus, to touch is, in some way, to perceive, while to be touched is to be perceived.

Being seen by another, being recognized as fully human, has the potential to counter toxic shame. Recognition that leads to acceptance fosters a sense of worth that contradicts such shame. This progression transpires in the field of exposure. Touch intensifies the "I see you" in the observation of the self by the other as it eradicates distance upon which the visual field relies. Further, in shame, one may escape or withdraw; touch necessarily refuses corporeal retreat. Withdrawal in shame, which entails hiding, becomes more difficult, because one is already grasped, obliterating distance between the self and the observing other.

In the eradication of distance between two people during touch, interest-excitement is present. Shame requires interest for its emergence. Thus, under the surface of interest lies affective shame. However, if interest-excitement continues unabated, shame remains regulated. To touch in interest, then, is obliquely to touch shame, confronting the possibility of shame's emergence while ratifying it. Touch and shame intertwine when touch establishes a connection. Thus, in both touch and shame, attachment becomes central.

As an affective "shaper of modern life," shame influences the social environment and interpersonal bonds indicating the greatest fear—of failure, for instance—and also the greatest attachment.[24] As shown, interest-excitement is a precondition of the shame response. Thus shame, in its action of truncating interest-excitement, effectively serves to indicate affective bonds.

Yet the experience of shame emerges as a result of severed attachment, and the self perceives itself alone. Touch has the potential to contradict this experience of aloneness in shame. Shame above all, Probyn asserts, "illuminates our intense attachment to the world, our desire to be connected to others, and the knowledge that, as merely human, we will sometimes fail in our attempts to maintain those connections."[25] The dynamic of and need for touch shares these qualities of shame.

However, when shame becomes interred, repressed, or maladaptive, it inspires behaviors of withdrawal and hiding that exacerbate distance, eradicating the possibility for connection or touch. Hiding comes in many forms; the body hides from others through literal isolation or by dissociating all or parts of the self, thereby curtailing affect and full participation in any particular event. Thus, the person in shame may be physically present in the flesh but dissociated or not fully present consciously. Dangerously, in cases of dissociation, the affective impact of touch has the potential to further bury shame, instead of making possible its release.

Trauma

Inherent in touch lurks the possibility of danger or risk highlighted in the case of trauma. The intimacy of touch allows for flesh to exceed boundaries and threatens its becoming unwanted, abusive touch. In such cases, touch itself maintains its feature of altering affect, but positive affect stimulated by the touch transmutes to terror. In order for touch, and for the events in Christian praxis that incorporate touch, to participate in the disinterment of shame, especially shame resulting from bad touch, the shame of trauma has to be negotiated, realized, and acknowledged. Shame must be brought up from the depths of the body and negotiated in terms of trauma. The challenge of this in any environment is ensuring that shame stays regulated to avoid intrusive traumatic memory and subsequent dissociation.

Contemplating the potential of touch for theology demands taking trauma into account. The touch that instills shame often manifests as some sort of violence, often in the form of physical or sexual abuse. In *Torment Me, but Don't Abandon Me*, Léon Wurmser demonstrates abusive touch as a double bind. Wurmser discusses a child's inherent and natural longing for the caregiver's nurturing touch. A lack of touch leads a child to imagine that something is inherently wrong with him or her; thus, the child feels shame. In order to combat the pain of not being touched, which typically manifests in the anxiety of being abandoned, a core fantasy develops that relates to Perry and Szalavitz's idea of "skin hunger." Afraid of loss indicative of a lack of physical contact, the child wishes for any type of touch, including abusive touch. This dynamic emerges in the lamentation, "Torment me but don't abandon me; punish me and forgive me then, but never leave me again."[26] This quotation elucidates the idea that the pain of punishment, or the painful touch, becomes "the avenue of union," where union signifies the natural inclination to connect to others.[27] This phenomenon manifests as the ambivalent longing in shame to reconnect with the person that harmed us, evidenced, for instance, in victims of child abuse who find themselves in abusive relationships in adulthood.[28] However, union to the source of pain generates shame. The longing for attachment communicated by touch, and the ultimate quest for the good and nurturing touch, takes precedence in such cases when individuals tolerate abusive touch, leading to shame. Thus, to be without touch, or to long for touch even if it is abusive, both facilitates and triggers shame.

Another problem inherent in touch, as it relates to shame, has to do with the blurring of boundaries between who touches and who is touched. The person applying touch possesses power over the other's body even insofar as the applied touch elicits an immediate affective response stimulating the body. The sense of touch, touching another, makes indistinct the boundaries between a "me" and a "you." Touch renders "us" as one; dualities extinguished, agency and passivity morph into an indistinguishable exchange of holding and enfolding. Such exchanges indicate individual vulnerability.

Touch also functions as a tool, conveying dominance and exacerbating the shame of the subordinated. Judith Herman reports that the most shame inducing forms of torture involve the body and touch used to ensure obedience: control of bodily functions, isolation, degradation, and enforced participation in atrocities.[29] Another legalized form of touch that supports both the dynamic of dominance and submission, as well as serves as a kind of public shaming, is New York's controversial stop-and-frisk program, also known as the Terry Stop. The dominating force of touch emerges in a routine procedure where one party is rendered publically powerless, and touching assumes the key to power in the exchange. Suspects are stopped, and outer garments are searched. While the law states that an officer "may search such a person," the qualification or form of touch employed remains undefined itself.[30] More ubiquitous forms of touch, just as damaging if not more so because of their insidiousness, include sexual abuse, domestic violence, forms of bullying, and sexual harassment. All of these also employ touch to denounce, humiliate, and control. Shame emerges at such moments of violence when the person touched becomes inferior. Subordinated and disempowered, this person is shamed into silenced.

The flight/fight/freeze response to a traumatic event of touch, and part of the impulse in shame to hide from view, renders the person as object of the touch speechless. This physiological response to extreme stress takes place in the sympathetic nervous system communicating to the body a need to escape, feign death, or exert violence. Affectively, these urges can be articulated as a shame response in the form of withdrawal, avoidance, or attack. According to Babette Rothschild, shame constitutes the affect that renders individuals speechless in the fight/fight/freeze response, but shame also disables the ability to either refute or respond to touch. In the case of abusive or intrusive touch, the trauma survivor interprets the experience of freezing, or "going dead," as a failure to act; the experience of shame accompanies this perception of failure. This situation emerges in cases of rape, torture, and physical/sexual violence and abuse, where survivors fault themselves for somehow causing the attack and for being unable to respond to attackers in any form of defense.[31]

Thus, in trauma, the proximity and sense of closeness that eases shame becomes inaccessible because that very thing constitutes a threat. A trauma survivor who has experienced the boundary crossing of touch in a damaging way cannot access the good qualities of touch, which becomes inaccessible because of fear or due to feelings of unworthiness. Paradoxically, the "good" touch communicates love and can potentially provide healing from the "bad" and shaming touch. This brings to bear the reality of healing touch. The intimacy of touch signifies attachment, giving touch the unique potential both to engender and dispel shame precisely because it can restore the interest and connection that shame initially truncated.

What is at stake in touch and corporeal practices, here in Christian praxis, rests within the interpretations of touch as good, bad, or confusing. Touch, so often intertwined with somatic issues around trauma that simultaneously link to shame, is potent and subjective. It blurs the boundaries between participants, conferring the power to elicit affective response from the person who is being touched. It amplifies the notion of exposure inherent in the shame event, obliterating the distance between the self and the observing other. It implies a closeness that has the potential to elicit shame. In situations where touch has been a factor of the trauma, for instance, in rape, torture, violent attacks, and child abuse, touch violates bodies, leaving them hyper- or hypo-aroused, ultimately dysregulated. In addition, the motive of touch questioned or misunderstood leads to self-questioning, doubt, and self-blame, which translates into an affective experience of shame.

Compounding this issue, motives to touch can have a variety of interpretations, and sometimes intention is not met with the spirit in which a touch was given. For instance, someone comes up behind another person to offer affection, a hug or a pat on the back, and the affective response to the gesture emerges based on the receiver's prior experience with touch. She might jump at being approached from behind, laugh at being surprised, or simply receive the touch that is given. Alternatively, the receiver might interpret a gesture meant to be warmhearted as offensive, or alternately perceive an offensive gesture as innocuous depending on personal history; for instance, many victims of childhood sexual abuse often cannot distinguish qualities of touch because their experience with touch has been so polluted by past trauma.[32]

Work on affect regulation, which relates to body awareness, is crucial to trauma survivors. Rothschild corroborates this, but she warns about situations where people have little tolerance for touch as a result of abusive histories. For instance, she reports of a client petrified of casual touch, especially in public situations. This client asks her never to give her a pat on the shoulder on her way out of the door. Thus, Rothschild points out that working with the body and touching the body after trauma are not necessarily synonymous; in fact, she asserts that often *not touching* preserves bodily integrity.[33] Not touching indicates a respect of the boundaries merged in touch and allows for trust to build between two parties. In addition, not touching in these cases communicates respect and therefore provides an opportunity for the disinterment of shame. An awareness of this appreciation of boundaries is critical to Christian officiants, who impose touch, not the least of which because they are situated within positions of power.

However damaging touch can be, Rothschild considers it a critical aspect of recovery from trauma. In her client's case, she aimed to increase the client's tolerance and positive affect at the moment of touch.[34] In therapeutic environments, teaching the tolerance of touch generally begins with helping clients gain body awareness and even tolerance of touching their own bodies.[35]

As these examples reveal, the effects of touch are complex and multifaceted. A good touch indicates friendship, care, love, or interest-excitement and intimates welcomed proximity. Alternatively, a bad touch is unwanted, rejected, perhaps even painful. The confusing touch complicates both of these because it signifies a painful touch from someone who represents love and protection. This could be from an abusive parent, or from another kind of authority figure whose role is to protect: the priest, the doctor, a day care worker, a close friend, a partner, or spouse. Further, during the experience of being touched, simple categories often disintegrate, making the moment of touch affectively charged and perhaps full of meaning yet difficult to decipher.

Part of the potency of touch resides in its ability to inter shame, especially in cases of abuse that provoke types of dissociation. However, touch, especially informed touch, also has the potential to disinter shame. This is because shame does not have the same emotional expression or release as other affects—for example, the ability to scream when angry or to cry when sad. Rothschild asserts that although shame does not appear to discharge from the body "acceptance and contact" relieve shame.[36] Inhibitory and interred shame thus dissipates under "very special circumstances – the nonjudgmental, accepting contact of another human being."[37] Ultimately, shame's disinterment and the amelioration of the detrimental conditions that interred shame perpetuates demand safe connections with other people. Such connections have specific qualities as non-judgmental contact. The iteration of liturgical practices of touch provides a unique forum for this type of physical connection needed precisely for the disinterment of shame.

The Potential of Touch to Disinter Shame

Touch is, above all, intimate.[38] Through touch, a body senses another body's nearness, presence, even its warmth. Although touch has the capacity to seriously harm and shame, it also represents the vital contact between bodies required to address shame. So indispensable, touch contains within it the possibility to participate in shame's disinterment. First, touch transforms affect, accounting also for its amplification in any particular encounter; this includes morphing negative affect into positive forms of affectivity.[39] Nurturing and non-judgmental touch stimulates the interest that shame truncates, rendering a body both present and vulnerable or exposed. The restoration of interest or positive affect opens up the potential for the transformation of a traumatic past narrative about shame. Second, touch of this sort validates, affirms, and acknowledges the self, constituting being. In this sense, the haptic expands the conception of the optic radiating a somatic message that one is perceived and recognized in the world. Furthermore, touch's inherent relationality and the way that it constitutes a distinct form of empathy enables the formation of bonds and affiliations so essential to bringing shame into full view. Without such connection, the hidden body in shame prevails. Approaching these distinct ways that touch operates to reveal shame, disempowering its detrimental effects, facilitates a potential pathway of disinterment through touch, providing—by transforming affect and acknowledging a person's being—at least two means through which shame can be potentially repaired. This is not to say that touch creates a dramatic change in shame immediately but rather to assert that the body responds to touch, and if shame is interred in the body as an affect, touch can potentially help release shame from its toxic grip on an individual. When considering a Christian practice of touch, examining what touch actually achieves adds another element for consideration.

Transforms Affect

One of the most compelling and intriguing aspects of touch is its ability to alter an individual's affective state. The organ, as skin, touched, elicits a somatosensory perception that leads to neural networks in the brain perceiving a change. When the body is touched, "the brain constructs a transient representation of local body change, different from the previous representation of that area."[40] The processing of constitutional changes "rapidly triggers a wave of additional body-state changes which further deviate the overall body state from the base range."[41] Therefore, not restricted solely to the part of the body being touched, touch affects the whole body, or the organ of flesh, as well as its interior.[42] Signifying an affective encounter, touch stimulates neural networks, triggering affect, and within this encounter, the physical—flesh—and affective—neurobiological response—converge.

Aristotle's strongest argument for the importance of touch comes at the end of his treatise, *On the Soul*. He privileges the haptic over the visual, insisting on the foundational and critical aspects of touch, which provide affective charges, what Aristotle calls "sensation."

> But if a body has sensation, it must be either simple or compound. And simple it cannot be; for then it could not have touch, which is indispensable. This is clear from what follows. An animal is a body with soul in it: every body is tangible, i.e. perceptible by touch; hence necessarily, if an animal is to survive, its body must have tactual sensation. All the other senses,

> e.g. smell, sight, hearing, apprehend through media; but where there is immediate contact the animal, if it has no sensation, will be unable to avoid some things and take others, and so will find it impossible to survive.[43]

In this passage, Aristotle asserts what research in psychology, affect theory, and neuroscience has come to support—that existence depends upon touch. He ratifies touch as vital, even urgent, as it connects not only one body to another but also the body to itself. He writes, "Flesh is 'the medium' of touch," not the organ, "the real organ being situated further inward."[44] The soul perceives the movement, contingency, and sensation of touch, and being so moved, it is altered. He adds, furthermore, that "all sense-perception is a process of being so affected."[45] Thus, touching stimulates affect, and while affect constitutes sensation for Aristotle, it is a sensation perceived by the soul.

Touch establishes an external connection between two people as flesh meets flesh, which also offers an internal union, for Aristotle at the soul level. The sensory, somatic response to the touch collides in such a moment with the social, external human interaction. Although the harmful effects of touch cannot be denied, research has shown that even brief skin-to-skin contact procures a positive affective incitement.[46]

In addition, the undeniable and positive affective impact of touch occurs with or without conscious awareness. In research conducted by Jeffrey D. Fisher and Marvin Rytting Richard Heslin, subjects handed a library card were touched during the exchange; some subjects knew ahead of receiving the card that a touch would occur, while others did not. The results of this exchange showed that "a casual touch of a very short duration in a Professional/Functional situation had positive consequences for the recipient."[47] In addition, the affective response of the recipients who were *not* prompted, that is they were not told that they would be touched, reacted similarly. Both those who knew they would be touched, and those who were touched and had no knowledge that touch was a part of the research, reacted positively to the touch. Thus, whether or not the touch was perceived, it generally had a positive effect on the recipient's affective responses.[48] In this case, "a touch (of less than one second) had the power to make people feel better,"[49] whether they realized it or not.

Affective encounters of this sort, bypass consciousness at first meeting and have the capacity to create a new experience, startling the self and drawing the body into the present moment. This physical jolt has the potential to detach the moment of touch from past meaning. While this potential is not always realized, especially for survivors of trauma, plausibly, touch offers opportunities for critical moments of transformation, disrupting and subsuming the present immediately, totally. Thus, touch makes a cognitive and somatic fissure in present occurrences, drawing attention to the body as well as to the connection that transpires between two people in the act of the touch.

Recent research in the neurosciences shows that shared representations of the experience of touch, and pain, occur in the human brain; touch increases these empathetic responses.[50] The "observation of tactile stimuli delivered to other individuals" induces activity in an observer's somatosensory cortical areas.[51] This means that not only being touched but also watching someone else being touched can activate an area of the brain sensitive to touch. Therefore, watching someone being touched elicits a similar affective response and transformation to that experienced by the one actually touched.[52] The neurobiological research on touch affirms that touch, even casual and unrecognized touch, makes an impact, a potentially positive impact on people even if the touch is merely observed. This has ramifications for practices of touch conducted in ecclesial settings.

However, an important factor to recall about shame when discussing the positive impact of touch and empathetic responses to the touch of another is that shame inhibits empathy. The person in shame avoids attention and empathetic connection even though these ameliorate shame. In order to cognitively process and then produce empathetic behavior, the body must necessarily somatically process, replicate, or perceive the other; shame interferes with this phenomenon, even though shame relies on connection and empathy for amelioration.[53] Again, shame presents the double bind. Even so, the empathetic connection fostered through touch provides an opportunity for shame's disinterment, in part because casual touch can produce positive affect, even if in some cases access to that touch is inhibited. Disinterring shame depends on connection. Touch at least offers a moment where such connection is possible.

Touch as Acknowledgment

To touch a person is to recognize their presence. In *Metaphysics*, Aristotle asserts that to touch has significance as the capacity to name, to indicate, and to acknowledge. For example, touching a person dignifies him or her by recognizing existence, therefore, supporting and endorsing life. At its most basic then, touch acknowledges being, human *being*.

For Aristotle, touch signifies multiple dimensions of being. This notion of touch redresses the diminished sense of self-worth in shame, as it confers respect through acknowledgement.

The quality that touch possesses to ratify existence, and which is highlighted by Aristotle, also figures in the Bible where Thomas touches the wounds of Christ to know that Christ is real. Similarly, Jesus appears to the disciples in Luke 24: 36–49, imploring their touch, to verify his presence and gain their trust. He says to them, "Why are you frightened, and why do doubts arise in your hearts? Look at my hands and my feet; see that it is I myself. Touch me and see; for a ghost does not have flesh and bones as you see that I have."[54] Therefore, biblically, touching ratifies being in a way that intensifies the notion of establishing presence through sight. Touching substantiates existence and solidifies the essence of being.

Thus, the result of affective transformation in touch amplifies and validates a person's being. Touch communicates being and presence by communicating, "You are here to me." In this way, touch confirms the visual realm. Conversely, to refuse to see, name, or touch another signifies a failure to recognize that person's existence or presence. Not to be touched is to remain unrecognized. This is the predicament of the neglected child. However, in the case of past trauma, if a person does not want to be touched, respecting that wish creates a similar result of acknowledging that person with respect and worthiness.

Authentic recognition begins to combat the feelings of diminished worth so characteristic of shame through touch. Thus, met through touch, a person relates to another person. This tactile part of relating defies embodied shame that communicates a body's unbelonging. Authentic and nurturing touch ratifies belonging conveying relationship and reestablishing the interest that shame truncated in the first place.

Belonging is a key component in the Christian community. Jesuit Priest Dennis Smolarski remarks in his book *Sacred Mysteries: Sacramental Principles and Liturgical Practice* that inherent in sacraments and multiple practices within the liturgy, "Human communication mediated through touch is a mystery, part of the mystery of human flesh and spirit created in the image and likeness of God."[55] Touch thus brings to bear the *Imago Dei* affording an opportunity to recognize the Christian self, reflecting back to Augustine's notion that there is no shame in wearing the cross, and that the cross in fact blesses such shame.

The Imposition

The imposition of a cross on the forehead on Ash Wednesday, the initiation of Lent, provides one entrance point for an analysis of shame and touch in the tradition. Repeated yearly, the practice elucidates what Lange considers in *Trauma Recalled*, the liturgical event as a ritual remembering, a constant return both to the traumatic events that happened to Christ on the cross and the joy inherent in Christ's resurrection.[56] Later, I show how this practice, along with touch and shame, has implications for a theological interpretation of Christ and the cross.

Lange argues that the iteration of liturgy is not simply a ritualistic return to the ineffable event, captured initially in written form, but rather "a continual return of that which cannot be captured in the event."[57] The liturgical iteration then, for Lange, cannot be fully grasped, as it refers to something that is essentially present only in memory. Thus, in practice, with the Christian entering into the Christian narrative through liturgical participation, some "force" returns "in the celebration to disrupt anew."[58] Lange calls this present unsettling by a past memory a "rupture," which continually intrudes upon the present moment.[59] Lange's analysis narrates the Christ events as sharing the inexplicability of trauma, which the liturgy also bears. This means that within the liturgy moments of rupture exist that bring the past immediately into the present, while constituting the present in a formidable way.

Taking the imposition of ashes as a moment of touch that both constitutes and intensifies Lange's concept of a rupture of some present force or memory calls into question whether the imposition of the ashes literally extends shame, whether the gesture is a form of writing shame on the body, connecting to Christ's experience of shame. This writing of shame onto the body in ash reflects Lange's notion of writing as signification of something passive emerging and which illustrates the impossibility of language in the traumatic event. At the moment of imposition, the haptic also converges with other affective experiences to witness that event. A prayer is recited as the touch is imposed, and in each prayer a trace of the Edenic narrative remains, including its preoccupation with sin, guilt, and death.[60] What happens to the body, or how is the body shaped, when the haptic, phonic, and optic meet in intentional and meaningful ways? As in each case of touch, the affective encounter—the implicit, non-verbal, somatic aspect to interrelating—remains.[61] When the voluntary encounter with God is made with the body, then the somatic experience of touch can be seen to take on a pivotal role in Christian practice.

Ashes

The first day of Lent, Ash Wednesday marks Jesus's initial forbearance in the desert where Satan tempts him prior to the crucifixion. Traditionally a day of fasting, Ash Wednesday initiates a period of penance, which culminates in Easter, the celebration of Christ's resurrection. At its best, the liturgy of Ash Wednesday purposively seeks to join the Christian self with the Christ story. This provides a forum for facing and naming shame in Christian practice. The provision for the acceptance and subsequent disinterment of shame happens in two ways. First, the liturgy encourages the recognition and acceptance of humanity as fragile and mortal. Part of this condition, as Augustine continually asserts, includes a full affective life of which shame is an indelible part. However, the commemoration of Ash Wednesday also provides a forum for mourning and grieving Christ's own mortality. Through this mourning, the aspects of pain and suffering that result from shame can also be processed. Second, in shame, always lies the loss of connection; affectively, this is the loss of interest-excitement. In Augustine, it constitutes the severing of the divine tie. Yet, while the ashes mark the lonely sinner of the Christian tradition, inherent in this practice, the promise of new life also persists—that is, a renewed life into a community of those similarly marked. Such reflection and renewal provided by practices in which the Christian participates year after year offer a pathway to the disinterment of shame.

Nowhere better than in the prayers recited during the receipt of ashes are these themes reflected. According to the old (1969) liturgy, the words from Genesis 3:19 accompany the imposition: "Remember, you are dust and to dust you shall return." These words echo those that Adam and Eve hear after eating from the fruit of the forbidden tree, and they foretell the mortification and death of Jesus's mortal self on the cross. With these words, the recipient of the ashes joins the Edenic narrative, entering into mortification, admitting a humble mortal status and renouncing pride. Current recitations that accompany the imposition of ashes in the Catholic liturgy employ a moderated version of the Genesis event. Although less explicit than Genesis 3:19, the message is similar: "Turn away [or repent] from Sin and be faithful to the Gospel." In other services, Mark 1:15 may be recited: "Repent and believe in the good news!" This version emphasizes the promise of rebirth and renewal. Ultimately, each recitation communicates the ways in which the Christian self understands herself in the world, as mortal and susceptible to suffering, but always engaged in the possibility of renewal.

Mortality and Mourning

According to the Baltimore Catechism, ashes "keep us in mind of our humble origin" and signify the necessity of penance inherent in human life, presumably as a result of the first sin.[62] The more recent *Directory on Popular Piety and the Liturgy*, updated by the Vatican in 2001, states that "the act of putting on ashes symbolizes fragility and mortality, and the need to be redeemed by the mercy of God."[63] Harking back to the symbolic palms of Palm Sunday the year before that have been burnt, or destroyed, the ashes illustrate a necessity for reflection on mortality. Mortality reflects human nature biologically, but it also connects—at least for Augustine—directly to the punishment Adam and Eve suffer in their affected bodies. The image of the ash operates as both a stain and a signification of such loss and eventual death. As Augustine tells readers again and again, after the Fall, human life finds itself doubly mortal, as inherently suffering both shame and death.

The perception of ashes as signaling mourning has historical roots that relate to Christian practice, the Genesis event, and to Christ's death. Thus, the practice of mourning reflects grieving that constitutes multiple types of losses: the loss of some aspect of self; the loss of immortality, which makes death and imperfection a natural part of human life; and the reality of suffering, also a part of life, but amplified in Christ's own suffering and subsequent death on the cross. Mourning is also critical for the disinterment of shame because it allows a cleansing of the body. Grieving loss disempowers the shame associated with loss and pathology, so that what remains can be transformed into something different, something closer to the more primal shame of attachment.

Thus, aligned with death, the ashes recall Christ's suffering and death. If liturgy is the participation of the individual Christian in a story, as the ashes come from the celebration that inaugurates the suffering and subsequent loss of Christ's human body, then the recipient also mourns this loss. It is not simply a loss of Christ's human body; it also constitutes a loss of the human body's dignity and signifies the shame experience.

The ashes on the forehead also refer to suffering: the suffering of Adam and Eve, of Christ, and of human life always directed toward death. Ashes on the forehead as the seat of shame, tied to suffering, shed light on the complicated relationship between shame and mourning. In the case of this event, it is mourning for the loss of perfection in Eden, the loss of Jesus, and the loss of heavenly perfection. Mourning is also bound up with the image of the cross, implying Jesus's death and his own shame.

While the ashes mark "mortality" and "fragility" as suffering, signifying shame, paired with Augustine's notion of the cross on the forehead as covering and touching shame, they also communicate that witnessing pain and shame elicits no shame. In such a way, the cross of ash indicates that shame persists, and even aligned with Christ and Christ's pain, there is no shame in attachment.

Renewal

While Ash Wednesday marks the mortification into which the Christian enters during Lent, the ashes also signify a promise of renewal. The Vatican asserts, "The faithful who come to receive ashes should be assisted in perceiving the implicit internal significance of this act, which disposes them towards conversion and renewed Easter commitment."[64] According to the catechism, a *conversion of the heart*[65] must always accompany the external act of imposing ashes. The touch functions as an "indispensable" component of conversion during the imposition of the ashes on Ash Wednesday. The ashes always make contact with the forehead, Augustine's seat of shame, and are always perceptible. Thus, the ashes serve as a persistent reminder of shame naturally held in the self.

Renewal thus signifies the interior conversion which constitutes the pathway to disinterment that touch both initiates and seals. Within the Christian community, the ash indicates that individuals do not bear shame alone. The ashes expose shame as shared as a part of life capable of being ameliorated through touch and relationship, though not eradicated or discarded because the experience of shame indicates the attachment to the community in the first place. Thus assimilated within this community, the ashes acknowledge that shame is a natural and blessed part of human affective life.

The Implications for Christology

The imposition of ashes foreshadows the suffering and death of Christ at the site of the affective body. Where does participating in the imposition of ashes on the forehead take the Christian in relation to Christ? Primarily, the event, emphasized by the moment of touch, takes the Christian to the affected and affective body in shame. The practice of the touch emphasizes the body, including Christ's body, individual Christian bodies, and the body of the Christian community conceived of as church. In this instant of touch, the bodies collide to reveal shame in a new somatic and affective way.

First, the attention to body, affectivity, and mortality assists Christian recipients of the touch in taking incarnation seriously. The touch reinforces the importance of incarnation through which Christ is known as fully human, his shame constituting part of that humanity. This is not the toxic shame and humiliation of his suffering but rather the true, natural shame that Augustine places on the face. Furthermore, "Taking the embodiment of Jesus seriously draws attention to Jesus's relationality, his touching and healing of people."[66] This Jesus, as the affected one, touches and is touched in love. Affect in this case, the true shame presaged by interest-excitement evident in the healing touch, takes on the notion given to it by Julia Kristeva when she says, "affect," while acknowledging lack, "gives greater importance to the movement toward the other in mutual *attraction*."[67] In this sense, the affected, incarnated Christ participates affectively with humanity in mutual attraction.

A duality in touch and shame emerges affectively in that what must be taken into account is that Christ as incarnated, touching and healing, is also Christ crucified, suffering in shame. What Christ experiences in this time is not only the true shame, affectively located at the low intensity end of Tomkins shame-humiliation pair, but the very intense humiliation that relates to Christ's suffering. That he undergoes shame publicly, willingly, notwithstanding tremendous suffering emphasizes the importance of facing and sharing shame despite the difficulty and pain.

While feminist critiques often move away from Christ's suffering as a useful narrative, Sharon Betcher actually moves toward it. Betcher claims that staying with suffering and pain is crucial for a theology of disability, especially true since the central image of Christianity is wounded body and victim of imperial power.[68] She views Christ affectively, developing a Christology that allows a "remaining" with Jesus in his shame and suffering as a model for staying with others in pain.[69] She writes, "instead of assuming the crucifixion of Jesus as an ontologically unique moment within a historically realist perspective and therefore a metaphysical truth to be believed toward salvation (that is, toward the 'anesthetizing of pain'), we read Christianity as a practice that allows suffering to speak."[70] To this, I would add that this posture allows shame to come to the fore, where it can be disinterred. Although it is not the totality of Christ's time on the cross, drawing attention to the suffering involved in facing shame recognizes suffering as a part of revealing shame. In the moment, Christ models the facing and sharing of shame. Thus, he refutes shame's interment.[71]

In the refusal to hide, to withdraw in shame, Christ also reveals his affected body and his vulnerability, unveiled, serving figuratively as a counter figure to Adam and Eve's cover-up.[72] Attention is drawn to Christ as body, in the mortal flesh. By doing this, his shame comes into view, not in a derogatory way, but in a way that connects to our most primal self. This is the potential of the shamed and humiliated Christ; attachment and love are possible even amidst suffering. This is the bodily connection that occurs through touching shame on the forehead. Through touch, bodies connect with the shame of Christ's most human self. The Ash Wednesday experience permits a facing shame, in a very intimate way, by imposing the cross on the forehead in community. The Christian recipient steps into a bodily knowing of shame at the imposition of ash on the forehead. The juxtaposition brings to the forefront—on the forehead in ash—shame's dependence on relationality, while toxic shame acts against that relationality.

The humiliated, publically shamed body of Christ also functions as an affective site of political struggle. Christ is the social agent that regulates affect. His is an affected body that affects other bodies, stimulating those bodies. In the case of shame, the withdrawal away from or attachment to God either increases or decreases shame but does not save it. "Affect is inherently political: bodies are part of an ecosocial matrix of other bodies, affecting them and being affected by them; affect is part of the basic constitution of bodies politic."[73] Once again, Christ exemplifies the duality in shame—both the toxic shame suffered at the extreme of humiliation and the acceptance of shame as a part of the self that binds us to one another as our most vulnerable selves. One narrative is agonizing, the other mutually empowering. The latter is Christ in connection to God.

The Cross

The cross is a fraught symbol in Christian thought. Some theologians problematize the discourse of suffering related to Christology. Recent scholarship especially related to trauma and issues of race and gender have critiqued ideas of redemptive suffering aligned with the crucifixion.[74] Even though the cross perpetuates suffering, even giving a reason for suffering, and even though it has been used to justify war and violence, people still love it. Christians kiss the cross, adore and adorn the cross, and wear the mark on their foreheads as a reminder of their finitude, along with the possibility of eternal life. The cross reveals a connection and attachment to Christ; part of the love toward it relates to what particular work people envision happening at the site of the cross, whether that be salvation, reconciliation, or forgiveness. While exploring the work of the cross is critical, the focus in this text remains on examining the connection and attachment to Christ and the cross as both relate to affect.

The imposition of ashes on the forehead brings shame to the fore and demonstrates the paradox of the cross: that the cross along with shame both binds the Christian self to what it most loves and partially severs the self from that same object. The duality that both attracts and repels is reflected in the dynamics surrounding the cross. Furthermore, this twofoldness emerges in the symbol of the cross itself. Mark C. Taylor points out what he calls the "paradoxical nonbinary (a)logic" of the symbol of the cross: "As the threshold of absolute passage, the cross marks the intersection of ascent and descent that is the 'marriage of heaven and hell,'" symbolized on the way to Golgotha.[75] This paradox continues perpetuating the symbol of the ash, itself a symbol of the path to death. The question becomes: what does the imposition of ashes reveal about a theology of the cross that can both inter and disinter shame?

The yearly return to the cross imposed on the forehead of the lonely sinner is, in some degree, the return to the problem in the tradition where guilt and sin eclipse shame. When this happens, shame is easily forgotten and denied. Eclipsed by guilt, shame goes unaddressed and concealed by a narrative that makes the Christian guilty for Christ's death. This narrative, explored extensively in theologies of atonement, cannot get at the pernicious or binding nature of shame; thus, shame becomes not only interred in the self but also buried in a particular rhetoric.

Interment of shame also occurs in the justification of suffering that permits the cycles of shame, mentioned by feminist critiques that refer to the cross's justifying violence. An affective reading of the cross shares feminist theologians' concerns that lifting up salvation through suffering is problematic as it relates to shame, because it condones the tolerance of toxic shame. As Rita Nakashima Brock and Rebecca Ann Parker argue, the cross has been used as a symbol to perpetuate suffering. This concern is also shared by womanists like Delores Williams who have contended that given black women's experiences of surrogacy in the USA, any links between suffering and salvation should be broken.[76] For instance, when the cross is interpreted by James Cone as "the burden we must bear in order to attain freedom," the link is perpetuated.[77] Redemptive suffering perpetuates shame, and instead of working at naming shame to promote empathy, justifies the pain of shame which instead works to undermine both human flourishing and relationality.

A different critique of this stance emerges in Shelly Rambo's *Spirit and Trauma* where she locates the promise not in the paradox of the cross as Cone does, but in the cross's "excess."[78] Her point is particularly compelling when placed within a haptic and affective frame. She asserts that the "theological meaning" of the cross "cannot be found in turning away or turning to the cross, but, instead, in the turning itself, the movements between that acknowledge a more tenuous relationship between death and life."[79] Acknowledgement of human experience lies at the fulcrum of this movement. Rambo's conception of turning emerges in the turn toward God, in our shame, reflected in Augustine's receipt of the cross on the forehead. It is this movement that connects participants both to one another and to God. The turning rather than being stagnant, or ever completed, always happens. The touch corroborates this, as Karmen Mackendrick states, "touch moves," as in being touched or moved by language.[80]

Also, Rambo asserts, "If we look between cross and resurrection, we are directed to a new way of being, to a form of life that is not triumphant. Instead, it is life configured as remaining."[81] Shame is figured in this step as a part of remaining that is neither mired in trauma nor relegated to promises of healing. Affectively this holds. It also corroborates Augustine's notion of Christ as an embodied bridge, remaining, between the two worlds Augustine envisions, connecting us to both, and with that connection, holding, touching our shame.

Affectively Attuned Theology

Augustine understands the dualism in the idea of the cross on the forehead—that it is both his story and a shared story, and that neither his faith nor his own shame is something to feel ashamed about. Augustine also understands that this shame resides in the body. Denying shame represents a futile act; embracing it, and placing the cross upon it, or allowing shame to converge with a story about love and promise allows for the message of the Christian tradition as Augustine conceives of it to be more fully realized. Augustine asks for the cross to cover his shame, not to mask it, but to bless it, so that he may reach ever toward God and participate in the divine.

Fully aware of how trying to rid the self of shame leads to its harmful interment and theologically allows for its misinterpretation, Augustine welcomes shame promoting a theological anthropology where shame can function naturally as an affect that binds people to God and to others. Further, an affectively attuned theology understands that human life is made up of fractious affects, and that practice offers hope for renewal and conversion, not in order to purify and cleanse, but in order to become fully participating members of the Christian community who all bear shame. But to achieve this end, there always exists a need for conversion, marked by the yearly return in liturgy to Ash Wednesday. No perfect ending evolves; it all begins again, always repeating.

Conclusion: Returning to the Practice

On Ash Wednesday, in a structure similar to the communion ceremony, each person walks toward the altar. The priests and Eucharistic ministers hold small glass and ceramic bowls of black ash. Ominous in their own right, the ashes convey a paradoxical message, that life is both full of joy and full of grief. Walking toward the altar, reverent and in a posture of shame, the procession of congregants mirrors Jesus's journey to the desert.

And each bows his or her head to receive the cross of ash of the forehead. Augustine's words convey the convergence of shame and the residue of the touch in the form of a cross, critical to Christian formation. "In no secret place do I keep the Cross of Christ, but bear it on my forehead," "because the forehead is the seat of the blush of shame." In this moment of touch on Ash Wednesday, shame is seen, touched, blessed, and conjoined with death and mourning, but also with love, mercy, and bounty.

The body presents itself joining with the travails and trials of Christ's body; the corporeal reflects in the recitation, "Remember that you are dust and to dust you shall return." In the moment of touch, the body joins with the ashes, the past, the Jesus story, shame, and the reality of individual death but always, at once, in this life also joins in the promise of renewal. The renewal exists in the human touch, in the potential for rejoinder, for intimate connection, that exists in this touch. Touch makes one immediately known and not alone, recognizing individual self-worth and disinterring shame. The shame that remains, an inevitable and inherent part of affective life, is shared and not borne alone; instead, as it emerges, an entire ecclesial history subsumes it.

Within the movement of touch as an affective encounter, at the moment of touch in the imposition of ash on the forehead, shame both hinders and fosters human relating. The moment of touch, the affective element of touch, and touch's role embedded in practice are multidimensional bodily experiences fraught with risk and possibility. As moments in which a mark of ash is made upon the body, this touch draws bodies both actually and symbolically into the Christian narrative. The mark has an implicit message about the Christian character reflecting the idea that in liturgy, a particular effort exists to form bodies. Each moment of touch assumes Lange's "present" which reflects practice that attempts to create a Christian character engaging in mortification while also seeking the promise of renewal in connection to God and the other. In each case, bodies are marked and formed, branded, figured, and reinforced in that conception. Reflected in the mark is not only what is remembered but also what is absent. The symbol of the cross of ash on the forehead reflects not only Christ's death but also his suffering and shame. The ash corroborates and reinforces the connection. The touch marks the return to the Christ event, embodies the remembering, while disrupting rote repetition, with its physical immediacy and its symbolic saliency established by both Christian texts and embodied Christian practice.

Understanding the potential for touch to offer bodily transformation emphasizes the concept of embodied practice, but it also addresses the whole person. The whole of the Christian thus engages in practice, the body both human and divine, with the touch of ash corroborating this. Clarifying where shame emerges and specifically addressing it, rather than allowing it to continue to be obscured by guilt and sin, allows the tactile affective encounter; that is, it allows for shame to be touched and so touched, named. Ultimately and most significantly, approaching shame and the body in this way allows for a more unified self—mortal, divine, and with shame. This admission fosters acceptance in the Christian community of everyone and every part of the self, and "If one feels whole [*heil*] then the good," available throughout the Christian tradition, "serves to give joy, not to hide shame."[82] Touch in Christian praxis has to the potential to facilitate this good, promoting self-worth, love, and therefore disinterring shame.

Notes

1. The touch of ash as praxis takes on different forms. For example, in some countries outside of the USA, ashes are sprinkled onto the forehead instead of being imposed as a cross on the forehead. Generally, English-speaking countries use the imposition of ashes with wet paste and a cross on the forehead; in Italy and Spain, for instance, often officiates sprinkle dry ash on the forehead; see Father Edward McNamara, "Laypeople Distributing Ashes," *Zenit*, last modified February 5, 2008, accessed May 2014, http://www.zenit.org/en/articles/laypeople-distributing-ashes

2. Keith F. Pecklers, S.J., "The Liturgical Year and Popular Piety," in *The Directory on Popular Piety and the Liturgy: Principles and Guidelines*, eds. Peter C. Phan and Robert J. Brancatelli (Collegeville, MN: Liturgical Press, 2005), 92. Here Pecklers talks about the imposition of ashes as a Roman Ritual, used by Lutheran and Anglican churches, but also having recently been more frequently adapted into Methodist and Presbyterian Ash Wednesday Services.
3. Teresa Swan Tuite, "Tactile Engagements in Christian Understanding," (PhD diss., Yale, 2008), 7.
4. Swan Tuite, "Tactile Engagements," abstract.
5. Saint Augustine, *Confessions*, trans. Henry Chadwick (Oxford: Oxford University Press, 1991), X.xxvii.38: 201.
6. Saint Bonaventure, *The Journey of the Mind to God*, trans. Philotheus Bohner, O.F.M. (1956; reprint, Indianapolis: Hackett Publishing Company, 1990), 24.
7. Marguerite Porete, *Mirror of Simple Souls*, trans. Ellen L. Babinsky (Mahwah, NJ: Paulist Press, 1993), 80.
8. Swan Tuite, "Tactile Engagements," 9.
9. Bryan P. Stone, *Evangelism after Christendom: The Theology and Practice of Christian Witness* (Grand Rapids, MI: Brazos Press, 2006), 26.
10. See Dirk G. Lange, *Trauma Recalled: Liturgy, Disruption, and Theology* (Minneapolis: Fortress Press, 2010). Lange's analysis of Luther's writing, informed by trauma theory, provides a useful model as it opens up new ways to understand liturgy.
11. St. Augustine of Hippo, *Exposition on the Book of Psalms: Psalms LXXIII-CL*, ed. Paul A. Böer, Sr. (1886; reprint, Dublin: Veritatis Splendor Publications 2012), 562–563.
12. Tomkins, *Affect, Imagery, Consciousness*, 123.
13. See Judee K. Burgoon, "Relational Message Interpretations of Touch, Conversational Distance, and Posture," *Journal of Nonverbal Behavior* vol. 15, no. 4 (1991), 246–247. It should be mentioned that this is a Western study, and it does not take into account cultural variations of touch.
14. Josephine W. Lee and Laura K. Guerrero, "Types of Touch in Cross-Sex Relationships Between Coworkers: Perceptions of Relational and Emotional Messages, Inappropriateness, and Sexual Harassment," *Journal of Applied Communication Research* vol. 29, no. 3 (2001): 210.
15. Lee and Guerrero, "Types of Touch," 201.
16. Tomkins, *Affect, Imagery, Consciousness*, 359.
17. Ashley Montagu, *Touching: The Human Significance of the Skin* (New York: Harper & Row, 1986), 3.
18. Montagu, *Touching*, 4.
19. Perry and Szalavitz, *The Boy Who Was Raised Like a Dog*, 64–66.

20. Kaufman, *The Face of Shame*, 36.
21. Perry and Szalavitz, *The Boy Who Was Raised Like a Dog*, 92.
22. Perry and Szalavitz, *The Boy Who Was Raised Like a Dog*, 92.
23. Perry and Szalavitz, *The Boy Who Was Raised Like a Dog*, 96 and 138.
24. Nathanson, *Shame and Pride*, 147–153.
25. Probyn, *Blush*, 14.
26. Wurmser, *Torment Me but Don't Abandon Me*, 137.
27. Wurmser, *Torment Me but Don't Abandon Me*, 137.
28. Kaufman, *The Face of Shame*, 19.
29. Judith L. Herman, "PTSD as a Shame Disorder," Webinar, International Society for Traumatic Stress Studies, October, 13, 2014.
30. "N.Y. CPL 140.50," FindLaw, accessed January 16, 2014, http://codes.lp.findlaw.com/nycode/CPL/TWO/H/140/140.50
31. Rothschild, *The Body Remembers*, 11.
32. See Karen A. Olio and William F. Cornell, "Therapeutic Relationship As the Foundation for Treatment with Adult Survivors of Sexual Abuse," *Psychotherapy: Theory, Research, Practice, Training* vol. 30, no. 3 (1993): 512–523.
33. Babette Rothschild, *The Body Remembers: The Psychophysiology of Trauma and Treatment* (New York: W.W. Norton & Company, 2000), xiv.
34. Rothschild, *The Body Remembers*, 144–155.
35. Fisher, "Sensorimotor Approaches to Trauma Treatment," 172–175.
36. Rothschild, *The Body Remembers*, 62.
37. Rothschild, *The Body Remembers*, 62.
38. See Peter J. Marston, Michael L. Hecht, & Tia Robers, " 'True Love Ways': The Subjective Experience and Communication of Romantic Love," *Journal of Social and Personal Relationships* vol. 4, no. 4 (1987); Marston et al. show that touch is one of the greatest indicators of partner's expression of love, second only to the words, "I love you."
39. Tomkins, *Affect, Imagery, Consciousness*, 1024.
40. Damasio, *Descartes' Error*, 263.
41. Damasio, *Descartes' Error*, 263.
42. Chrétien, *The Call and Response*, 92–93.
43. Aristotle, *On the Soul*, II.11.
44. Aristotle, *On the Soul*, II.11.
45. Aristotle, *On the Soul*, II.11.
46. Jeffrey D. Fisher and Marvin Rytting Richard Heslin, "Hands Touching Hands: Affective and Evaluative Effect of and Interpersonal Touch," *Sociometry* vol. 39, no. 4 (1976).
47. Fisher and Heslin, "Hands Touching Hands," 419.
48. Fisher and Heslin, "Hands Touching Hands," 420.
49. Fisher and Heslin, "Hands Touching Hands," 420.

50. See Michael J. Banissy and Jamie Ward, "Mirror-Touch Synesthesia Is Linked with Empathy," *Nature Neuroscience* vol. 10 (2007): 815–816; Keysers C, Wicker B, Gazzola V, Anton JL, Fogassi L, Gallese V., "A Touching Sight: SII/PV Activation During the Observation and Experience of Touch," *Neuron* vol. 42, no. 2 (2004): 335–346; Blakemore S.J., Bristow D, Bird G, Frith C, Ward J., "Somatosensory Activations During the Observation of Touch and a Case of Vision—Touch Synaesthesia," *Brain* vol. 128 (2005):1571–1583; Schaefer M., Flor H., Heinze H.J., Rotte M., "Dynamic Modulation of the Primary Somatosensory Cortex During Seeing and Feeling a Touched Hand," *Neuroimage* vol. 29 (2006): 587–592.
51. Ilaria Bufalari, Taryn Aprile, Alessio Avenanti, Francesco Di Russo, and Salvatore Maria Aglioti, "Empathy for Pain and Touch in the Human Somatosensory Cortex," *Cerebral Cortex* (2007), 2554.
52. Vittorio Gallese and Corrado Sinigglia, "What Is So Special About Embodied Simulation," *Trends in Cognitive Sciences* vol. 15, no. 11 (2011): 1.
53. Schulte-Rüther et al., "Theory of Mind Mechanisms," 1368. Studies have shown that mere observation of another person performing an action recruits partly the same "circuitry" elicited by the execution of the observed action. More specifically, this circuitry involves supplementary motor area (SMA), pre-SMA, pre-motor cortex, the supramarginal gyrus, intraparietal sulcus, and the superior parietal lobe; see Singer, "The Neuronal Basis and Ontogeny of Empathy and Mind Reading," 857. There are also studies that cite fault with this phenomenon.
54. Luke 24:38–39.
55. Dennis C. Smolarski, S.J., *Sacred Mysteries: Sacramental Principles and Liturgical Practice* (New York: Paulist Press, 1995), 18.
56. Lange, *Trauma Recalled*, 1–2.
57. Lange, *Trauma Recalled*, 132.
58. Lange, *Trauma Recalled*, 10.
    Lange, *Trauma Recalled*, 141.
59. Lange, *Trauma Recalled*, 1 and 142.
60. I turn to the *Baltimore Catechism Three* (Charlotte, NC: Saint Benedict Press, 2010) used primarily before Vatican II, and to the United States Catholic Church, *Catechism of the Catholic Church* (New York: Doubleday, 1994) based on Vatican II principles and employed primarily after 1985. The catechisms are useful, together and separately, as both tools of learning and as underlying the primary assumptions enacted in the practice of Ash Wednesday.
61. I use this term in accordance with the neurobiological description detailed in relationship to right brain processing in Margaret Wilkinson's *Changing Minds in Therapy: Emotion, Attachment, Trauma, and Neurobiology*

(New York: W.W. Norton & Co., 2010), 85–102. The term is also interestingly a key theological expression in Shelly Rambo's *Spirit and Trauma: A Theology of Remaining* (Louisville: Westminster John Knox Press, 2010).

62. *Baltimore Catechism Three,* Lesson Twenty-Seventh, Q1077: 251.
63. "Directory on Popular Piety and the Liturgy: Principles and Guidelines," The Holy See, accessed September 7, 2013, http://www.vatican.va/roman_curia/congregations/ccdds/documents/ rc_con_ccdds_doc_20020513_vers-direttorio_en.html#Chapter%20Two
64. "Directory on Popular Piety and the Liturgy."
65. United States Catholic Church, *Catechism of the Catholic Church*, Part Two, Section Two, Chapter Two, Article 4, 1430: 399.
66. Riet Bon-Storms, "A Challenge to Change Developments in Feminist Theology and Feminist Christology," *HTS* vol. 61, no. 1&2 (2005), 58.
67. Julia Kristeva, *Tales of Love*, trans. Leon S. Roudiez (New York: Columbia University Press, 1987), 155.
68. Sharon Betcher, *Spirit and the Obligation of Social Flesh* (New York: Fordham University Press, 2013), 70–71.
69. Betcher, *Spirit and the Obligation of Social Flesh*, 70–71. See also Rambo, *Spirit and Trauma,* 68, as mentioned, "remaining" is a key term in Rambo's theology of spirit.
70. Betcher, *Spirit and the Obligation of Social Flesh*, 93.
71. Tomkins, *Affect, Imagery, Consciousness*, 454 and 480.
72. This is problematized by Mark D. Jordan, who discusses the shame in talking about Christ's genitals, see *Telling Truths in Church: Scandal, Flesh, and Christian Speech* (Boston: Beacon Press, 2003), 87.
73. John Protevi, *Political Affect: Connecting the Social and the Somatic* (Minneapolis: University of Michigan Press, 2009), 50.
74. See, for instance, Rambo, *Spirit and Trauma: A Theology of Remaining* and Jones, *Trauma and Grace.* See also Rita Nakashima Brock and Rebecca Ann Parker, *Proverbs of Ashes: Violence, Redemptive Suffering, and the Search for What Saves Us* (Boston: Beacon Press, 2001); Delores Williams, *Sisters in the Wilderness: The Challenge of Womanist God-Talk* (Maryknoll: Orbis Books, 1993); Joann Terrell, *Power in the Blood? The Cross in the African American Experience* (Maryknoll: Orbis Books, 1998); Marit Trelstad, ed. *Cross Examinations: Readings on the Meaning of the Cross Today* (Minneapolis: Augsburg Press, 2006); William Cavanaugh, *Torture and Eucharist: Theology, Politics, and the Body of Christ* (Oxford, UK: Blackwell Publishers, 1998).
75. Mark C. Taylor, *Erring: A Postmodern A/Theology* (Chicago: University of Chicago Press, 1984), 13.
76. Delores Williams, *Sisters in the Wilderness* (Maryknoll: Orbis Books, 1993), 148.

77. James Cone, *The Cross and the Lynching Tree* (Maryknoll: Orbis Books, 2013), 148.
78. Rambo, *Spirit and Trauma*, 158.
79. Rambo, *Spirit and Trauma*, 158.
80. Karmen Mackendrick, *Word Made Skin* (New York: Fordham University Press, 2004), 61.
81. Rambo, *Spirit and Trauma*, 127.
82. Wurmser, *Torment Me but Don't Abandon Me*, 79.

CHAPTER 6

Empathic Engagement

Couples dancing is a form of expression and connection. Eye contact increases the intensity of the exchange, displaying a profound sense of affinity. Coordinating movement requires resonance and rhythm, an interplay that allows each person not only to experience himself or herself in motion but also to understand the kinesthetic intentions of the other. The pair does not unify but corresponds and synthesizes. They join together to convey the strength and beauty of a couple. The couple experiences this as a balance among contrasts: power corresponds with yielding, tenderness steadies passion, and sharp reactions are met with equally sensitive ones.

The coordination of affect and energy during couple dancing replicates the modulation of communication and imagination necessary in empathy. Empathy entails presence and deep listening, while envisioning another's experience. Shared between partners, coordination, harmony, and reciprocity are essential. Fostered by a sense of self-worth that expands and enables the self to understand another, empathic exchange includes shared affect: friends express mutual joy upon meeting, or undergo the pangs of loss at the account of suffering. In the dance, partners respond to each other's bodies through a reliable and fluid connection; in empathy, responding affectively, equally as reliable, honors another person's selfhood and dignity. As a steadfast, non-judgmental approach to the other, empathy counters the shame experience. However, shame itself, subversive to self-worth, interferes with the capacity for coordinated, affective communication. Shame interrupts balance between two people as it draws us to the other only to impede connection, yet it is precisely this other,

S.N. Arel, *Affect Theory, Shame, and Christian Formation*,
DOI 10.1007/978-3-319-42592-4_6

and the support provided through empathy, that repairs shame. Thus, empathy, while it is restricted by shame, is an important part of shame's amelioration.

In the previous chapter, the discussion about touch provided a pathway for analyzing empathy as an automatic, and often unconsciously recognized, neurobiological phenomenon involved with mirror neurons. The work of mirror neurons is understood as a component of cognitive empathy. We observe bodies move—our bodies respond in kind. We watch an Olympic gymnast perform on television, or a sports team nearly make a final goal. The body tenses or may even move in a manner similar to the athlete's on the screen because the same neurons that fire for the individual performing or receiving action fire for the observer. Thus, this aspect of empathy functions as a mirroring mechanism correlating with the embodiment of action and the transfer of skills.

While mirror neuron mechanisms illustrate a neurological component or starting point for empathy, another more affective or sensory level transpires in the limbic system. Like mirror neuron activity, the functions of the limbic system precede the language-generating system of the neocortex. Thus, limbically based communication patterns are composed of sensory experiences—including both touch and sight—that moderate the internal system with the external environment. Related to emotion, memory, and motivation, the limbic system is responsible for pleasure and pain. It moderates fear responses to threatening stimuli, just as it triggers the impulse to connect—through talk or touch—with another person who evokes immediate attraction.[1] Thomas Lewis, Fari Amini, and Richard Lannon identify what happens neurologically in this part of the brain as "limbic resonance."[2] Defined as "a symphony of mutual exchange and internal adaptation whereby two mammals become attuned to each other's inner states," limbic resonance assumes the qualities of a dance.[3] Empathetic harmony arises from the limbic system, which works rapidly to make identifying a "kindred spirit" a relatively easy cognitive task.[4]

In affect theory, this empathetic communication is expressed as "affective resonance," defined as "the sharing of emotion that accounts for much of the quality of adult interpersonal relationships."[5] Initiated by Tomkins's category of interest-excitement, empathy emerges in the reflective and responsive face of the caregiver to the child, whether to reflect joy or to commiserate, as when a child experiences pain and the caregiver assumes a facial expression that mimics the child's. Primordial and crucial, as Perry and Szalavitz continually assert in *The Boy Who Was Raised Like a Dog*, the empathic exchange is an "essential part of human health."[6]

The empathetic child-caregiver dyad is a fundamental model for similar incidences of interest-excitement in adulthood. Without such interest, the self experiences, instead of love, a world of shame. The cognitive components and neurological foundations of empathy account for its ease in performance, illustrating the absolute human need for connection. However, efforts at empathic attunement are also influenced by affect and socialization which emerge as *habitus* and scripts. For instance, shame scripts that partially truncate interest-excitement account for an adverse effect on attunement. Yet, how and to what extent does shame impede empathy? Exploring how shame inhibits empathy, along with how empathy can be encouraged to address shame, reveals the necessity to attend to shame to espouse empathy. Probing how shame and empathy intertwine is thus significant for interpreting Christian self-understanding.

Empathy facilitates an ability to tolerate and intentionally engage in painful affects such as shame.[7] The ability to hold shame without interring it, without its becoming detrimental, requires commitment from the self to remain both introspective and attentive to the world and the other. This self reflexivity is not only a psychological phenomenon but can also be conceived of as a theological or spiritual practice. Edith Stein's *On Empathy* provides a theological and philosophical platform for delving into empathy as a capacity that impedes and ameliorates shame—for both the self and the other. In fact, Stein envisions empathy as interwoven into the "psycho-physical" and spiritual becoming of the self, who is in a continual process of growth or, as Stein puts it, "unfolding."[8]

So while empathy is a neurological and affective phenomenon, it is also, according to Stein, a spiritual one. The self evolves through the development of empathy. Facilitating an exploration of this dimension of empathy defined as the "perceptual consciousness in which foreign persons come to givenness for us,"[9] Stein's work offers ways of thinking and rethinking what it means to relate to others and the world. She proffers a theory that insists that empathic connection, along with what it demands, is critical to the development of the "psychophysical" and spiritual self. The emphasis in the empathetic connection to the other ameliorates shame as it establishes interest-excitement. Yet, encountering the other and fostering "affective resonance" demands a presence of the self that is lost in the shame experience. Stein understands this, affirming the importance for persons to understand themselves as worthy in order to empathically connect.

Empathy and Attachment

Tracing the multidimensional capacity of empathy consists first in examining its affective origins. As "affective resonance," empathy emanates from visceral sensations that draw people toward each other. This affective source of empathy correlates with shame's primal roots. At the basis of both lies the human need for attachment that requires no words and is sensually communicated. However, unlike shame, empathy is not an individual affect, even though affects and the attunement of affect facilitate empathic connection. Affects, as the biological expression of emotions, are what is shared in the empathic exchange. Empathy constitutes an ability to attend and respond to an affect or constellation of affects. A deeper look at the attachment phenomenon, referred to elsewhere in the text as secure/regulated, insecure/dysregulated, clarifies aspects of the development and function of empathy.

In the 1970s, Mary Ainsworth developed a way to measure attachment through a procedure titled "The Strange Situation."[10] In an effort to replicate the interactions of children and caregivers at home in a laboratory setting, this procedure measures the quality of attachment between a child and a caregiver. The experiment intends to place stress on the child in order to measure what researchers label "the reunion" of the caregiver (in this study the mother) with the child. In the first part of the experiment, the caregiver and child are introduced to an experimental room. The child explores and plays in the presence of the caregiver who remains present yet not engaged. Then a stranger enters the environment. The child continues to play, and the stranger attempts to interact with the child. The mother is cued to leave the room. Generally, the response from the child is one of negative affect. The stranger attempts to comfort the child in vain. Then the mother returns, and scientists record how the child reacts. A second part of the experiment includes leaving the child alone in the room. Then the stranger returns. The mother follows. The stranger subsequently departs, and the reunion of caregiver and child is measured again. Scientists recorded three types of behavior patterns emerging in the reunion periods, labeled as three distinct attachment styles: secure, ambivalent, and avoidant. To these, subsequent research has added a fourth: disorganized.[11] The styles indicate the nature of the attachment between the primary caregiver and the child, which has come to be an effective predictor for attachment styles in adulthood.[12] Each style influences all subsequent relationships and, imbricated some way with shame, makes an impact on the capacity for empathy.

In secure attachment, when the mother returns, the child seeks her support, love, and care, but then, once affectively regulated, departs again from the mother's embrace to play and explore the surroundings. This provision of care and support leads to the ability to self-regulate, express positive emotion to others, develop and communicate compassion, tolerate vulnerability, and to both sustain and flourish in the intimacy of interpersonal relationships.[13] As such, shame, when it emerges, is met with positive affect such as interest-excitement and therefore ameliorated. Caregiver-child attunement or "affective resonance" that modulates shame and negative affect provides the blueprint for the development of empathy that continues into adulthood. Such "affective resonance" is disturbed in the insecure attachment types, which are thus made more susceptible to toxic shame. For instance, the avoidant child fails to respond to the caregiver, may resist physical contact, and explores less than the securely attached child impeding the regulation of negative affect.[14] The ambivalent child may cling to the caregiver, showing "extreme reliance" on her, exhibiting dysregulated affect—tears and fits—and then alternately rejecting her.[15] In disorganized attachment, the child often responds with intense fear upon separation and may either be warm and caring to the returning caregiver or punitive; this attachment style is evident in cases of dissociation of which shame plays a major role.[16]

Attunement between caregiver and child mitigates shame and, as a powerful force in nature, constitutes deep, genuine connections. From this place of "resonance" we are aware of and responsive to another. This affinity provides the essential means for the mastery of negative affect. Secure attachment enables a general sense of trust, developed in the initial attachment relationship, which ensures that susceptibility to negative emotional experiences does not result in damage to the self or others. In fact, the ability to tolerate negative affect leads to trust of the other and of the self. Secure attachment fosters confidence in the constructive responses of others and instills the assurance that negative affective states can be integrated into the self; therefore, these are not denied or repressed.[17]

Affects can, thus, be interpreted as normal, natural, and even *safe* aspects of human life, even if they are negative. Affects—positive and negative—compose human experience, enriching it despite their intractability. Stein helps us understand affective life as a part of self-formation that includes affect as substantiating the body and ratifying our being "alive."[18] Affects, for Stein, are feelings experienced in their purity.[19] Pure joy, pure interest, pure love that conjoins us leads to mutual reciprocity, buttressing empathy. They provide the basis for empathic exchange, immediately shared through facial expressions.

But empathy is dimensional, and interpreted as supported by attachment, it constitutes a complex and dynamic phenomenon. One dynamic in empathy relates to being seen. For instance, in the Strange Situation, attenuating negative affect occurs in the visible presence of the caregiver. Thus, attachment, and subsequently empathy, takes place in the field of exposure. Functioning within the visual realm, even as it endures affectively or somatically based, empathy requires at least the perception of one other. Stein calls this "co-seeing."[20] Co-seeing takes place in the field of sensation between the self and the foreign other. "I see" the other, a foreign "sensing living body."[21] This seeing composes the beginning of the empathetic connection, serving as a dual introduction, of the self to the self and of the other to the self. "I see" the "sensing living body" of the foreign other and "empathically project myself into it."[22] This develops a new image, a new understanding through the empathic projection that reveals something more about the self. Or as Stein puts it, "I see myself as another or as another sees me. This makes empathy possible for me."[23]

Practically, "co-seeing" challenges us because of the intimacy it evokes. Mutual gazing makes us vulnerable to the other—we attach. Tomkins considers this concept of seeing as radically intimate: "The closest approximation to the shared look," he writes, "is sexual intimacy, in which analogously pleasure is simultaneously given and received by the same act."[24] The mutuality of the gaze in interest intensifies in the intimate encounter with another, sexual or otherwise. And in this mutuality, we can see the other, more deeply, profoundly. When such an exchange occurs, the instrumentation of empathy is made possible. The exchange instigated by sight is heightened by touch. As Stein states, "the tactile and visual senses … call each other as witnesses."[25] Thus, in empathy, we are always exposed, especially so. Attaching to someone or connecting to someone to instigate the capacity to empathize requires vulnerability, disclosure, and expression of our most defenseless self.

This capacity demands engagement of the self and the toleration of the other. As illustrated by the Strange Situation, empathy necessitates affective regulation of shame in at least one party. Someone who is affectively regulated, who is not hyperaroused, is thus capable of expressing empathy to another who suffers or experiences shame. Furthermore, the ability to imagine the feelings of another requires self-introspection on one hand and a willingness to be susceptible on the other. Both of these are impeded by a diminished sense of self-worth indicative of shame.

Empathy and Shame

Empathy illustrates the human capacity to harmonize. Neurological, cognitive, and affective, empathic connection is foundational to human growth and health. Stein distinguishes empathy as necessarily visceral and spiritual, as a co-seeing. Empathy in the attachment phenomenon, perceived in part by what Ainsworth termed the "reunion," is significantly influenced by shame. Shame undermines self-worth, contributes to withdraw, or provokes negative affects such as anger impeding empathy. A closer investigation of how empathy attenuates shame and how shame conversely interferes with empathy illuminates the consequences of shame on Christian formation.

Secure attachment provides the basis for healthy, attuned adult relationships and the capacity for empathy. Shame interferes with this. For instance, elements of insecure attachment styles typify shame. The ambivalently attached child longs for connection, and this need is always on "high."[26] However, shame evolves when the love this child expresses—often manifested as a desperate need—fails to be responded to by the caregiver.[27] Similarly, the avoidant type is immersed in shame and is often blatantly disliked or emotionally disregarded by the caregiver.[28] This child refuses to open him/herself up to vulnerability. Rage and anger at the parent follow.[29] In disorganized attachment, the primary caregiver is "a source of unremitting shame" generally associated with trauma.[30] In this attachment style, the inclination to attune competes with the fear of being humiliated, and the desire for love that results in attachment is met equally with the refusal to attach.

The "reunion" episode of the Strange Situation that captures attachment styles can also be understood in terms of the affect interest-excitement, which partially truncated, signals shame. Restoring the interpersonal connection when the caregiver returns reinstates interest-excitement, thereby decreasing the shame affect. But failure at reconnection signals trouble. For instance, if a child expresses a desire to attach and the desire fails to be met with an equitable response, the child withdraws in shame from the thing or person capturing interest. The capacity to attach and to reinstate positive regulated affect mitigates shame establishing the grounds for "affective resonance" or empathy.

Secure attachment provides the necessary tools to manage or regulate shame and to build empathic connections. However, insecure attachments promote interred and toxic shame preventing such connection. Further, shame responses, and shame-prone individuals, locate the self at the center of a particular experience instead of focusing on the affective experience of the other. Thus, shame inspires the self to turn away. Motivated by a belief that the self is deficient in some way, the turn away exemplifies the bind in shame to be seen as shameful. Self-worth diminished leads to the belief that the self is not "good" enough to connect to the other. At the root then of empathic connection lies the need for an inherent sense of value in the self, that means, an amelioration of shame which paradoxically requires empathy for its amelioration.

Shame Impedes

Shame represents a belief that the self is not worthy of love. At base, this presumption constitutes the formation of a stigmatized self, which has some inherent and impassable defect. The ensuing logic is that something is wrong with the self, which as discussed earlier, contrasts with the logic of guilt that assumes fault in behavior or action, not the core self. The recognition of action—not the self—as the greatest component in wrongdoing inspires remorse in lieu of the visceral recoil in shame. Research has repeatedly shown that experiencing guilt has a positive correlation with the capacity for empathy, while the experience of shame asserts the inverse.[31] This is in part because shame motivates the self to both turn away and turn inward. The reduced sense of self-worth in shame compounds behaviors of withdrawal impeding remorse as a potential source of repair that relates empathy to guilt. Empathy helps us recognize "when our actions adversely affect others, and it motivates us to take corrective steps to remedy the situation."[32] However, shame hinders the ability to identify a precipitating action; instead, fault is directed toward the self, who believed deficient, can only remedy the situation by disappearing.

As mentioned, the shame-prone individual lacks empathy, while the guilt-prone is empathetic.[33] Guilt and empathy contribute to mutual growth, and the affective experience of guilt provokes remorse as a result of understanding the experiences of an injured other. Shame impairs the capacity for empathy, and the incapacity to have empathy is dangerous. Empathy curbs anger and aggression, while shame perpetuates these.[34] "Shamed people are less inclined toward empathy – empathy that might otherwise help curb their tendency to externalize blame and lash out in anger."[35] Further, shame perpetuates negative affect and additional shame, which rupture the harmony of empathic exchange, in part because the person in shame remains absorbed in his or her own experience and fails to imagine the affect of the other.

The inability to feel the pain of another, to imagine or absorb negative affect experienced as a result of the behavior of another, constitutes the absence of empathy. On a moderate level, this leads to the inability to engage in healthy relationships; on a more severe level, it can lead to extreme violence. Often motivated by a lack of love in childhood, shame as an impediment to empathy leads to what Michael Slote calls the "incapacity for emotional receptivity and responsiveness that characterizes sociopaths and certain sadists."[36] Similarly, in *The Boy Who Was Raised Like a Dog*, Perry and Szalavitz discuss Leon, a 16-year-old boy who brutally murdered two teenage girls and raped their dead bodies. The authors argue that Leon shows the markers of a lack of empathy, which was key to his violent actions. If empathy is the ability to understand the effects of one's "actions on others and connected with them," this demonstrates an obvious lack to the extreme.[37]

The capacity in empathy to recognize the pain another experiences as the result of hurtful action accompanies the concept of the apology, while the comparable ability to identify pleasure experienced as a result of kind action coincides with the concept of gratitude. Both apologizing and expressing thanks involve an affective exchange—disrupted by shame—intended to effect a particular response in the other—one to ameliorate negative affect, the other to increase positive affect. In shame, the experience of the self as unloved and unworthy constrains the capacity for both remorse and gratitude. Both expressions involve imagining the experience of another person which shame impedes. Slote argues that empathy emerges from a primal gratitude, the gratitude young children feel toward loving parents.[38] When shame interferes in this development it inhibits the tendency for gratitude to spread beyond its original context, emerging eventually as altruism, to spread itself over the larger world.[39]

Empathic contact implied by the "I am sorry" and "Thank you" relies on an interpretation of the self as worthy and as having agency. Stein addresses this. She writes, "Only he who experiences himself as a person, as a meaningful whole, can understand other persons."[40] The shame that undermines self-worth leads to the internalized belief that the self is not whole. This toxic shame inhibits the ability to recognize a need for contact that expresses remorse or gratitude; self-absorbed by the pain of understanding him/herself as deficient these words become nearly unspeakable. The self is therefore restricted from imagining or being present to the pain of another. Shame impedes affective receptivity, blocking both the sensation of the other and the perception of the other's needs. Obstacles to self-other connections, to "co-seeing," feed the negative affect of shame and often lead to its refusal in other affective forms. Along with impediments to remorse or gratitude, the self in shame, in an effort to break free from said shame, may turn to anger or rage in order to reestablish some sense of self-worth. This kind of grasping emerges in Gilligan's study where imprisoned men who felt "dissed" or shamed tried to eradicate the affect through violence, to reestablish pride.[41]

Pride thus intertwines with empathy, in this case inhibiting it and, worse, precipitating violence. The avaricious need to deny shame correlates with Augustine and Niebuhr's interpretations of pride that leads to sin—the pride of arrogance and *hubris*. However, the pride of self-worth, defined as pleasure in accomplishments or self-compassion, promotes, even allows empathic connection. As with gratitude, this has societal implications. For instance, Tangney and Dearing assert that "hubristic pride decreases empathy for stigmatized others, which leads to increased prejudice [and also violence]. On the other hand, authentic pride increases empathy for stigmatized others, which reduces prejudice."[42] In this case, empathy has an increased societal function. Empathy fosters the healing of prejudice which reduces violence and mitigates shame.

Empathy Attenuating Shame

Empathy offered by another allows for the address and redress of shame, disenabling its interment. Shame, treated as natural, only impartially truncates the interest-excitement that indicates attachment, what has now been established as undergirding the empathic connection. Yet, empathy is a necessary condition for shame.[43] Tomkins states that "if there is insufficient interest in the other, shame through empathy is improbable."[44] He implicates empathy and attachment in his further assertion regarding the importance of showing a child that shame need not be disastrous.

This means assisting the child in the regulation of the shame affect. Socialized in such a way, children learn that empathy assists in the "mastery of shame and defeat" which are subsequently attenuated through secure attachment or empathic connection.[45]

Shame in the securely attached self is accepted as an inherent part of life, processed, faced, addressed, and then incorporated into the self, as a worthy self. The experience of shame as a denigration of self-worth is therefore fleeting and regulated. In this case, shame does not complicate the empathic connection; in fact, it enhances the empathic connection because the experience of addressed shame before another indicates deep trust.

How then does empathy make a positive impact on shame? Depending on the intensity of the shame experience, the empathy that ameliorates a damaged sense of self-worth originates from someone not in the throes of shame. For instance, the therapist offers a client a holding environment for damaging shame and responds to it compassionately. In this case, what occurs is that the person in shame experiences himself or herself as able to risk exposure and to tolerate the affect enough to address it rather than turning away or lashing out. The visceral, non-verbal aspect of shame thus becomes seen.

The last chapter showed that touch ratifies the notion that being seen and acknowledged has the potential to mollify the shame response. Both being seen and touched are therefore important to experiencing and developing empathy. Furthermore, shame constitutes a withdrawal from the field of exposure; whether that be actual or performed by gestures such as the impulse to avert the eyes, the self can still be accessible through touch. Stein writes supporting touch as a means of empathic connection that can access the self where seeing cannot: "Things that withdraw from the glance," Stein writes, "are accessible to touch."[46] Part of touch's impact relates to its ability to stimulate positive affect, at variance of negative affects such as shame.

Another example of the instillation of positive affect to combat shame is through joy manifested as laughter. Shared laughter, like touch, immediately connects two people through affective behavior. Laughter thus represents one of the purest ways of facilitating an empathic exchange. Furthermore, laughing at an embarrassing or shameful event fosters human connection that can immediately eradicate the shame affect. "Good-humored or affectionate laughter, almost always dispels shame," Scheff asserts.[47] On a visceral level, laughter provides the infusion of joy that can, as affects do, immediately shift or alter the painful experience of shame.

Development of the Christian Self

Empathy is foundational to Christian formation. On the most obvious level, the Christian notions of guilt support the idea of fostering empathy. However, all too often the discourse around rue and contrition, guilt and sin, eclipses shame. Thus shame, as an affect operating in every self, goes unaddressed. The failure to name shame allows it to function surreptitiously and to subsequently be interred. Interred shame that becomes toxic undermines an individual's full participation in community, communal gathering, and communion. Christian formation and growth depends upon relationality, upon shared vulnerability, and, indeed, shared shame. Empathy is implied in this construction, but fostering empathy through gratitude for instance, along with an acute awareness of how shame inhibits empathy, can facilitate repair of shame.

A necessary step in this repair is to uncover where shame lies hidden in Christian rhetoric and practice. Identifying shame in this way provides the grounds from which shame's perpetuation and interment in selves and bodies can be arrested. Shame must also be addressed as a primordial experience that all individuals share, but that as a result of Christian teachings—for instance, about shameful *pudenda*—often becomes buried in the self. Further, unaddressed shame, embedded in ideas of sin and guilt, assumes the form of toxic shame. Each one of us has the potential to experience damaging levels of shame, and each one of us, in the pursuit of empathic connection, bears the responsibility, at least from a Christian sensibility, to confront shame. This confrontation does not simply constitute a logical or cognitive encounter; it is a visceral one.

Understanding that the solvent to shame is connection remains critical and lies at the root of the Christian ideal of love. And yet while connection fosters empathy and impedes shame, self-knowledge must also be a priority. Self-knowledge is both the *apriori* condition that enables empathy as well as the result of empathy: as Kohut states, "introspection and empathy *as an essential constituent*" are pivotal in psychic and psychological development.[48] Stein corroborates this as she sees empathy a critical avenue to constituting the person. Through empathy, Stein writes, "what is 'sleeping' in us develops,"[49] while the other is constituted in "empathetically experienced acts."[50] For instance, recognizing the other through affect, corporeally communicated as a laugh or a glance offers a way of conceiving that person's core—the person's "soul."[51]

For Stein, empathy itself brings one into the realm of spirit.[52] This subsists as the realm of "pure sensations" and "pure consciousness," in the "I" of the living body. Empathy evolves from the living body, the sensing body, the affective body, which is also always a spiritual body. For Stein, feelings make us present, constitute us, and comprehending the feeling of another brings us into the realm of spirit.[53] The spiritual enters through the body for Stein: "We meet the spirit ... always bound to a physical body."[54] And "a spiritual subject empathetically seizes another and brings its operation to givenness of itself."[55] This sense of "givenness" as wholeness operates as an emollient to shame, complementing the formation of a flourishing Christian self.

Empathy can also be expanded by fostering a sense of gratitude. This might be for what is occurring in one's own daily life but expands to include the other promoting an activity whereby that other becomes recognized and seen. This recognition provides a pathway to undermining detrimental shame. Furthermore, since gratitude operates, according to such philosophical assumptions, *via processes of empathy*, it also facilitates self-reflection, reflection on reflection, and a reflection of the self related to the other.[56] Stein would not call this simply reflection, which implies an outwardness in the act of empathy. Reflection interpreted thusly becomes objective, a mere observance. Yet, neither does Stein call reflection an inner perception. Instead, she uses the term an "inner-intuition" "for the comprehension of our own and foreign experience."[57] Thus, intuition implies a grounded self, experienced as a whole self who has shame but who still comes to an awareness of and concern for the other.

Furthermore, Stein's use of intuition draws us back toward affect—to immediate experience—further ratifying the body and physicality as the root of the spiritual experience of empathy. Thus, shame is essential to the self. Shame lives alongside joy and anger making up what Stein calls "psycho-physical unity."[58] She presses this aspect of self, not separate from spiritual life but essential to it. In this interpretation, Stein locates the psychological and affective as indispensable to Christian spiritual formation. In fact, fostering this unity transitions into the ability to perceive a foreign consciousness—empathy.[59]

Conclusion

This discussion of the imbrication of empathy and shame challenges theologians and religious leaders to implement practices that foster empathic connection, not to merely talk about them. And yet it is not as simple as that. First, shame itself needs to be addressed, as an affect, as a biological and neurological phenomenon that is both present naturally in the self, and often detrimental to the self. Detrimental shame takes root in the self when that self believes that it is unlovable for some reason. Shaming of any type undermines the feeling of lovability and has pernicious effects including self and other directed violence. But not shaming is not enough. Church leaders benefit from understanding the dynamics of shame and other negative affects so that they may not only help those in shame but also educate people about their experiences in shame and therefore foster empathic connection and intimacy.

Loving one another is a basic tenet of the Christian faith. Christian growth takes place in community, in literal communion with others. Empathy underlies these principles. Empathy is critical for moral and societal development. Without empathy, the world is devoid of loving, caring, and emotionally engaged human beings, a critical need for humanity and the planet. In empathy, as in faith, love is not one directed toward another's action, it is directed toward the person as he or she is. This love constitutes an adjudication of a person's value. The natural self has inherent value and, as Stein says, we love a person for her own sake.[60] This comprises the formative process for the spiritual person. The accountability for the Christian then is to love, but to love without a standard—to love as a spiritual practice that fosters another's coming into their full self and supports human dignity.

Highlighting the important role theologians and religious leaders play in fostering empathy emphasizes the need for a deeper understanding of shame and attachment. That shame impedes empathy, but that empathy also attenuates shame, presses theology and theologians to recognize where shame is elided, repressed, neglected, and interred so that they can contribute to shame's repair. Shame poses a challenge because it's painful and difficult to grasp, but the efforts to reveal where shame lurks attempt to pave a pathway to developing a critical but constructive theological voice in addressing the multiple contentions that emerge as a result of toxic shame. Resources in theology offer new visions and understandings of shame that, instead of perpetuating its toxic effects, bolster empathy and foster gratitude, attending to shame as an innate, even essential, part of human experience.

Notes

1. See Jean-Marc Fellous, "The Neuromodulatory Basis of Emotion," *The Neuroscientist* vol. 5, no. 5 (1999).
2. Thomas Lewis, Fari Amini, and Richard Lannon, *A General Theory of Love* (New York: Random House, 2001), 61.

3. Lewis, Amini, and Lannon, *A General Theory of Love*, 63.
4. Lewis, Amini, and Lannon, *A General Theory of Love*, 54.
5. Nathanson, *Shame and Pride*, 45. Donald Nathanson uses this term frequently, but the concept of resonance at the level of affect is developed first in Silvan Tomkins's *Affect, Imagery, Consciousness.*
6. Bruce D. Perry, and Maia Szalavitz, *Born for Love: Why Empathy Is Essential and Endangered* (New York: William Morrow Paperbacks, 2011), 1.
7. Schore, *Affect Regulation and the Origin of the Self*, 351.
8. Edith Stein, *On Empathy*, trans. Waltraut Stein (Washington, DC: ICS Publications, 1989), 111.
9. Stein, *On Empathy*, 96.
10. Mary D. Salter Ainsworth, Mary C. Blehar, Everett Waters, and Sally N. Wall, *Patterns of Attachment: A Psychological Study of the Strange Situation* (New York: Halsted Press, 1978). See also a video displaying the experiment at http://bu.kanopystreaming.com.ezproxy.bu.edu/video/mary-ainsworth-attachment-and-growth-love.
11. See Mary Main and Judith Solomon, "Discovery of a New, Insecure-Disorganized/Disoriented Attachment Pattern," in *Affective Development in Infancy*, eds. T.B. Brazelton and M. Yogman (Norwood, New Jersey: Ablex, 1986): 95–124.
12. To understand the measurement of these, see C. George, N. Kaplan, and Mary Main, *The Adult Attachment Interview.* Unpublished, 1985. An illustrative document can be accessed at http://www.psychology.sunysb.edu/attachment/measures/content/aai_interview.pdf.
13. See Mario Mikulincer, Phillip R. Shaver, Omri Gilath, and Rachel A. Nitzberg, "Attachment, Caregiving, and Altruism: Boosting Attachment Security Increases Compassion and Helping," *Journal of Personality and Social Psychology* vol. 89, no. 1 (2005): 817–839.
14. Ainsworth et al., *Patterns of Attachment*, 94 and 124.
15. Ainsworth et al., *Patterns of Attachment*, 60 and 183.
16. Mary Main, "Introduction to the Special Section on Attachment and Psychopathology: 2. Overview of the Field of Attachment," *Journal of Consulting and Clinical Psychology* vol. 64, no. 2 (1996): 239. For the relationship between shame and dissociation, see Herman, "Shattered Shame States."
17. Mario Mikulincer and Phillip R. Shaver, *Attachment in Adulthood: Structure, Dynamics, and Change* (New York: Guilford Press, 2007), 191–192.
18. Stein, *On Empathy*, 8.
19. Stein, *On Empathy*, 50.
20. Stein, *On Empathy*, 57.
21. Stein, *On Empathy*, 61.
22. Stein, *On Empathy*, 69.

23. Stein, *On Empathy*, 63.
24. Tomkins, *Affect, Imagery, Consciousness*, 385.
25. Stein, *On Empathy*, 41.
26. Robert Karen, *Becoming Attached: First Relationships and How They Shape Our Capacity to Love* (Oxford: Oxford University Press, 1998), 221.
27. Karen, *Becoming Attached*, 232.
28. Karen, *Becoming Attached*, 239
29. Karen, *Becoming Attached*, 239.
30. Herman, "Shattered Shame States," 3.
31. Tangney and Dearing, *Shame and Guilt*, 86.
32. Tangney and Dearing, *Shame and Guilt*, 79.
33. Tangney and Dearing, *Shame and Guilt*, 86.
34. Tangney and Dearing, *Shame and Guilt*, 95.
35. Tangney and Dearing, *Shame and Guilt*, 94.
36. Michael Slote, "The Roots of Empathy," in *Cultivating Virtue: Perspectives from Philosophy, Theology, and Psychology*, ed. Nancy E. Snow (Oxford: Oxford University Press, 2014), 69.
37. Perry and Szalavitz, *The Boy Who Was Raised Like a Dog*, 133.
38. Slote, "The Roots of Empathy," 73.
39. Slote, "The Roots of Empathy," 65–86.
40. Stein, *On Empathy*, 116.
41. See Gilligan, *On Violence*.
42. June Price Tangney and Jessica L. Tracy, "Self-Conscious Emotions," in *Handbook of Self and Identity*, eds. Mark R. Leary and June Price Tangney (New York: Guilford Press, 2012), 461.
43. Tomkins, *Affect, Imagery, Consciousness*, 409.
44. Tomkins, *Affect, Imagery, Consciousness*, 409.
45. Tomkins, *Affect, Imagery, Consciousness*, 454.
46. Stein, *On Empathy*, 41.
47. Thomas J. Scheff, *Microsociology: Discourse, Emotion, and Social Structure* (Chicago: University of Chicago Press, 1990), 172.
48. Heinz Kohut, "Introspection, Empathy, and Psychoanalysis: An Examination of the Relationship Between Mode Observation and Theory," *Journal of the American Psychoanalytic Association* vol. 7, no. 3 (1959): 459 and 469.
49. Stein, *On Empathy*, 116.
50. Stein, *On Empathy*, 109.
51. Stein, *On Empathy*, 110.
52. Stein, *On Empathy*, 92.
53. Stein, *On Empathy*, 92.
54. Stein, *On Empathy*, 117.
55. Stein, *On Empathy*, 93.

56. Slote, "The Roots of Empathy," 71.
57. Stein, *On Empathy*, 34.
58. Stein, *On Empathy*, 54.
59. See Stein, *On Empathy*, 57–79.
60. Stein, *On Empathy*, 102.

CHAPTER 7

Conclusion

Shame lies at the core of the self. It exposes who and what the self loves most, but it also inhibits love, because steeped in toxic shame, the self feels unlovable. This state of shame emerges when shame lies interred in the body, concealed by other affects and experiences. The affective body in shame comes into view as vulnerable, compelled to turn away, hide, or escape from view. Rooted in the most primal self, shame as preverbal needs no words for expression. Shame informs the body, even as it often renders its bearer speechless before the eyes of a real or imagined other. Thus, shame viscerally draws bodies away from human and divine connection, emerging as a "sickness of the soul."[1]

However detrimental shame might be, its primitive, more primal presentation in the self directs that self to its greatest attachments. Interest, excitement, and even joy ground the affective experience of shame, discontinuing abruptly when shame emerges. Severing the most viable connections, shame erupts from the core of the self to arrest these positive experiences, truncating them, and leaving the self exposed. But only through further exposure, turning to the other or to God in shame, only through facing the shame in reconnection with another, does repair occur.

Looking through the lens of affect theory and trauma studies highlights shame's role in attachment, uncovering how in shame, without the availability of trusting human connection, part of the self escapes from view, cut off, and denied, itself buried away as bad or disgusting. Damaging attempts at alleviating shame emerge, engendering cycles of more shame

S.N. Arel, *Affect Theory, Shame, and Christian Formation*,
DOI 10.1007/978-3-319-42592-4_7

or even rage. The desperate grasp at pride and use of rage that pretend to alleviate shame, only do so momentarily, if at all. Extraordinary attempts are made to diminish and bury shame in expressions of violence by those seeking to restore the pride of self-worth stolen by shame. However, these behaviors and choices fail to ameliorate shame, serving only to sever attachments needed for shame's repair. Alternatively, behaviors of withdrawal, avoidance, and pulling away eliminate the possibility of both repair and empathic connection.

Uncovering the nature of shame to expose how it operates both inside and on bodies emerges in Augustine's notion of shame, both recognized and named in his theology. Augustine places shame both *on* the body as *pudenda* and *in* the body as concupiscence linked to original sin. A cycle of shame occurs in his rhetoric, perpetuated by the *pudenda*, for which humanity, according to Augustine, should feel more shame. This is expressed in his prescription that Adam and Eve, along with their progeny, "cover up." Thus, Augustine grieves shame's presence. However, in his efforts to veil shame, he also conceals the primal, prelapsarian shame he initially recognizes. This shame, like the preverbal shame of affect theory, signals attachment and binds humans one to the other, in theological terms, to God. This is the shame that reveals something to the bearer and points to what is loved.

Necessary attachment to God occurs in Niebuhr's work as well, but when he writes *Nature and Destiny of Man*, the historical trajectory and natural human tendency to conceal shame have been well under way. In Niebuhr, shame makes an implicit appearance under the guise of other affects. Niebuhr laments what he sees as the deterioration of human society in the wake of World War II, faulting, as Augustine does before him, Christian laxity in the turn toward God. In his diagnosis, he conceals shame, expressing it through his formulations of pride, sensuality, guilt, sin, and anxiety. Reconstructed and made more explicit, Niebuhr's argument locates shame at the root of pride, as *hubris*, and sensuality, as escape or withdrawal from God. His perception of ontological anxiety framed through the lens of affect theory uncovers a more corrosive problem. Niebuhr understands that violence to the self and others derives from a need to counter a sense of worthlessness that is shame's derivative and pride's motivation.

However, Niebuhr's slippage in languaging shame perpetuates its toxicity. Providing the fodder for more shame, Niebuhr isolates the guilty sinner figured in Adam, suggesting remorse and repentance for what he calls guilt and anxiety but which actually appears as dysregulated shame. By separating this figure from others in shame, he dangerously perpetuates a sense of diminished self-worth and fails to get at the motivational structure of violence that is shame, even though throughout his work he presses the need to eliminate violence. He urges desire and commitment to God, but his rhetoric often contributes to the dynamic inherent in the shame of the unlovable self.

The shame interred in the unlovable self interferes with repair, and in shame, the Christian practitioner cannot participate fully in the event of Ash Wednesday. Focusing particularly on the moment of touch in the imposition of ashes on the forehead punctuates the affective encounter as having potential to begin to disinter shame by naming and acknowledging it. Shame in this moment can keep a participant from connecting to Christ through a misinterpretation of shame or a narrow view that it makes him or her undeserving. However, what is truly needed, as it was in Adam and Eve's case, is to reveal one's shame to God. Modeled through Christ as the connection to the most primal self, shame can be faced and shared with one another.

Shame revealed allows shame to fulfill its normal social role of mediating relationships, and of indicating attachment. Shame also emerges in the capacity of empathy as it inhibits empathic connection while simultaneously indicating the interest-excitement empathy demands. Edith Stein understands the interplay of affects and empathy, but she also adds a spiritual dimension to empathy as critical to the "psycho-physical" and spiritual self. Empathy for Stein is the means through which we understand each other, but it is also the means through which we flourish as selves, a significant aspect of Christian formation and Christian tradition. This advocating of the whole self, in relationship with others and God, acknowledges shame, while also moderating it.

Uncovering the nature of shame, at once deleterious, primal, and shared exposes what is at stake for the Christian self in shame. Theological discourse and practice that leave shame unacknowledged or concealed by other terms and experiences allow for shame's interment. Although many factors contribute to this phenomenon, this project focuses on how theology figures into a construction of the self in shame, interpreting shame as an experience that severs *and* that connects. The challenge for theology relates to how it names shame, in order to foster disinterment and repair the pathologies that sever attachment in the first place.

Dangers of Interment

This brings us to the pivot point in shame, the crux of shame as an indicator of attachment. Whether that attachment is to God or to others, shame exhumed informs the self about who and what is most revered; it is a revelation. Touch informs this revealing. As a primary, non-verbal way of relating, touch regulates affects including shame in early attachment relationships. Touch is a conduit for the connection necessary to repair shame, even as it can perpetuate shame; both indicate attachment. Attachment and attunement repair shame, and unless theology understands and communicates this, the problem of violence cannot be fully addressed. To shame, or to ignore shame, is to communicate that one is unworthy of love. This is detrimental because, as Léon Wurmser deftly expresses, "Unlovability is the core experience of shame. It comes together with desolate loneliness and sadness, and with that, almost inevitably, a wish to gain power over what seems to have been lost."[2]

Examining how shame is buried in the self promotes a theological awareness of the complexities of sin and guilt and how they so frequently disguise shame, which unrecognized, has deleterious effects. The consequences of shame concealed by guilt have gone relatively unexplored in the Christian tradition. Further, the traditional understanding of guilt and sin allows shame to be bypassed, masked, and unattended. This leads to shame's dangerous interment, but more fundamentally, it often results in a lack of recognition that shame functions as part of the human condition.

For instance, in Niebuhr, the ideal Christian self feels anxious about original sin and, therefore, subjects the self to God. The remedy for the internal wound of original sin is repentance and submission. However, if human experience is described and understood in this way, while the experience of shame continues to go unaddressed or masked by guilt, both theoretically and practically, access to repair remains blocked; thus, the self remains isolated and lonely. As affect theory shows, unnamed, interred shame interferes with remorse, empathy, attachment, and its own regulation. I believe that the theoretical and rhetorical use of guilt and sin, therefore, needs to be continually revisited in order to further understand how language about guilt eclipses shame and leads to the toxic interment of shame in the body.

The stigma of original sin as an inherent wrong in the self supports the idea that the human experience includes shame, but used malignantly, it supports an image of the Christian self as stigmatized, and again, ultimately isolated. The situation is complicated further by the focus on guilt, in both Niebuhr and in the liturgy of Ash Wednesday, where the shame of original sin lies beneath a veil of guilt, creating the image of the guilty sinner who is actually the self stigmatized by shame.

Obscuring human shame with the image of the lonely sinner in guilt is not productive to disinterring shame and extricating the root of violence, which is, in fact, interred shame. When the belief exists that some part of the self is injured, deficient, or bad, the self is cut off or dispelled, believing itself unworthy of love. In order to combat internal shame as an inner sense of worthlessness, people hide themselves or escape from view, anesthetize themselves, or use violence in vain attempts to restore dignity and eradicate shame. This unlovable self fights for what it has lost, either claiming love from the wrong sources or using aggression to take back the pride of self-worth. Both Augustine and Niebuhr understood that this inner sense of worthlessness provoked dangerous behavior and that both recommended that a turn toward God as a vulnerable human would ameliorate the situation, but the person in shame confronts a deeper, darker problem. Shame interred, while it points to attachment, inhibits attachment, impeding empathy and the connection even to God.

Acknowledging explicitly that shame as foundational to human existence and human bonding retrieves shame from pathology and alleviates, at least to some degree, the shame for feeling shame. Augustine approaches this notion of shame as he celebrates the imposition of the cross on the forehead in Psalm 141. Recognizing shame as a biological affect releases shame from its role as stigmatizing, permitting an additional acceptance of the body as an epistemological source. Shame, partially truncating interest-excitement, viscerally communicates to the self both attachments to others and to God. The body, thus, knows through the experience of shame that it longs to connect to something other than itself: another body, another story, a divine tie. Shame, which emerges on the face, for Augustine on the forehead, presents itself on Ash Wednesday where ashes are imposed on the forehead. The innate, shared shame the faithful wear on their foreheads is, thus, through the imposition of the cross both held and touched.

Furthermore, since touching practices are abundant in Christian praxis, understanding what is at stake in touch is critical. This constitutes having an awareness of the traumatized body that cannot tolerate touch, as well as understanding that touch, even the observation of it, fosters empathy. The painful state of shame can unfold and morph as a result of empathy "into a renewed sense of closeness to others."[3] Touch amplifies this sense of closeness. Shame, especially through touch, can create the sense of being undone or fragmented; both also peculiarly unite the self with others. The willingness to be vulnerable in shame creates an extraordinary level of relation and intimacy that can only be experienced when shame is faced.

This presses theology to work toward a disentangling of the bind between shame and sin so as to disinter shame in order that it might return to its innate social function of shame in relation. In the imposition of the cross on the forehead, shame occurs within what I call the logic of exposure, related to sight, which is emphasized through the haptic. The Christian narrative comes to fruition in the haptic, colliding with the forehead—Augustine's seat of shame. The cross itself brings to the individual being touched the reality of participation in the Christian community; this individual faces shame alongside Christ. Christ offers a glimpse of who we really are through grace, through touch, and through connection with others. In a very unique way then, the moment of touch confers, evokes, and blesses shame.

Ultimately, shame cannot be eradicated, but it can be approached, addressed, and therefore disinterred. In Augustine's words, shame can be ameliorated by grace. In Niebuhr's work, what takes on the nature of shame—anxiety and sin—cannot be entirely altered, but these can be faced, confronted, and then turned toward God. And the language of guilt and sin, specifically actual sin, need not be dismissed in a theology of shame. This is because empathic connections assuage shame; in addition, guilt fosters empathy. Thus, both guilt and shame operate in the self and contribute to a robust theological anthropology. Guilt as a response to a wrong act, repaired through remorse, disentangled from the perception of wrong in the self, encourages relationship, bonding, and empathetic connection. While shame confused with wrongdoing inters shame in the self and inhibits empathic connections, regulated shame serves to point to attachment and indicates interest-excitement, promoting social bonding and repairing shame.

The Most Vulnerable Self

Through the lens of affect theory and trauma studies, this book explores how shame functions in Christian formation to move toward a more distinct theological understanding of shame. Throughout the writing process, the project both expanded and narrowed, revealing aspects of shame that have far more implications for theology than initially imagined. Shame is interred in the body, initially as a result of its propensity to be repressed and denied by the self or traded for other affects or experiences, such as guilt. Past trauma exacerbates these dynamics. However, shame has a far more common and mundane role in human social life. Shame informs the self about its most intimate human relating, raising deeper questions about shame's role in attachment. Exploring shame becomes less about delineating it from guilt and more about discerning how it functions both to connect humanity to each other and to God and to rupture this connection. Unearthing shame from theological rhetoric and practice is thus less about diagnosis of pathology and more about understanding that being seen by the other in shame connects an individual to his or her most primal self and to what he or she loves most.

Stepping into a terrain of theological anthropological literature through Augustine and Niebuhr, who intend purposively to diagnose the human condition, to disentangle their rhetoric uncovers the role of shame in their works. Both do this diagnostic work in historical contexts rife with human suffering and violence. Etiologists and theologians at once each wrestles with the Eden scene in his or her attempt to discern and demarcate human pain while relying on discourse about sin and guilt. Analysis of their works leads to the excavation of shame in their writing, a shame that can emerge as toxic, but also a shame that originates in the body betraying attachment and the need for connection. For Augustine, this is a prelapsarian shame. For both Augustine and Niebuhr, a turn toward God in shame but seeking reattachment initiates repair.

The dual concept of shame, as toxic or innate, unfolds and has implications for theology in terms of its conceptions of sin as a stigma or imperfection, its inconspicuous role underlying the guilt-ethic, and in its perceived amelioration through violence or eradication. When shame contributes to violence, the problem is toxic, unregulated shame, not innate shame that binds Christians to each other.

Delving deeper into shame uncovered a dual conception of humility. Although affectively, humility, prescribed by both Augustine and Niebuhr, shares some characteristics with toxic shame, a "true humility" emerges and includes a sense of self-worth characteristic of innate shame that toxic shame undermines. This humility, modeled by Christ, embodies the beauty of the revelation of shame, which returns us to the most primal attachments. Although probing deeper into humility exceeded the frame of this project, disentangling humility from pride and shame begins to reveal a more reparative notion of its function in Christian theology. This notion of humility does not lead to the embodiment of a traditionally perceived low view of oneself shared with toxic shame but rather points to the recognition of oneself as innately connected to God, or the divine, in Christian life to Christ. This starting point for innate shame has implications for the psychology of religion and theology in research concerning humility, shame, and pride.

The work to be done is daunting; the confusion around shame as deleterious while still playing an important role in attachment necessarily needs to be elucidated for theology to contribute to the growing problem of violence. For instance, challenges must be made to the promotion of the lonely sinner in guilt; instead, a more fruitful focus would be on the Christian self as possessing shared, innate shame, which connects Christians to both others and to God. To face shame and start to destabilize the motivational structures of violence is more than a challenge. Toxic shame as an impediment to human bonding has far-reaching implications, even more than this text portrays. Excavating innate shame that can be tolerated and regulated, not interred, and which indicates attachment is a process that needs further exploration by scholars in psychology and religion and pastoral theology. Developing theological anthropologies that take account of the whole person demands sophisticated and thorough interdisciplinary analyses, drawing from the new and rapidly changing fields of affect theory and neurobiology.

A general theological recognition and acceptance of where and how shame appears in theology has far-reaching and practical implications for the role of the body and sexuality in Christian life, for the acceptance of marginalized bodies, for the resistance to violence, for the traumatized body, and for social justice. Avowing the presence of shame, along with its potential to do harm and good, enables a more comprehensive theological anthropology. Named and embraced, shame increases empathetic connections and fosters the ability for a more integrated participation in Christian life: when the shamed part of self is not damned, it is free to engage in relationships, exposing vulnerability, flesh, and humanness.

Notes

1. Tomkins, *Affect, Imagery, Consciousness*, 387.
2. Wurmser, *Torment Me, but Don't Abandon Me*, 198.
3. Block Lewis, "Introduction," 26.

Bibliography

Abraham, Nicholas and Maria Torok. *The Shell and the Kernel.* Translated by Nicholas T. Rand. Chicago: University of Chicago Press, 1994.

Agamben, Giorgio. *Potentialities: Collected Essays in Philosophy.* Edited and translated by Daniel Heller-Roazen. Stanford: Stanford University Press, 1999.

Agamben, Giorgio and Monica Ferrando. *The Unspeakable Girl: The Myth and Mystery of Kore.* Translated by Leland De La Durantaye and Annie Julia Wyman. London: Seagull Books, 2014.

Ahmed, Sara. *The Cultural Politics of Emotion.* New York: Routledge, 2004.

Ainsworth, Mary D. Salter, Mary C. Blehar, Everett Waters, and Sally N. Wall. *Patterns of Attachment: A Psychological Study of the Strange Situation.* New York: Halsted Press, 1978.

Allen, David F. *Shame: The Human Nemesis.* Bahamas: Eleuthera Publications, 2010.

Althaus-Reed, Marcella. *Indecent Theology: Theological Perversions in Sex, Gender and Politics.* New York: Routledge, 2000.

"Anointing with Chrism." The Catholic Liturgical Library, 1970 Missal. Accessed September 7, 2014. http://www.catholicliturgy.com/index.cfm/fuseaction/Textcontents/index/4/subindex/67/textindex/7.

Aristotle. *The Art of Rhetoric.* Translated by Hugh Lawson-Tancred. London: Penguin Books Limited, 1991.

—. *The Nicomachean Ethics.* Translated by R.W. Brown. London: Penguin Classics, 2003.

—. *On the Soul.* Translated by J.A. Smith. Stilwell, KS: Digireads.com Publishing, 2006.

Armour, Ellen T. and Susan M. St. Ville, eds. *Bodily Citations: Religion and Judith Butler.* New York: Columbia University Press, 2006.

S.N. Arel, *Affect Theory, Shame, and Christian Formation*,
DOI 10.1007/978-3-319-42592-4

Augustine, Saint, Bishop of Hippo. *Concerning the City of God against the Pagans.* Translated by Henry Bettenson. London: Penguin Books, 2003.

—. *Confessions.* Translated by Henry Chadwick. Oxford: Oxford University Press, 1991.

—. *Exposition on the Book of Psalms: Psalms LXXII-CL,* edited by Paul A. Böer. 1886. Reprint, Dublin: Veritatis Splendor Publications, 2012.

—. "On Genesis: A Refutation of the Manichees." In *On Genesis,* edited by John E. Rotelle, O.S.A., translated by Edmund Hill, O.P., 25–104. Hyde Park, NY: New York City Press, 2002.

—. "The Literal Meaning of Genesis." In *On Genesis,* edited by John E. Rotelle, O.S.A., translated by Edmund Hill, O.P., 155–506. Hyde Park, NY: New York City Press, 2002.

—. "Sermon 228." In *Sermons (184-229z) on the Liturgical Seasons,* edited by John E. Rotelle, O.S.A., translated by Edmund Hill, O.P., 257–59. Vol. III/7 of The Works of Saint Augustine: A Translation for the 21st Century. New Rochelle: NY: New City Press, 1993.

—. "Sermon 376." In *Sermons (341–400) on Various Themes,* edited by John E. Rotelle, O.S.A., translated by Edmund Hill, O.P., 346–8. Vol. III/10 of The Works of Saint Augustine: A Translation for the 21st Century. Hyde Park: NY: New City Press, 1993.

—. "The Unfinished Literal Commentary on Genesis." In *On Genesis,* edited by John E. Rotelle, O.S.A., translated by Edmund Hill, O.P., 105–54. Hyde Park, NY: New York City Press, 2002.

Ayers, Mary. *Mother-Infant Attachment and Psychoanalysis: The Eyes of Shame.* New York: Brunner-Routledge, 2003.

Bacevich, Andrew. "Illusions of Managing History: The Enduring Relevance of Reinhold Niebuhr." *Historically Speaking* vol. 9, no. 3 (2008): 23–5.

—. *The Limits of Power: The End of American Exceptionalism.* New York: Holt Paperbacks, 2009.

Baltimore Catechism Three. Charlotte, NC: Saint Benedict Press, 2010.

"The Baptismal Covenant." Service for Baptism (2013) Christian Reformed Church. Accessed September 7, 2014. http://www.crcna.org/resources/church-resources/liturgical-forms-resources/baptism-children/service-baptism-2013.

Banissy, Michael J. and Jamie Ward. "Mirror-touch Synesthesia is Linked with Empathy." *Nature Neuroscience* vol. 10 (2007): 815–6.

Benedict, Ruth. *The Chrysanthemum and the Sword.* New York: Meridian Books, 1946.

—. *Patterns of Culture.* New York: Houghton Mifflin, 1934.

Berlant, Lauren, ed. *Compassion: The Culture and Politics of an Emotion.* New York: Routledge, 2004.

—. *Cruel Optimism.* Durham: Duke University Press, 2011.

—. "Eve Sedgwick, Once More." *Critical Inquiry* vol. 35, no. 4 (2009): 1089–91.
—. *The Queen of America Goes to Washington City*. Durham: Duke University Press, 1997.
—. *Sex, or the Unbearable*. Durham: Duke University Press, 2013.
Beste, Jennifer. *God and the Victim: Theological Reflections on Evil, Victimization, and Forgiveness*. Grand Rapids: Eerdman's, 1999.
Betcher, Sharon. *Spirit and the Obligation of Social Flesh*. New York: Fordham University Press, 2013.
Bewes, Timothy. *The Event of Postcolonial Shame*. Princeton: Princeton University Press, 2011.
Blake, John. "How Obama's First Favorite Theologian Shaped His First Year in Office." CNN.com. Last modified February 5, 2010. Accessed August 15, 2014. http://www.cnn.com/2010/POLITICS/02/05/Obama.theologian/.
Blakemore S.J., Bristow D., Bird G., Frith C., and Ward J. "Somatosensory Activations during the Observation of Touch and a Case of Vision – Touch Synaesthesia." *Brain* vol. 128 (2005): 1571–83.
Boesel, Christopher and Catherine Keller. *Apophatic Bodies: Negative Theology, Incarnation, and Relationality*. New York: Fordham University Press, 2010.
Bonaventure, Saint. *The Journey of the Mind to God*. Translated by Philotheus Bohner. 1956. Reprint, Indianapolis: Hackett Publishing, 1990.
Bon-Storms, Riet. "A Challenge to Change Developments in Feminist Theology and Feminist Christology." *HTS* vol. 61, no. 1&2 (2005): 45–63.
Bourdieu, Pierre. *The Logic of Practice*. Translated by Richard Nice. Stanford: Stanford University Press, 1992.
—. *Masculine Domination*. Translated by Richard Nice. Stanford: Stanford University Press, 1998.
—. *Pascalian Meditations*. Translated by Richard Nice. Stanford: Polity Press, 2000.
Brandstetter, Gabriele, Gerko Egert, and Sabine Zubarik, eds. *Touching and Being Touched: Kinesthesia and Empathy in Dance and Movement*. Berlin: De Gruyter, 2013.
Brennan, Teresa. *Transmission of Affect*. New York: Cornell. University Press, 2004.
Breugelmans, Seger and Ype H. Poortinga. "Emotion without a word: Shame and guilt with Rarámuri Indians and Rural Javanese." *Journal of Personality and Social Psychology* vol. 91, no. 6 (2006): 1111–22.
Brison, Susan. *Aftermath: Violence and the Remaking of the Self*. Princeton: Princeton University Press, 2002.
Brock, Rita Nakashima and Rebecca Ann Parker. *Proverbs of Ashes: Violence, Redemptive Suffering, and the Search for What Saves Us*. Boston: Beacon Press, 2001.

Brooks, David. "Obama, Gospel, and Verse." *New York Times,* April 26, 2007. Accessed August 15, 2013. http://www.nytimes.com/2007/04/26/opinion/26brooks.html?_r=2&.

Brown, Peter. *Augustine of Hippo.* Berkeley: University of California Press, 1967.

—. *The Body and Society: Men, Women, and Sexual Renunciation in Early Christianity.* New York: Columbia University Press, 1988.

Brown, Peter and Michael Fiedrowicz. Introduction to *On Genesis,* by Saint Augustine, edited by John E. Rotelle, O.S.A., translated by Edmund Hill, O.P., 13–22. Hyde Park: New York City Press, 2002.

Bufalari, Ilaria, Taryn Aprile, Alessio Avenanti, Francesco Di Russo, and Salvatore Maria Aglioti. "Empathy for Pain and Touch in the Human Somatosensory Cortex." *Cerebral Cortex* (2007): 2553–61.

Burgoon, Judee K. "Relational Message Interpretations of Touch, Conversational Distance, and Posture." *Journal of Nonverbal Behavior* vol. 15, no. 4 (1991): 232–59.

Burnell, Peter. "Concupiscence and Moral Freedom in Augustine and Before Augustine." *Augustinian Studies* vol. 26, no. 1 (1995): 49–63.

Burrus, Virginia. "Bodies, Desires, Confessions: Shame in Plotinus, Antony, and Augustine." In *Shame between Punishment and Penance: The Social Usages of Shame in the Middle Ages and Early Modern Times*, edited by Bénédicte Sère and Jörg Wettlaufer, 23–48. Firenze: Sismel, 2013.

—. *Saving Shame: Martyrs, Saints, and Other Abject Subjects.* Philadelphia: University of Pennsylvania Press, 2008.

Burrus, Virginia and Catherine Keller, eds. *Towards a Theology of Eros.* Fordham University Press, 2006.

Burrus, Virginia, Mark D. Jordan, and Karmen MacKendrick, eds. *Seducing Augustine: Bodies, Desires, Confessions.* New York: Fordham University Press, 2010.

Butler, Judith. "Introduction." In *Bodies That Matter: On the Discursive Limits of 'Sex,'* 1–17. New York: Routledge, 1993.

Bynum, Caroline Walker. *The Resurrection of the Body: In Western Christianity,* 200–1336. New York: Columbia University Press, 1995.

Cahill, Lisa. "Catholic Sexual Ethics and the Dignity of the Person: A Double Message." *Theological Studies* vol. 50 (1989): 120–50.

Calfhill, James. *An Answer to John Martiall's Treatise of the Cross.* Edited by Richard Gibbings. Cambridge: Parker Society, 1846.

Caruth, Cathy, ed. *Trauma: Explorations in Memory.* Baltimore: Johns Hopkins University Press, 1995.

—. *Unclaimed Experience: Trauma, Narrative, and History.* Baltimore: Johns Hopkins University Press, 1996.

CatholiCity. "The Baltimore Catechism." The Baltimore Catechism Revised Edition (1941). Accessed August 15, 2014. http://www.catholicity.com/baltimore-catechism/.

Cavanaugh, William T. *Torture and Eucharist: Theology, Politics, and the Body of Christ.* Malden: Blackwell, 1998.
Cho, Grace. *Haunting the Korean Diaspora: Shame, Secrecy, and the Forgotten War.* Minneapolis: University of Minnesota Press, 2008.
Chrétien, Jean-Louis. *The Call and Response.* Translated by Anne A. Davenport. New York: Fordham University Press, 2004.
Christ, Carol P. and Judith Plaskow, eds. *WomanSpirit Rising – A Feminist Reader in Religion.* 1979. Reprint, New York: Harper Collins, 1992.
Clark, Elizabeth. "1990 Presidential Address: Shame, Sex, and Rhetoric: En-Gendering Early Christian Ethics." *Journal of the American Academy of Religion* vol. 59, no. 2 (1991): 221–45.
—, ed. *St. Augustine on Marriage and Sexuality.* Washington, D.C.: The Catholic University of America Press, 1997.
Clough, Patricia Ticineto and Jean Halley, eds. *The Affective Turn: Theorizing the Social.* Durham: Duke University Press, 2007.
Comstock, Gary David and Susan E. Henking, eds. *Que(e)rying Religion: A Critical Anthology.* New York: Continuum, 1997.
Cone, James. *The Cross and the Lynching Tree.* Maryknoll: Orbis Books, 2013.
Cooper, Terry D. *Reinhold Niebuhr and Psychology: The Ambiguities of the Self.* Macon: Mercer University Press, 2009.
Copeland, M. Shawn. *Enfleshing Freedom: Body, Race, and Freedom.* Minneapolis: Fortress Press, 2010.
Cressy, David. *Birth, Marriage, and Death: Ritual, Religion, and the Life-Cycle in Tudor and Stuart England.* Oxford: Oxford University Press, 1999.
Cvetkovich, Ann. *An Archive of Feelings: Trauma, Sexuality, and Lesbian Public Cultures.* Durham: Duke University Press, 2003.
Damasio, Antonio. *Descartes Error: Emotion, Reason and the Human Brain.* London: Penguin Books, 1994.
—. *The Feeling of What Happens: Body and Emotion in the Making of Consciousness.* Orlando: Harcourt, 1999.
Darwin, Charles. *The Expression of Emotions in Man and Animals.* Edited by Joe Cain and Sharon Messenger. 1872. Reprint, London: Penguin Books, 2009.
Davidson, Jonathan R. T. and Edna B. Foa, eds. *Posttraumatic Stress Disorder: DSM-IV and Beyond.* Washington, D.C.: American Psychiatric Press, 1993.
Dearing, Rhonda L. and June Price Tangney, eds. *Shame in the Therapy Hour.* Washington, D.C.: American Psychological Association, 2011.
Deleuze, Gilles. *The Fold: Leibniz and the Baroque.* Translated by Tom Conley. Minneapolis: University of Minnesota Press, 1993.
Deleuze, Gilles and Féliz Guattari. *A Thousand Plateaus: Capitalism and Schizophrenia.* Translated by Brian Massumi. Minneapolis: University of Minnesota Press, 1987.
Delumeau, Jean. *Sin and Fear: The Emergence of the Western Guilt Culture, 13th–18th Centuries.* New York: Palgrave Macmillan, 1990.

Derrida, Jacques. *Writing and Difference*. Translated by Alan Bass. Chicago: The University of Chicago Press, 1978.

Dickerson, Sally S., Tara L. Gruenewald, and Margaret E. Kemeny. "When the Social Self is Threatened: Shame, Physiology, and Health." *Journal of Personality* vol. 72, no. 6 (December 2004): 1191–216.

"Directory on Popular Piety and the Liturgy: Principles and Guidelines." The Holy See. Accessed September 7, 2013. http://www.vatican.va/roman_curia/congregations/ccdds/documents/ rc_con_ccdds_doc_20020513_vers direttorio_en.html#Chapter%20Two.

Doehring, Carrie. *The Practice of Pastoral Care: A Postmodern Approach*. Louisville: Westminster John Knox Press, 2006.

Dorrien, Gary J. Introduction to *The Children of Light and the Children of Darkness: A Vindication of Democracy and a Critique of its Traditional Defense*, by Reinhold Niebuhr, ix–xxvi. Chicago: University of Chicago Press, 2011.

—. *The Making of American Liberal Theology: Idealism, realism, and Modernity 1900–1950*. Louisville: Westminster John Knox Press, 2003.

—. *The Obama Question: A Progressive Perspective*. Lanham, MA: Rowman & Littlefield, 2012.

Douglas, Kelly Brown. *Sexuality and the Black Church: A Womanist Perspective*. New York: Orbis Books, 1999.

Dues, Greg. *Catholic Customs and Tradition*. Ellicot City, MD: Twenty-Third Publications, 1992.

Dunfee, Susan Nelson. *Beyond Servanthood: Christianity and the Liberation of Women*. Lanham, MD: University of American Press, 1989.

—. "The Sin of Hiding." *Soundings* vol. 65, no. 3 (Fall 1982): 316–27.

Ekman, Paul, Wallace Friesen, Maureen O'Sullivan, Anthony Chan, Irene Diacoyanni-Tarlatzis, Karl Heider, Rainer Krause, William Ayhan LeCompte, Tom Pitcairn, Pio E Ricci-Bitti, Klaus Scherer, Masatoshi Tomita, and Athanase Tzavaras. "Universals and Cultural Differences in the Judgments of Facial Expressions of Emotion." *Journal of Personality and Social Psychology* vol. 53, no. 4 (1987): 712–17.

Eribon, Didier. *Insult and the Making of the Gay Self*. Translated by Michael Lucey. Durham: Duke University Press, 2004.

Erickson, Erik. *Childhood and Society*. 1950. Reprint, New York: W. W. Norton and Company, 1993.

—. *Identity and the Life Cycle*. 1959. Reprint, New York: W. W. Norton and Company, 1980.

Eubanks, Dan. "Unresolved Guilt in the Church." *Gospel Advocate*, April 2011. Accessed April 2014, http://www.gospeladvocate.com/Magazines/GA/0411GAguilt.pdf.

Fairbairn, William Ronald Dodds. *Psychoanalytic Studies of the Personality*. 1952. Reprint, London: Routledge, 1986.

Fairweather, Eugene R. *The Message and Meaning of Lent*. New York: Harper & Brothers, 1962.

Fanon, Franz. *Wretched of the Earth*. Translated by Richard Philcox. English Edition. New York: Grove Press, 2004.

Father Edward McNamara. "Laypeople Distributing Ashes." Last modified February 5, 2008. Accessed May 2014. http://www.zenit.org/en/articles/laypeople-distributing-ashes.

Fellous, Jean-Marc. "The Neuromodulatory Basis of Emotion." *The Neuroscientist* vol. 5, no. 5 (1999): 283–94.

Felman, Shoshana and Dori Laub, M.D. *Testimony: Crisis of Witnessing in Literature, Psychoanalysis, and History*. New York: Routledge, 1992.

Fischer, Jeffrey D., Marvin Rytting, and Richard Heslin. "Hands Touching Hands: The Effect of Interpersonal Touch." *Sociometry* vol. 39, no. 4 (1976): 416–21.

Fisher, Janina. "Sensorimotor Approaches to Trauma Treatment." *Advances in Psychiatric Treatment* vol. 17, no. 3 (2011): 171–7.

Flanagan, Kieran. *The Enchantment of Sociology: A Study of Theology and Culture*. Basingstoke: Macmillan Press, 1996.

Fonagy, Peter. *Affect Theory and Psychoanalysis*. London: Karnac, 2004.

Foucault, Michel. *Discipline & Punish*. Translated by Alan Sheridan. 1975. Reprint, New York: Second Vintage Books, 1995.

—. *The History of Sexuality: An Introduction*. Vol. 1. Translated by Robert Hurley. New York: Vintage Books, 1990.

Freud, Sigmund. *Beyond the Pleasure Principle*. Translated by James Strachey. 1920. Reprint, New York: W.W. Norton and Company, 1990.

—. *Civilization and its Discontents*. Translated by James Strachey. 1929. Reprint, New York: W.W. Norton, 1962.

—. *Five Lectures on Psychoanalysis*. Translated by James Strachey. 1910. Reprint, New York: W.W. Norton, 1961.

—. *The Ego and The Id*. Edited by James Strachey. Translated by Joan Riviere. New York: W.W. Norton & Company, 1960.

—. *New Introductory Lectures on Psychoanalysis*. Translated by James Strachey. 1933. Reprint, New York: Liveright, 1989.

—. *Moses and Monotheism*. Translated by Katherine Jones. 1937. Reprint, New York: Vintage, 1955.

Freud, Sigmund and Joseph Breuer. *Studies in Hysteria*. Translated by James Strachey. 1955. Reprint, New York: Basic Books, 2000.

Gadamer, Hans-Georg. *Truth and Method*. Translated by Joel Weinsheimer and Donald G. Marshall. 2nd ed. New York: Continuum, 2003.

Gallese, Vittorio and Corrado Sinigglia. "What is so Special about Embodied Simulation." *Trends in Cognitive Sciences* vol. 115, no. 11 (2011): 512–9.

Gennep, Arnold van. *The Rites of Passage*. 1960. Reprint, Oxford: Routledge, 2004.

George, C., N. Kaplan and Mary Main. *The Adult Attachment Interview*. Unpublished, 1985. http://www.psychology.sunysb.edu/attachment/measures/content/aai_interview.pdf.

Gilkey, Langdon. *On Niebuhr: A Theological Study*. Chicago: University of Chicago Press, 2001.

—. *Violence: A National Epidemic*. New York: Putnam, 1996.

Gilligan, James. "Shame, Guilt, and Violence." *Social Research* vol. 70, no. 4 (2003): 1150–80.

Goffman, Erving. *Asylums: Essays on the Social Situation of Mental Patients and Other Inmates*. New York: First Anchor Books Edition, 1961.

—. *Interaction Ritual*. 2nd ed. Brunswick: Transaction Publishers, 2005.

—. *Stigma: Notes on the Management of Spoiled Identity*. New York: Simon and Schuster, 1963.

Graham, Elaine L. "A Remembrance of Things (Best) Forgotten: the 'Allegorical Past' and the Feminist Imagination." *Feminist Theology* vol. 20, no. 1 (2012): 58–70.

—. "Practical Theology as Transforming Practice." In *The Blackwell Reader in Pastoral and Practical Theology*. Edited by James Woodward and Stephen Pattison, 104–17. Malden: Blackwell, 2000.

—. *Transforming Practice: Pastoral Theology in an Age of Uncertainty*. 1996. Reprint, Eugene: Wipf & Stock Publishers, 2002.

Graham, Elaine L. and Anna Rowlands, eds. *Pathways to the Public Square: Practical Theology in an Age of Pluralism*. Munster: Lit Verlag, 2005.

Graham, Elaine, Heather Walton, and Frances Ward, eds. *Theological Reflections: Methods*. London: SCM, 2005.

Grand, Sue. *The Reproduction of Evil A Clinical and Cultural Perspective*. New York: Taylor and Francis, 2002.

Gregg, Melissa and Gregory J. Seigworth, eds. *The Affect Theory Reader*. Durham: Duke University Press, 2010.

Grimes, Ronald L. *Deeply into the Bone: Re-Inventing Rites of Passage*. Berkeley University of California Press, 2000.

Hamilton, Kenneth Morris. *The Doctrine of Humanity in the Theology of Reinhold Niebuhr*. Ontario: Wilfrid Laurier University Press, 2013.

Harper, Kyle. *From Shame to Sin: The Christian Transformation of Sexual Morality in Late Antiquity*. Cambridge: Harvard University Press, 2013.

Herman, Judith Lewis. "Posttraumatic Stress Disorder as a Shame Disorder." In *Shame in the Therapy Hour*. Edited by Ronda L. Dearing and June Price Tangney, 261–75. Washington, D.C.: American Psychological Association, 2011.

—. "PTSD as a Shame Disorder." Webinar. International Society for Traumatic Stress Studies. October, 13, 2014.

—. "Shattered Shame States and their Repair." Presentation, The John Bowl by Memorial Lecture from Harvard Medical School, Cambridge, Saturday March 10, 2007.

—. *Trauma and Recovery*. New York: Basic Books, 1992.

Holder, Ward and Peter B. Josephson. *The Irony of Barak Obama: Barak Obama, Reinhold Niebuhr and the Problem of Christian Statecraft*. Burlington: Ashgate, 2012.

Hollywood, Amy. "Performativity, Citationality, Ritual." In *Bodily Citations: Religion and Judith Butler*. Edited by Ellen T. Armour and Susan M. St. Ville, 225–75. New York: Columbia University Press, 2006.

Hooker, J.T. "Homeric Society: A Shame Culture?" *Greece & Rome* vol. 34, no. 2 (1987): 121–25.

Huffer, Lynne. *Mad for Foucault: Rethinking Foundations of Queer Theology*. New York: Columbia University Press, 2009.

Inki Ha, Francis. "Shame in Asian and Western Cultures." *The American Behavioral Scientist* vol. 38, no. 8 (1995): 1114–31.

Irvine, Christopher. *The Art of God: The Making of Christians and the Meaning of Worship*. Great Britain: Liturgy Training Publications, 2006.

Isherwood, Lisa and Elizabeth Stuart, eds. *Introducing Body Theology: Introductions in Feminist Theology*. New York: T&T Clark, 1998.

Jensen, Robin M. *Living Water: Images, Symbols, and Setting in Early Christian Baptism*. London: Brill, 2011.

Johnson, Erica L. and Patricia Moran. *The Female Face of Shame*. Bloomington: Indiana University Press, 2013.

Johnston, Adrian and Catherine Malabou. *Self and Emotional Life: Philosophy, Psychoanalysis, and Neuroscience*. New York: Columbia University Press, 2013.

Jones, Serene. *Trauma and Grace: Theology in a Ruptured World*. Louisville: Westminster John Knox Press, 2009.

Jordan, Mark D. *Recruiting Young Love: How Christian's Talk about Homosexuality*. Chicago: Chicago University Press, 2011.

—. *Telling Truths in Church: Scandal, Flesh, and Christian Speech*. Boston: Beacon Press, 2005.

Jantzen, Grace M. *Becoming Divine: Towards a Feminist Philosophy of Religion*. Bloomington: Indiana University Press, 1999.

Karen, Robert. *Becoming Attached: First Relationships and How They Shape Our Capacity to Love*. Oxford: Oxford University Press, 1998.

Kauffman, Jeffrey. *The Shame of Death, Grief, and Trauma*. London: Psychology Press, 2010.

Kaufman, Gershen and Lev Raphael. *Coming Out of Shame: Transforming Gay and Lesbian Lives*. New York: Doubleday, 1996.

—. *The Psychology of Shame*. 2nd ed. New York: Springer, 1996.

Keller, Catherine. *God and Power*. Minneapolis: Augsburg Fortress Press, 2005.

Keysers, C., B. Wicker, V. Gazzola, J.L. Anton, L. Fogassi, and V. Gallese. "A Touching Sight: SII/PV Activation During the Observation and Experience of Touch." *Neuron* vol. 42, no. 2 (2004): 335–46.

Kohut, Heinz. "Introspection, Empathy, and Psychoanalysis: An Examination of the Relationship between Mode Observation and Theory." *Journal of the American Psychoanalytic Association* vol. 7, no. 3 (1959): 459–83.

Konstan, David. "Shame in Ancient Greece." *Social Research* vol. 70, no. 4 (2003): 1031–60.

Kovacs, David. "Shame, Pleasure, and Honor in Phaedra's Great Speech (Euripides, Hippolytus 375–87)." *The American Journal of Philology* vol. 101, no. 3 (1980): 287–303.

Kristeva, Julia. *New Maladies of the Soul.* Translated by Ross Guberman. New York: Columbia University Press, 1995.

—. *Powers of Horror: An Essay of Abjection.* Translated by Leon S. Roudiez. New York: Columbia University Press, 1982.

Lacan, Jacques. *Anxiety: Seminar of Jacques Lacan, Book X.* Edited by Jacques-Alain Miller. Malden: Polity Press, 2014.

Lange, Dirk G. *Trauma Recalled: Liturgy, Disruption, and Theology.* Minneapolis: Fortress Press, 2010.

Leary, Joy DeGruy. *Post-Traumatic Slave Syndrome: America's Legacy of Enduring Injury and Healing.* Baltimore: Uptown Press, 2005.

LeDoux, Joseph E. "Emotional Circuits in the Brain." *Annual Review of Neuroscience* vol. 23 (March 2000): 155–84.

Lee, Boyung. "Caring-Self and Women's Self Esteem: A Feminist Reflection on Pastoral Care and Religious Education of Korean-American Women." *Pastoral Psychology* vol. 54 (2006): 337–53.

Lee, Jacob Hee Cheol. "Shame and Pastoral Care: Implications from an Asian Theological Perspective." *Pastoral Psychology* vol. 57 (2009): 253–62.

Lee, Josephine W. and Laura K. Guerrero. "Types of Touch in Cross-Sex Relationships Between Coworkers: Perceptions of Relational and Emotional Messages, Inappropriateness, and Sexual Harassment." *Journal of Applied Communication Research* vol. 29, no. 3 (2001): 197–220.

Lee, Sang Hyun. *From a Liminal Place: An Asian-American Theology.* Minneapolis: Fortress Press, 2010.

Lefkowitz, Mary R. and Maureen B. Fant. *Women's Life in Greece and Rome: A Source Book in Translation.* 3rd ed. Baltimore: The Johns Hopkins University Press, 2005.

Levine, Peter A. *Waking the Tiger – Healing Trauma.* Berkeley: North Atlantic Books, 1997.

Lewis, Helen Block. "Introduction: Shame – The 'Sleeper' in Psychopathology," In *The Role of Shame in Symptom Formation.* Edited by Helen Block Lewis, 1–28. London: Psychology Press, 1987.

—. *The Role of Shame in Symptom Formation.* London: Psychology Press, 1987.

—. *Shame and Guilt in Neurosis.* New York: International Universities Press, Inc., 1971.

—. "Shame and the Narcissistic Personality." In *The Many Faces of Shame*. Edited by Donald L. Nathanson, 93–132. New York: Guilford, 1987.

Lewis, Michael. *Shame: The Exposed Self.* New York: The Free Press, 1992.

Lewis, Thomas, Fari Amini, and Richard Lannon. *A General Theory of Love*. New York: Random House, 2000.

The Liturgy Archive. "Mass: Ash Wednesday." Accessed August 15, 2014. http://www.liturgies.net/Lent/ashwednesdayrc.htm.

Loughlin, Gerard, ed. *Queer Theology: Rethinking the Western Body.* Malden: Blackwell Publishing, 2007.

Lynd, Helen Merrell. *On Shame and the Search for Identity.* New York: Harcourt, Brace & World, 1958.

McClintock, Jessica. *Imperial Leather: Race, Gender, and Sexuality in the Colonial Conquest*. New York: Routledge, 1995.

McNish, Jill L. *Transforming Shame: A Pastoral Response*. New York: Routledge, 2004.

MacKendrick, Karmen. *Fragmentation and Memory: Meditations on Christian Doctrine*. New York: Fordham University Press, 2008.

—. *The Word Made Skin*. New York: Fordham University Press, 2004.

Magai, Carol and Susan H. McFadden. *The Role of Emotions in Social Personality Development: History, Theory, Research*. New York: Plenum, 1995.

Main, Mary and Judith Solomon. "Discovery of a New, Insecure Disorganized/Disoriented Attachment Pattern." In *Affective Development in Infancy.* Edited by T. B. Brazelton and M. Yogman, 95–124. Norwood, New Jersey: Ablex, 1986.

Main, Mary. "Introduction to the Special Section on Attachment and Psychopathology: 2. Overview of the Field of Attachment." *Journal of Consulting and Clinical Psychology* vol. 64, no. 2 (1996): 237–43.

Marston, Peter J., Michael L. Hecht, and Tia Robers. "'True Love Ways': The Subjective Experience and Communication of Romantic Love." *Journal of Social and Personal Relationships* vol. 4, no. 4 (1987): 387–407.

Martos, Joseph. *Doors to the Sacred: A Historical Introduction to Sacraments in the Catholic Church.* Liguori, MO: Liguori Publications, 2001.

Massumi, Brian. "Autonomy of Affect." *Cultural Critique,* no. 31 (1995): 83–109.

—. *Parables of the Virtual: Movement, Affect, Sensation.* Durham: Duke University Press, 2002.

May, Melanie. *A Body Knows: A Theopoetics of Death and Resurrection.* New York: Continuum, 1995.

Menninger, Karl A. *Whatever Became of Sin.* New York: Bantam Books, 1988.

Merleau-Ponty, Maurice. *Phenomenology of Perception.* New York: Routledge, 2002.

Michl, Petra, Thomas Meindl, Franziska Meister, Christine Born, Rolf Engel, Maximilian Reiser, and Kristina Hennig-Fast. "Endogenous Cortisol Level Interacts with Noradrenergic Activation in the Human Amygdala." *Neurobiology of Learning and Memory* (November 2012): 1–8.

Mikulincer, Mario and Phillip R. Shaver. *Attachment in Adulthood: Structure, Dynamics, and Change*. New York: Guilford Press, 2007.

Mikulincer, Mario, Phillip R. Shaver, Omri Gilath, and Rachel A. Nitzberg. "Attachment, Caregiving, and Altruism: Boosting Attachment Security Increases Compassion and Helping." *Journal of Personality and Social Psychology* vol. 89, no. 1 (2005): 817–39.

Miles, Margaret R. *Reading Historical Theology: Before, During and After Augustine*. Eugene, Oregon: Cascade Books, 2008.

—. "Sex and the City (of God): Is Sex Forfeited or Fulfilled in Augustine's Resurrection of the body?" *Journal of the American Academy of Religion* vol. 73, no. 2 (2005): 307–27.

Mills, Rosemary S.L. "Taking Stock of the Developmental Literature on Shame," *Developmental Review* vol. 25, no. 1 (2005): 26–63.

Mollica, Richard. *Healing Invisible Wounds: Paths to Hope and Recovery in a Violent World*. New York: Harcourt Books, 2006.

Montagu, Ashley. *Touching: The Human Significance of the Skin*. New York: Harper & Row, 1986.

Moore, Patrick. *Beyond Shame: Reclaiming the Abandoned History of Radical Gay Sexuality*. Boston: Beacon Press, 2004.

Mount-Shoop, Marcia W. *Embodied Prayer of Confession*. Academia.edu. Accessed March 8, 2013. http://www.academia.edu/2989633/Embodied_Prayer_of_Confession.

—. *Let the Bones Dance: Embodiment and the Body of Christ*. Louisville: Westminster John Knox Press, 2010.

Nancy, Jean-Luc. *Corpus*. New York: Fordham University Press, 2008.

—. "Rühren, Berühren, Aufruhr: Stirring, Stirring up, Uprising." Translated by Christine Irizarry. In *Touching and Being Touched: Kinesthesia and Empathy in Dance and Movement*. Edited by Gabriele Brandstetter, Gerko Egert, Sabine Zubarik, 13–22. Berlin: De Gruyter, 2013.

Nash, Roy. "Bourdieu on Education and Social and Cultural Reproduction." *British Journal of Sociology of Education* vol. 11, no. 4 (1990), 431–47.

Nathanson, Donald L., ed. *The Many Faces of Shame*. New York: Guilford Press, 1987.

—. Prologue to *Affect, Imagery, Consciousness*, Vols. 3 and 4, by Silvan Tomkins, xi–xxvi. New York: Springer Publishing Company, 2008.

—. *Shame and Pride: Affect, Sex, and the Birth of the Self*. New York: W. W. Norton & Company, 1992.

Nelson, Susan. "For Shame, For Shame, The Shame of it All: Postures of Refusal and the Broken Heart." In *The Other Side of Sin: Woundedness from the*

Perspective of the Sinned-Against. Edited by Andrew Sung Park and Susan Nelson, 71–86. Albany, NY: State University of New York Press, 2012.

Neusner, Jacob. *The Social World of Formative Christianity and Judaism: Essays in Tribute to Howard Clarke Kee.* Philadelphia: Fortress Press, 1988.

Neyrey, Jerome H. *The Social World of Luke-Acts: Models of Interpretation.* Peabody: Hendrickson Publishers, Inc., 1991.

Niebuhr, Reinhold. *Christian Realism and Political Problems.* New York: Charles Scribner's Sons, 1953.

—. *The Nature and Destiny of Man: Vol. 1, Human Nature.* 1943. Reprint, Louisville: Westminster John Knox Press, 1996.

Nietzsche, Fredrich. *On the Genealogy of Morality.* Translated by Maudemarie Clark and Alan Swensen. Indianapolis: Hackett Publishing, 1998.

Nisula, Timo. *Augustine and the Function of Concupiscence.* Boston: Brill, 2012.

Noland, Carrie. *Agency and Embodiment: Performing Gestures/Producing Culture.* Cambridge: Harvard University Press, 2010.

Nussbaum, Martha. *Hiding from Humanity: Disgust, Shame, and the Law.* Princeton, NJ: Princeton University Press, 2004.

"N.Y. CPL 140.50." FindLaw. Accessed January 16, 2014. http://codes.lp.findlaw.com/nycode/CPL/TWO/H/140/140.50.

Odegard, Holtan P. *Sin and Science: Reinhold Niebuhr as Political Theologian.* Yellow Springs: Antioch Press, 1956.

Olio, Karen A. and William F. Cornell, "Therapeutic Relationship As the Foundation for Treatment with Adult Survivors of Sexual Abuse." *Psychotherapy: Theory, Research, Practice, Training* vol. 30, no. 3 (1993): 512–23.

Oort, Johannes van. *Jerusalem and Babylon: A Study into Augustine's City of God and the Sources of his Doctrines of the Two Cities.* New York: Brill, 1991.

Park, Andrew Sung and Susan Nelson, eds. *The Other Side of Sin: Woundedness from the Perspective of the Sinned-Against.* Albany: New York, 2012.

Pattison, Stephen. *Shame: Theory, Therapy, and Theology.* Cambridge: Cambridge University Press, 2000.

Pecklers, S.J. and Keith F. "The Liturgical Year and Popular Piety." In *The Directory on Popular Piety and the Liturgy: Principles and Guidelines.* Edited by Peter C. Phan and Robert J. Brancatelli, 77–100. Collegeville, MN: Liturgical Press, 2005.

Pembroke, Neil. *The Art of Listening: Dialogue, Shame, and Pastoral Care.* New York: T&T Clark/Handsel Press, 2002.

Perry, Bruce D. and Maia Szalavitz. *Born for Love: Why Empathy is Essential and Endangered.* New York: William Morrow Paperbacks, 2011.

—. *The Boy who was Raised as a Dog.* New York: Basic Books, 2006.

Piers, Gerhart and Milton B. Singer. *Shame and Guilt: A Psychoanalytic and Cultural Study.* New York: W. W. Norton and Company, 1971.

Pilario, Daniel Franklin E. *Back to the Rough Grounds of Praxis: Exploring Theological Method with Pierre Bourdieu.* Leuven: Leuven University Press, 2005.

Pinn, Anthony B. and Dwight N. Hopkins, eds. *Loving the Body: Black Religious Studies and the Erotic.* New York: Palgrave Macmillan, 2004.

Plaskow, Judith. *Sex, Sin and Grace: Women's Experience and the Theologies of Reinhold Niebuhr and Paul Tillich.* Lanham, MD: University Press of America, 1980.

Porete, Marguerite. *Mirror of Simple Souls.* Translated by Ellen L. Babinsky. Mahwah, NJ: Paulist Press, 1993.

Probyn, Elspeth. *Blush: Faces of Shame.* Minneapolis: University of Minnesota Press, 2005.

—. "Shame in the Habitus." In *The Editorial Board of the Sociological Review.* Edited by Lisa Adkins and Beverley Skeggs, 223–48. Malden: Blackwell Publishing, 2004.

Protevi, John. *Political Affect: Connecting the Social and the Somatic.* Minneapolis: University of Michigan Press, 2009.

Rambo, Shelly. *Spirit and Trauma: A Theology of Remaining.* Louisville: Westminster John Knox Press, 2010.

Retzinger, S.M. "A Theory of Mental Illness: Integrating Social and Emotional Aspects." *Psychiatry* vol. 152, no. 3 (1989): 325–35.

Reuther, Rosemary Radford. "Augustine: Sexuality, Gender, and Women." In *Feminist Interpretations of Augustine.* Edited by Judith Stark, 47–67. University Park, PA: Pennsylvania State University Press, 2007.

Ricoeur, Paul. *Symbolism of Evil.* Translated by Emerson Buchanan. Boston: Beacon Press, 1969.

Riley, Hugh M. *Christian Initiation: A Comparative Study of the Interpretation of the Baptismal Liturgy in the Mystagogical Writings of Cyril of Jerusalem, John Chrysostum, Theodore of Mopsuestia, and Ambrose of Milan.* Washington D.C.: The Catholic University Press, 1974.

Rothschild, Babette. *The Body Remembers: The Psychophysiology of Trauma and Treatment.* New York: W.W. Norton & Company, 2000.

Rushdie, Salman. *Shame: A Novel.* New York: Random House, 1983.

Saiving, Valerie. "The Human Situation: A Feminine View." In *WomanSpirit Rising – A Feminist Reader in Religion.* Edited by Carol P. Christ and Judith Plaskow, 25–42. 1979. Reprint, New York: Harper Collins, 1992.

Sands, Kathleen M. *Escape from Paradise: Evil and Tragedy in Feminist Theology.* New York: Fortress Press, 1994.

Sanghera, Jasvinder. *Shame.* London: Hodder & Stoughton, 2007.

Sartre, Paul. *Being and Nothingness.* Translated by Hazel E. Barnes. New York: Washington Square Press, 1993.

Scarry, Elaine. *The Body in Pain.* New York: Oxford, 1985.

Schaefer M., Flor H., Heinze H.J., and Rotte M. "Dynamic modulation of the primary somatosensory cortex during seeing and feeling a touched hand." *Neuroimage* vol. 29 (2006): 587–92.

Scheff, Thomas J. *Microsociology: Discourse, Emotion, and Social Structure.* Chicago: University of Chicago Press, 1990.

—. "The Shame-Rage Spiral: A Case Study of an Interminable Quarrel." In *The Role of Shame in Symptom Formation*. Edited by Helen Block Lewis, 109–49. London: Psychology Press, 1987.

Schore, Allan N. *Affect Regulation and the Origin of the Self.* Hillsdale, NJ: Lawrence Erlbaum Associates, Publishers, 1994.

—. *Affect Regulation and the Repair of the Self.* New York: W.W. Norton & Company, 2003.

Schulte-Rüther, Martin, Hans J. Markowitsch, Gereon R. Fink, and Martina Piefke. "Mirror Neuron and Theory of Mind Mechanisms Involved in Face-to-Face Interactions: A Functional Magnetic Resonance Imaging Approach to Empathy." *Journal of Cognitive Neuroscience* vol. 19, no. 8 (2007): 1354–72.

Sedgwick, Eve Kosofsky. "A Poem is Being Written." In *Tendencies,* 177–21. Durham: Duke University Press, 1993.

—. *Tendencies.* Durham: Duke University Press, 1993.

—. *Touching Feeling: Affect, Pedagogy, Performativity.* Durham: Duke University Press, 2004.

Sedgwick, Eve Kosofsky and Adam Frank, eds. *Shame and Its Sisters: A Silvan Tomkins Reader.* Durham: Duke University Press: 2005.

Segal, Charles. "Shame and Purity in Euripides' Hippolytus." *Hermes* vol. 98, no. 3 (1970): 278–99.

Sère, Bénédicte and Jörg Wettlaufer, eds. *Shame between Punishment and Penance: The Social Usages of Shame in the Middle Ages and Early Modern Times.* Firenze: Sismel, 2013.

Sifton, Elisabeth. Interview by Krista Tippett. Radio Interview. Minneapolis, MN, December 7, 2004.

—. *Serenity Prayer: Faith and Politics in Times of Peace and War.* New York: W.W. Norton & Company, 2003.

Singer, T., Seymour, B., O'Doherty, J., Kaube, H., Dolan, R.J., and Frith, C.D. "Empathy for Pain Involves the Affective but not the Sensory Components of Pain." *Science* vol. 303 (2004): 1157–62.

Singer, Tania. "The Neuronal Basis and Ontogeny of Empathy and Mind Reading: Review of Literature and Implications for Further Research." *Neuroscience and Biobehavioral Reviews* vol. 30 (2006): 855–63.

Slote, Michael. "The Roots of Empathy." In *Cultivating Virtue: Perspectives from Philosophy, Theology, and Psychology.* Edited by Nancy E. Snow, 65–86. Oxford: Oxford University Press, 2014.

Smith, John. "Obama inaugurated as President." Cable News Network. Accessed February 1, 2009. http://www.cnn.com/POLITICS/01/21/obama_inaugurated/index.html.

Smolarski, Dennis C., S.J. *Sacred Mysteries: Sacramental Principles and Liturgical Practice.* New York: Paulist Press, 1995.

Spinoza, Benedict de. *Ethics.* Translated and edited by Edwin Curley. London: Penguin Classics, 2005.

Stark, Judith, ed. *Feminist Interpretations of Augustine*. University Park, PA: Pennsylvania State University Press, 2007.

Starkey, A. Denise. *The Shame that Lingers: A Survivor-Centered Critique of Catholic Sin-Talk*. New York: Peter Lang Publishing, 2009.

Stegeren, Anda van, Oliver Wolf, Walter Everaerd, Philip Scheltens, Frederik Barkhof, and Serge Rombouts. "Endogenous Cortisol Level Interacts with Noradrenergic Activation in the Human Amygdala." *Neurobiology of Learning and Memory* 87 (2007): 57–66.

Stein, Edith. *On Empathy*. Translated by Waltraut Stein. Washington, D.C.: ICS Publications, 1989.

Stewart, Kathleen. *Ordinary Affects*. Durham: Duke University Press, 2007.

Stockitt, Rodin. *Restoring the Shamed: Toward a Theology of Shame*. Eugene: Cascade Books, 2012.

Stockton, Kathryn Bond. *Beautiful Bottom, Beautiful Shame: Where "Black" Meets "Queer."* Durham: Duke University Press, 2006.

Stone, Bryan P. *Evangelism after Christendom: The Theology and Practice of Christian Witness*. Grand Rapids, MI: Brazos Press, 2006.

Suchocki, Marjorie. "The Symbolic Structure of Augustine's 'Confessions,'" *Journals of the American Academy of Religion* vol. 50, no. 3 (September 1982): 365–78.

Surprenant, Céline. "Freud and Psychoanalysis." In *Literary Theory and Criticism: An Oxford Guide*. Edited by Patricia Waugh, 199–211. Oxford: Oxford University Press, 2006.

Supriya, K.E. *Shame and Recovery: Mapping Identity in an Asian Women's Shelter*. New York: Peter Lang, 2002.

Swan Tuite, Teresa. "Tactile Engagements in Christian Understanding." PhD diss., Yale, 2008.

Tangney, June Price and Ronda L. Dearing. *Shame and Guilt*. New York: The Guilford Press, 2002.

Tangney, June Price and Jessica L. Tracy. "Self-Conscious Emotions." In *Handbook of Self and Identity*. Edited by Mark R. Leary and June Price Tangney, 446–80. New York: Guilford Press. 2012.

Tangney, June Price, Jeff Stuewig, and Logaina Hafez. "Shame, Guilt and Remorse: Implications for Offender Populations." *The Journal of Forensic Psychiatry and Psychology* vol. 22, no. 5 (2011): 706–23.

Taylor, Mark C. *Erring: A Postmodern A/Theology*. Chicago: University of Chicago Press, 1984.

Terr, Lenore. *Too Scared to Cry How: Trauma Affects Children and Ultimately Us All*. New York: Basic Books, 1992.

Terrell, Joann. *Power in the Blood? The Cross in the African American Experience*. Maryknoll: Orbis Books, 1998.

Tisseron, Serge. "De La Honte Qui Tue Á La Honte Qui Sauve: De La Catastrophe Á L'Affiliation." In *Shame between Punishment and Penance*. Edited by Bénédicte Sère and Jörg Wettlaufer, 389–404. Firenze: Edizioni del Galluzzo, 2013.

Thompson, Craig. *Blankets*. Marietta, GA: Top Shelf Productions, 2003.

Tomkins, Silvan S. *Affect, Imagery, Consciousness*. 4 vols. 1962. Reprint, New York: Springer Publishing Company, 2008.

—. *Exploring Affect*. Cambridge: Cambridge University Press, 1995.

—. "Shame." In *The Many Faces of Shame*. Edited by Donald L. Nathanson, 133–61. New York: Guilford, 1987.

Townes, Emilie M. *Womanist Ethics and the Cultural Production of Evil*. New York: Palgrave Macmillan, 2006.

Tracy, Jessica L., Richard W. Robins, and June Price Tangney, eds. *The Self-Conscious Emotions: Theory and Research*. New York: Guilford Press, 2007.

Trelstad, Marit, ed. *Cross Examinations: Readings on the Meaning of the Cross Today*, Minneapolis: Augsburg Press, 2006.

Trumbull, Henry Clay. *The Threshold Covenant or the Beginning of Religious Rites*. New York: Scribner's Sons, 1896.

Turner, Victor. *The Ritual Process: Structure and Anti-Structure*. London: Penguin Books Limited, 1974.

United States Catholic Church. *Catechism of the Catholic Church*. New York: Doubleday, 1994.

Viefhues-Bailey, Ludger H. *Beyond the Philosopher's Fear: A Cavellian Reading of Gender, Origin and Religion in Modern Skepticism*. Burlington: Ashgate, 2007.

Vos, Casparus. "Liturgical Language as Metaphorical Language: A Contribution to Spirituality and the Public Realm." In *Pathways to the Public Square: Practical Theology in an Age of Pluralism*. Edited by Elaine L. Graham and Anna Rowlands, 303–12. Munster: Lit Verlag, 2005.

Walton, Heather. *Imagining Theology: Women, Writing, and God*. London: T&T Clark, 2007.

—. *Literature, Theology, and Feminism*. Manchester: Manchester University Press, 2008.

Walton, Heather and Andrew Hass, eds. *Self/Same/Other: Re-Visioning the Subject in Literature and Theology*. London: T&T Clark, 2000.

Ward, Graham. *Christ and Culture*. Oxford: Blackwell, 2005.

—. *Cities of God*. London and New York: Routledge, 2000.

—. *The Politics of Discipleship: Becoming Postmaterial Citizens*. Grand Rapids: Baker Academic, 2009.

Welch, Edward T. *Shame Interrupted: How God Lifts the Pain of Worthlessness and Rejection*. Greensboro: New Growth Press, 2012.

West, Traci C. *Disruptive Christian Ethics: When Racism and Women's Lives Matter*. Louisville: Westminster John Knox Press, 2006.

"What Tomkins Said." The Tomkins Institute. Accessed August 15, 2014. http://www.tomkins.org/what-tomkins-said/introduction/what-we-learn-through-affects-becomes-programmed-as-scripts-which-govern-our-behavior/.

Wilkinson, Margaret. *Changing Minds in Therapy: Emotion, Attachment, Trauma, and Neurobiology.* New York: W.W. Norton & Co., 2010.

Williams, Bernard. *Shame and Necessity.* 1993. Reprint, Berkley: University of California Press, 2008.

Williams, Delores. *Sisters in the Wilderness: The Challenge of Womanist God-Talk.* Maryknoll: Orbis Books, 1993.

Wissinger, Elizabeth and Jean Halley. "Always on Display: Affective Production in the Modeling Industry." In *The Affective Turn: Theorizing the Social.* Edited by Patricia Clough, 231–60. Durham: Duke University Press, 2007.

Wong, Ying and Jeanne Tsai. "Cultural Models of Shame and Guilt." In *The Self-Conscious Emotions: Theory and Research.* Edited by Jessica L. Tracy, Richard W. Robins, and June Price Tangney, 209–23. New York: Guilford Press, 2007.

Woodward, James and Stephen Pattison, eds. *The Blackwell Reader in Pastoral and Practical Theology.* Malden: Blackwell, 2000.

Wu, Tianyue. "Shame in the Context of Sin: Augustine on the Feeling of Shame in the De Civitate Dei." *Recherches de Théologie et Philosophie Médiévales* vol. 74, no. 1 (2007): 1–31.

Wurmser, Léon. "Shame: The Veiled Companion of Narcissism" In *The Many Faces of Shame.* Edited by Donald Nathanson, 64–92. New York: Guilford, 1987.

—. *Torment Me, But Don't Abandon Me.* Lanham, MD: Rowman & Littlefield, 2007.

You, Young Gweon. "Shame and Guilt Mechanisms in East Asian Culture." *The Journal of Pastoral Care* vol. 51 (1997): 57–64.

Index

Note: Page numbers followed by "n" denote notes.

S.N. Arel, *Affect Theory, Shame, and Christian Formation*,
DOI 10.1007/978-3-319-42592-4

Printed by Printforce, the Netherlands